BEING BRITNEY

BEING BRITNEY

PIECES OF A MODERN ICON

A BIOGRAPHY BY
JENNIFER OTTER BICKERDIKE

NINE
EIGHT
BOOKS

NINE
EIGHT
BOOKS

NEB 003

First published in the UK in 2021 by Nine Eight Books
An imprint of Bonnier Books UK
4th Floor, Victoria House, Bloomsbury Square, London, WC1B 4DA
Owned by Bonnier Books, Sveavägen 56, Stockholm, Sweden

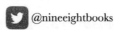 @nineeightbooks

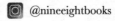 @nineeightbooks

Hardback ISBN: 978-1-7887-0523-3
Trade paperback ISBN: 978-1-7887-0524-0
eBook ISBN: 978-1-7887-0525-7
Audio ISBN: 978-1-7887-0526-4

A CIP catalogue record for this book is available from the British Library.

Publishing director: Pete Selby
Senior editor: Melissa Bond

Cover design by Luke Bird
Cover image © Mark Liddell/Getty Images
Typeset by IDSUK (Data Connection) Ltd
Printed and bound in Great Britain by Clays Ltd, Elcograf S.p.A

1 3 5 7 9 10 8 6 4 2

Every reasonable effort has been made to trace copyright-holders of material
reproduced in this book. If any have been inadvertently overlooked,
the publisher would be glad to hear from them.

Nine Eight Books is an imprint of Bonnier Books UK
www.bonnierbooks.co.uk

For some women I admire greatly:
Aunt Janet, Tami, Lynne, Julie, Andrea, Margareth

CONTENTS

INTRODUCTION

American Shame

The early life of Britney Spears plays perfectly into a familiar narrative deeply cherished in American culture – that of an individual coming from humble origins to attain meteoric heights of fame, success and wealth. In the beginning, Spears was beloved *because* she was so like us. Yet, once the marketing sheen had been dulled, a version of the singer who looked and acted a bit *too* much like a normal girl was revealed. Just as Britney had been held up as an aspirational virgin/vixen, she was then dragged down as the epitome of lowest-common-denominator America – a familiar but highly mediatised version of what many saw when looking honestly at themselves.

The more success Britney amassed, the more she longed to genuinely have the very normality that she was presented as personifying. As fame began to mould her character, she tried desperately to hang on to the threads of her previous life – the same life that she was exalted for escaping. This existence seemed increasingly appealing the further she went from it. When asked in an early interview with *Teen Celebrity* what the hardest part about her job was, Spears answered, 'Losing my identity and privacy,' adding, 'How fun can it be going out with your friends when your bodyguard is right there all the time?'[1]

Within just a few years of attaining global stardom, album sales, appearances and number ones started lacking importance to Britney. Instead, her focus became a desire to 'do what normal people do'. The longing to be anyone but Britney Spears became all-encompassing. A friend of the singer confided, 'She spoke about becoming a schoolteacher, a waitress – anybody other than who she was.'[2] This white-picket-fence dream was an idea Spears returned to repeatedly in interviews, telling a British television talk-show host in 2003 that she hoped to have 'five or six kids' and 'a beautiful home' by the age of forty.[3] This tension between what Britney saw as the aspiration of normality and her actual life began to manifest in panic attacks and low moods, raising concerns among Britney's inner entourage about her seemingly spiralling depression. Doctors prescribed the singer Prozac to aide with her mental health. However, instead of taking the medication daily as suggested by professionals, Spears would only pop a pill when she felt down, as though it were an aspirin for a headache. This only made her already precarious emotional stability worse.

At the start of her ascent to pop dominance, Spears was lauded and held up as being a decent southern Christian girl, an assumed mantle of apple-pie goodness. However, this trait was soon used against her as the young teen matured into an adult, with the press and public alike swarming to call Spears out on behaviour they framed as unacceptable. As her fame grew, Spears was lambasted for the very attributes for which she had originally been heralded. The classist media portrayal of Britney shifted from 'small-town girl done good' to 'crazed, drugged hillbilly somehow sneaking into prominence among the great and the fabulous'. Stories of her father, Jamie, hunting for dinner in the woods behind the family home when Britney was little flipped from being a tale of a struggling clan trying to feed themselves to one of backwater freaks using their fingers to eviscerate defenceless rabbits or squirrels at the kitchen table. Another article took it a step further, claiming that Britney's uncles dined on roadkill, while a 2008 *Rolling Stone* cover piece went so far as to quote an unnamed former manager of Spears, who alleged that the singer was 'the product of some very, very bad genetics'.[4]

Previously, Britney's modest beginnings had been celebrated; now they were reframed under the banner of 'white trash'. (The term 'white trash' is primarily associated with poor white Americans – most often located in rural and southern areas of the US – who 'live on the margins of society, largely divorced from accessing political or economic power'.[5]) Even in articles where the stamp of 'uncouth hick' is not explicitly applied to Spears, it is still implicitly there. 'Spears has always been like this,' wrote another *Rolling Stone* journalist in 2011, 'silly, sweet, humble. She has never been very articulate, but she always tries to be accommodating.'[6]

The tabloids were Britney's shadow, documenting her every movement, ready to pounce on any possible conceived slip-up, whether that be wearing trucker hats and smoking with an unravelling weave or emerging barefoot from a public toilet at a gas station in California. 'Britney Spears' poor hygiene reputation is taking another turn for the worse,' website Popdirt trumpeted in 2004.[7] Spears' various fashion choices – mainly cut-off denim shorts paired with slouchy woollen Ugg boots – did not help. While her look was common on many young women in the mid-2000s, it was deemed low-brow on Britney herself – a descent from the immaculately turned-out schoolgirl of her debut single. When Spears appeared alongside then-fiancé Kevin Federline in a top bearing the slogan 'I'm a virgin, but this is an old shirt', the media had a feeding frenzy over the woman they had once thrust forward into the spotlight, composing her plunge from darling to destitute.[8]

As if to underscore that Britney was just another descendant from a deeply damaged family tree, her grandmother's tragic suicide was hauled out as an example of a seeming predestined mental break looming on the singer's own horizon. Emma Jean, Jamie's mother, had been just thirty-one years old when she used the big toe of her right foot to pull the trigger on a 12-bore shotgun, taking her own life shortly before 4 p.m. on 29 May 1966. Her body was found at a cemetery 3 miles east of Kentwood, near the grave of her son, Austin Wayne, who had died nine years before. He had only lived for three days, but Emma Jean had never been able to come to terms with the loss, having already attempted suicide on three previous occasions.

All these stories about Britney and her family may be partially or even completely factual, but they were not the focus of the narrative until the young woman began to come undone – in public – from non-stop stress and potential postpartum depression. On 17 May 2021, an Instagram post on Spears' account stated: 'So many documentaries about me this year with other people's opinions about my life . . . These documentaries are so hypocritical . . . they criticize the media and then do the same thing?'[9] No one has to look very far to see that Spears rightly nails the irony and conundrum of being a public figure – the balance between actual news or information and the seemingly insatiable appetite for downfall and demise.

In the 2008 *Rolling Stone* cover article (dramatically titled 'The Tragedy of Britney Spears'), the subheading sensationally exclaims: 'She was a pop princess. Now she's in and out of hospitals, rehab and court. How Britney lost it all.' The piece goes on to relate an incident involving a fan approaching Spears for an autograph, to which the star responded, 'I don't know who you think I am, bitch, but I am not that person.'[10] In fact, Britney had never been 'that person'; it was the public who made her something 'superhuman'. Fans did not understand (or want to understand) that the very 'ordinariness' they so loved in Britney was actually a reflection of themselves – a reflection that they did not like as much when it was mirrored back at them.

For most of Spears' career, there has always been someone else speaking on her behalf. Articles claiming to have an 'exclusive line' to the singer's inner thoughts and feelings are instead laden with quotes from her record company, her managers, those working on the conservatorship or even random 'acquaintances', countless 'sources' and extraneous 'confidantes'. This created a vacuum; Spears was absent, voiceless. The person of focus was completely missing.

Then, on 23 June 2021, Britney made an unprecedented statement about her conservatorship, finally providing a glimpse into what she has experienced during her time under the legal mandate.

Britney Spears claims that, throughout her life and career, she has been abused, manipulated and deceived by those closest to her: family, romantic partners, managers and even the state of California. Yet, while many would have shut down completely under such circumstances, Britney has managed to remain both a creator and a creation. She is a conduit of culture who rarely gets the acknowledgement she deserves for being a unique catalyst for radical change and empowerment among countless fans; she is a businesswoman from unassuming roots who has come to dominate numerous areas of commerce; and she is the queen not only of reinvention but also of self-belief.

Britney may be held up as an icon for many things: her personality, her music, her looks, her work ethic. Even if you are someone who has never panted along to the chorus of 'I'm a Slave 4 U' while making dinner or pranced down the street in time to 'Gimme More' while walking the dog, what cannot be denied is that Britney Spears is a bad-ass, deserving of our admiration and respect for pulling through arguably some of the most intense and grotesque media scrutiny ever seen, one of the worst abuses of the legal system, and endless personal disappointments. Against all odds, Britney has been victorious – making records, building a perfume empire, flipping the economy of Vegas on its head, and so much more. Her triumph in the face of such indomitable challenges is a lesson in grace. Above all else, amid all the darkness and adversity, Britney Spears is a survivor, a touchpoint and a superheroine, showing us all how to be bloodied and bruised yet seemingly unbreakable, no matter how daunting the circumstances.

PIECE 1

Wish Upon a Star

When American TV show *Star Search* launched in 1983, it was groundbreaking. Premiering years before the countless deluge of reality fodder that is now omnipresent, *Star Search* was the forerunner by almost two decades of talent mainstays *American Idol* and *The X Factor*. With ten different categories (including dance, spokesmodel, comedy, female and male singer, teen and junior singer, and group vocal), it provided the unique opportunity for anyone to be plucked from total obscurity and splayed in front of a national audience, underpinning the great American pillar that 'anyone can make it' with enough hard work and gumption.

The process to get on the show was fairly straightforward. Potential contestants would audition for their appropriate category. If successful, they would then go head to head with the reigning champion before being marked by a panel of show judges, who would award up to four stars. The performer with the most stars won. If a performer won several shows in a row, they would proceed to the semi-finals. If they conquered *that*, they would advance to the extravaganza that was the championships, where a grand prize of $100,000 was up for grabs for the winners of the adult categories and $10,000 for the junior groups. Hosted by Ed McMahon, *Star Search* offered seemingly wholesome, aspirational viewing that the entire family could sit down and watch together.

The competition was edited to appear as though it took place over the course of several weeks; however, filming was completed in just a few days at a Los Angeles studio. Contestants were told to prepare enough songs and bring enough costume changes to make it seem like more time was passing between 'appearances'. In reality, it may have been just hours between takes. Performers and parents of artists under the age of eighteen were forced to sign nondisclosure agreements, forbidding them from revealing the results of their shows.

After being put forth to try out by her talent agent at the time, Britney Spears soared through the initial audition process and entered the junior singer category as a challenger. '*Star Search*, to us in Louisiana, is a big thing,' said a friend in a VH1 interview. Britney's mum, Lynne, concurred. 'That was probably the first major thing that we thought she had ever done.'

'The whole *Star Search* thing was such a big deal to her. She had always dreamed of it,' said another childhood pal, Cortney Brabham. Indeed, Britney's attainment of a spot on the show was a crucial part of the foundation to the relatable everygirl-ness of the Britney brand. 'I grew up with her. I know her,' says her friend. This feeling of 'growing up' with Britney would later be shared with millions around the world.

Britney's initial *Star Search* appearance shows the then-ten-year-old confidently marching onto the very barren stage. A lone figure in a sparkly black and white dress, she emotively performs the track 'I Don't Care', beating out the pint-size champion by half a star and scoring a winning overall mark of 3.75. After securing her first victory on a national stage, the young girl is asked how she feels. Britney responds, with a huge, genuine grin, 'I feel wonderful.' McMahon tells her, 'You are on your way.'

The next round, though set to hit airwaves the week after Britney's first performance, was actually taped just a few hours after Britney's initial win. This time, the show's producers assigned Britney the Grammy Award-winning song 'Love Can Build a Bridge', which she would sing in the show's grand finale. Britney's lack of familiarity with the track is already evident as she walks on stage to defend her title of champion. Unlike the self-assured stride she possessed for her *Star Search* premiere, she seems more subdued and unsure. When she sings, Britney sounds tentative, uncertain how to unfurl her vocal chops on the lyrics about hardship and longing. Thirty seconds in, how-ever, something changes: Britney comes alive. A powerful surge emanates from the lone figure that would be better suited to a church gospel singer than to a skinny kid with a big floppy bow in her hair.

Yet the sparkling end was not enough to secure victory. Also on the *Star Search* set that day was a young twelve-year-old upstart from Missouri by the name of Marty Thomas. 'I was looking at the competition, I was sizing them up,' Thomas recalls of the day. 'I knew it was going to be Britney or this other child I was competing against – both equally hateable,' he says with a laugh. After watching Britney, the pre-teen did not think he had much of a chance of beating her. 'She's a force of nature. The way that girl handles a microphone and handles the stage, it was obvious that she was damn good.'[11] Marty performed right after Britney. Resplendent in a string tie, grey suit and feathered blond hair, the 'challenger' sang a syrupy ballad. Years later, Marty recalled leaving the stage and thinking, 'She's going to beat me.'[12]

As the cameras pan to the show's judges casting their votes to seal the fate of the young crooners, a painful exchange between host McMahon and Britney occurs. McMahon tells the child that he's noticed her 'adorable, pretty eyes'. He then goes on to ask her if she has a boyfriend back home in Louisiana. When she replies, 'No, sir,' McMahon asks, 'Why not?' In a frightening foreshadowing of future events, young Britney says, 'Because they're mean.' McMahon asks if he would be a suitable boyfriend for her. This is the first glimpse of Britney being asked an uncomfortable and arguably inappropriate question yet responding with genteel grace. Countless more examples would follow. Less than a decade later, she would face endless questions about her virginity, her breasts and other very personal, intimate details, often in interviews with older men. During this encounter with McMahon, aged sixty-nine at the time, Britney looks embarrassed, but is still polite and charming, replying, 'It depends.'[13]

The marks are then revealed, with Marty edging out Britney, scoring a perfect four stars to surpass her 3.75. Britney maintains a big smile as she gives the winner a hug. Marty remembered being 'shocked out of [his] mind' when he actually won.[14] Fellow contestant Timothy Arbolida was on set that day when Britney came off stage. 'I felt bad and I walked over to her. She was curled up crying on the couch. She was upset that she had lost. I said, "I'm sorry, you know you were good."'

Lynne later recalled that her daughter was 'really hurt' when she was defeated and that she had really wanted to win.[15] However, Britney is just one of a long, long list of *Star Search* 'losers' who went on to become global icons. Not unlike more recent graduates of reality talent shows – notably One Direction – who have had massive success despite not snatching the final win, *Star Search* boasts an impressive list of well-known talent who did not finish first. Long before *Basic Instinct*, Sharon Stone was seen in homes across the US in the 'spokesmodel' category, while teenage comedian Dave Chapelle won two battles on the *Star Search* stage before being defeated. Canadian export Alanis Morissette and future pop royalty Beyoncé Knowles, Kelly Rowland and Usher were all dismissed before attaining finalist glory, too. Britney's fellow Mouseketeers Christina Aguilera and Justin Timberlake also graced the *Star Search* stage before joining Disney – the first at the tender age of nine; the latter as 'Justin Randall', aged eleven. Yet things did not go as hoped for either singer. Though Christina showcased her enviable ability by belting out Etta James, host McMahon stumbled over the pronunciation of her Ecuadorian surname. Challenger Timberlake/Randall had plenty of saucy attitude, donning a white cowboy hat, a colourful western shirt and an oversized belt buckle, but it was not enough to topple the then-champion, ten-year-old Anna Nardona. Nardona, now employed at a preschool in Connecticut, has great memories of her short-lived time on the show, recalling, 'I loved the attention, the audiences, the applause.' However, Nardona's reign ended when she was knocked out of the competition by a five-year-old – a blow that took away her confidence in performing. 'I was really embarrassed by it. And I lost it,' she said. 'I didn't lose my talent; I lost my interest. But I know deep down in my heart I'm meant to sing.'[16]

Britney victor Marty Thomas has continued to perform since first gracing TV screens on *Star Search*. He has worked steadily in New York City, adding Broadway productions of *Wicked* and *The Secret Garden* to his acting credentials. In more recent years, Marty has taken up hairdressing as a second career, operating a private salon and working with wigs for Disney International. Yet Marty still has his eyes on mainstream success. In a 2019 interview, he shared some advice given to him by mentor and fellow *Star Search* alum Billy Porter: 'He encouraged me to just do me and wait for the world to be ready for it.'[17]

Though he admits to not having 'been in touch directly with Britney in several years', Marty says that his parents and hers still keep in contact. When asked about Britney's public mental-health issues of the mid-2000s, Marty responds honestly, 'She went a little crazy for a minute, but I would have been butt-ass crazy by now if I were her. She has everything she needs to make a comeback.'[18]

PIECE 2

Mouseketears

It was a casual exchange in the school lunchroom that arguably changed the entire trajectory of Britney Spears' life. A friend gave her a newspaper clipping advertising an open audition in Atlanta, Georgia, for a new show on the Disney Channel, *The All-New Mickey Mouse Club*. Disney scouts were scouring America, making stops not only in Atlanta, but also in Dallas, Miami, New York, Detroit, Chicago and Los Angeles, trying to find 'an ordinary American kid with extraordinary talent' among the hordes of hopefuls. After convincing Lynne to undertake the gruelling 500-mile drive and the costs associated with such a trip, Britney set off. She had prepared her three-minute routine for the audition, which included the backflips and a rendition of jazz standard 'Sweet Georgia Brown'.

Britney's hard work paid off and she made a lasting impact on casting director Matt Casella. 'We saw her on the first day and she blew me away,' he later recalled. 'I could not believe this kid was just eight or nine years old. She commanded the stage with a comfort and authority that I didn't see in seasoned professional young performers twice her age. She scored tens across the board from everyone.'[19] Out of the thousands of kids who auditioned, Britney was one of just six asked to come back for a second go, which was to be filmed and viewed by Disney Channel executives and producers. Though her talent was obvious to those watching her pre-recorded performance, it was eventually decided that Spears, aged eight, was too young to join the show.

Her first attempt at being a Mouseketeer may not have been successful, but Spears had made a meaningful connection with Casella, who was deeply impressed by the young girl's abilities. Not wanting to let the promising kid sink back into obscurity, he had his assistant ring Nancy Carson. Carson – half of the Carson-Adler Agency – had already launched the careers of new and developing talent: other clients at the time included Ben Affleck and Matt Damon. Knowing that a recommendation from Casella was rare, Carson got in touch with Lynne Spears and went on to represent Britney until she was cast for *The All-New Mickey Mouse Club* three years later. Britney joined other new Disney recruits Ryan Gosling, Christina Aguilera and Justin Timberlake, all of whom were picked to don the mouse ears as they represented 'salt-of-the-earth, bread-and-butter all-American kids' (though Gosling is Canadian).[20]

Airing Monday to Thursday at 5.30 p.m., *The All-New Mickey Mouse Club* was the most popular afternoon series on the Disney Channel, reaching 5.6 million cable subscribers. A gruelling schedule was necessary to rehearse and deliver so many new episodes. Each week during the season comprised three days of rehearsals followed by two days of filming.[21] The on-set school provided lessons for the kids between show responsibilities. Britney, who was just eleven when she joined, quickly impressed the older cast members with her dancing skills. Tony Luca was seventeen when Spears came onto the scene and later recalled 'always ask[ing] Britney how the [dance] combinations went because she was really great at committing them to memory'. Fellow ex-Mouseketeer Nikki DeLoach commented that the entire experience of being on the show was 'like going to a graduate school for the arts at a really young age'. When asked in 2018 about her time as a Mouseketeer, Britney responded, 'It was a really good time . . . probably one of the most special times in my life.'[22]

The All-New Mickey Mouse Club was not the first iteration of the rodent-eared programme. Britney's series was the third outing for the show, which had initially graced television screens in 1955 and was then resurrected in 1977 with a contemporary disco flavour.

The timing of the inaugural series could not have been better to take advantage of the new purchasing power afforded to many Americans as the US experienced an unprecedented economic boom. People who would have once held blue-collar jobs now found themselves able to join the idealised, white, middle-class dream thanks to post-war prosperity. The 'mostly non-professional California kids' selected as Mouseketeers for the club embodied the hopeful, upwardly mobile mood of the nation.[23] Beamed into living rooms around the country, the hour-long show was broadcast every evening Monday to Friday. The format featured animation, newsreels, live performances by the Mouseketeers, and short films on kid-appropriate topics like health and safety. By the start of the second series, *The Mickey Mouse Club* had set a record for viewing audiences, with over 12 million children and 7 million adults religiously tuning in to the show.

The cultural tidal wave of *The Mickey Mouse Club* helped create the foundation for what would become Disney's merchandising goliath. The show not only acted as an advertisement for the corporation's cartoons, theme park and merchandise – like the best-selling mouse-eared beanies, as worn by the Mouseketeers – but also offered a glimpse into an entire value system and way of life. One breakout star in particular evoked these traits: Annette Funicello.

Hailing from a 'very solid, solid family background', Funicello embodied many of the attributes that would later help Britney rise to worldwide domination, with colleagues and peers alike describing her as having 'a wonderful innocence about her, no matter what adulation she got', and being 'a sweet, nice girl, very loving to the people around her'. Like Britney, the ingénue persona connected with a large audience; at one point, Funicello was getting more than 6,000 fan letters a day.

Funicello's ascension to fame has parallels with Britney's, with both young women encapsulating the American Dream of being plucked from obscurity via a combination of chance and determination. As a young girl, Funicello was enrolled by her mother in ballet lessons. The hope was that the classes would help the then-five-year-old get over her shyness – a trait that Spears has also admitted possessing. By the time she was twelve, Funicello was starring in a local production of *Swan Lake* when Walt Disney happened to be in the audience. Disney was so taken by the pre-teen's performance that he cast Annette as the twenty-fourth Mouseketeer on his soon-to-be-launched show. The budding mogul was 'a mentor' or 'second father' to Funicello, her friends later said in a documentary about the relationship between Disney and the actress.[24]

As the show got renewed each season, the stars themselves aged from adorable tweens to full-blown teenagers. The emergence of Funicello's bust was problematic as breasts were considered too provocative for television. The burgeoning bosom hinted at a sexually awakening young woman – a far cry from the virtuous child Disney had first spotted. Wanting to retain the young, untouched, pre-adolescent Funicello that America had fallen in love with for as long as possible, Disney allegedly insisted that the young woman's blossoming boobs be taped down in an attempt to make her look as child-like as possible.[25] Since the main portrayal of women everywhere was as a domestic, docile housewife, the idea that his main star could possibly be titillating as a sex symbol seemed unacceptable.

By the 1990s, when Spears donned the ears, more women held positions of power in big companies or had a voice in music, art and literature, coinciding with the worldwide promotion of 'girl power', as popularised by the Spice Girls. But the idea that equality had been reached during the decade was manufactured.

As women gained influence, they were simultaneously 'pushed back' and reduced 'to gruesome sexual fantasies and misogynistic stereotypes' where 'nothing was off limits' – a similar social atmosphere to the time when Funicello came of age before an entire country.[26] Funicello's natural adolescence had threatened a nation with the very idea that a sexually mature woman could be more popular – and, therefore, potentially more powerful – than her male counterparts. For Disney's purposes, Funicello presented the most viable product as an angelic virgin, hovering between childhood and her seemingly pre-destined role of obedient, unsoiled homemaker.

Forty years separated Funicello and Spears' respective tenures as Mouseketeers; however, it was not just the catchy opening jingle of 'M-I-C-K-E-Y' that Britney inherited from her predecessor. The show that once made 'Annette's jugs' (to quote Kenickie in *Grease*) a topic of obsession and longing also provided the launchpad for the ceaseless dissecting of every aspect of Spears' body and life, a price tag attached to anything Spears did or said – not unlike the very merchandise Disney hawked on the series, at their amusement parks and in shopping malls around the world. Dehumanised Britney was a product to be purchased, consumed and, inevitably, thrown away.

PIECE 3

The Max Factor

Though Britney Spears has worked with a number of era-defining musical collaborators throughout her career, one person will forever be synonymous with the peaks of her imperial reign: Swedish songwriter and super-producer Max Martin. The pair have created an entire canon of hits together, from early favourites '. . . Baby One More Time', '(You Drive Me) Crazy' and 'Oops! . . . I Did It Again' to more recent successes 'Hold It Against Me', 'Till the World Ends', 'I Wanna Go' and 'Criminal'. In the meantime, the unique vocal/production combination of Spears and Martin has become the culture-defining soundtrack of the past twenty-plus years, playing a huge part in ushering out the era of rock 'n' roll and birthing the now-omnipresent modern pop economy. The duo's collaboration history also charts the audio evolution of both artists: Martin went from working with developing artists on the Jive Records label to becoming an internationally renowned songwriter; Spears transformed from Louisiana high schooler to reigning pop icon.

In 1997, Max Martin – real name: Karl Martin Sandberg – was a teaboy and aspiring producer, working under the guidance of fellow Swede Denniz PoP. PoP had recently scored mega hits with singles 'All That She Wants' and 'The Sign', which Ace of Base (also Swedish) took to number one across the world. Martin wanted to follow in his mentor's footsteps, though his personal interest veered more towards the rock/metal end of the musical spectrum. 'I was a hard rocker at that time and listened to nothing but Kiss,' he told the Swedish documentarian Fredrik Eliasson, adding, 'I mean nothing but Kiss. It was like we belonged to a cult.' Inspired by the face-painted Americans, Sandberg – adopting the stage name 'Martin White' – took a turn as the frontman and principal songwriter of his own mid-'80s glam-metal outfit, the snappily titled It's Alive. Yet beneath the rocker exterior loomed a secret: 'White' was actually a pop fan (as illustrated by his confession in a later interview that the Bangles' 'Eternal Flame' is his all-time favourite song). Of course, revealing this passion to his head-banging pals was not an option.

However, things started to change when Martin connected with PoP in 1994. At the time, an unknown boy band called the Backstreet Boys had signed to Jive Records and needed a song. PoP and Martin teamed up to create the group's 1995 debut smash, 'We've Got It Goin' On', with Martin also providing the boys' fourth single, 1996's 'Quit Playing Games (with My Heart)'. When fifteen-year-old Britney signed with Jive (initially for a ninety-day development deal), Martin was brought in by the label to hopefully repeat his previous pop alchemy with the young singer.

Martin had a song in mind for Spears that he had been working on for a while. Composed with Rami Yacoub, a Swedish-Moroccan beatmaker, 'Hit Me Baby (One More Time)' had originally been written with R&B supergroup TLC in mind. The band rejected it due to their misunderstanding of the title's Swedish slang: for Martin and his friends, 'hit me' meant 'give me a call'; however, to American ears, the lost-in-translation line carried connotations of domestic violence. In a later MTV interview, TLC singer T-Boz recalled hearing the song while it was at demo stage, saying, 'I was like, "I like the song, but do I think it's a hit? Do I think it's TLC?" . . . Was I going to say, "Hit me, baby, one more time"? Hell, no!'

Another rebuff came from Robyn (joining our list of Swedes) before Martin shared the track with Spears. Though the pair clicked upon meeting, Britney's first impression of Martin was that she 'thought he was from Mötley Crüe or something'. Martin, meanwhile, recognised the teenager's talent from the start: 'She thought I was a fifty-year-old producer from the old school. I had really long hair at the time – I looked like Ozzy Osbourne. It was pretty obvious that she had something, even though she was very quiet and very shy.'[27]

Jive sent Spears to Sweden to work with Martin; they had six songs to record in a week. Martin was immediately impressed with the young performer's dedication. 'She was very well prepared,' Martin remembered of the sessions:

Since '. . . Baby One More Time' was the first song, we really didn't know where to take it. We just kept on recording. We tried a couple of different styles. After a while, I could hear her stomach growl in the microphone. I asked if she was hungry. We'd been going for eight hours. She said, 'No, I'm fine.' I said, 'Let's take a break,' and she had three burgers.

The Spears/Martin combination sparked magic, with Britney adding her own twist to what would become her iconic debut single. As Jive executive Barry Weiss recalled:

I remember when we got it back with Britney on it, she had that 'oh, BAY-BAY, BAY-BAY' – these ad libs. We thought it was really weird at first. It was strange. It was not the way Max wrote it. But it worked! We thought it could be a really good opening salvo for her.

Back-up vocalist NaNa Hedin had an equally positive reaction to the track:

I remember that I thought the song was for teenagers, but the production was filled with a grown-up attitude and with sounds that I really liked. I was so impressed by how a guy like Max and the other writers could write lyrics that spoke to teenage thinking . . . The magic is the attitude. Deep underneath the pop sound it has a sexy rock rebel attitude, from a young schoolgirl and her voice.[28]

Amid the positivity, however, there was still some pushback from the US market regarding the title of the song, as had been the case with TLC. Yet Martin refused to change the lyrics. With executives worried about taking a track with a potentially offensive name to radio promotion staff, the decision was made to lose the 'Hit Me' and shorten the title to the more palatable '. . . Baby One More Time'.

Though he has become a legend for his pop prowess, Martin's love for the big-haired bands of his youth is still evident, according to colleagues. 'A lot of songwriters and producers listen to the music of now and try to mimic it or make a version of it,' says singer-songwriter Sophia Somajo, another Swedish compatriot. (Somajo, who records as Soso, has co-written hits with Martin for Britney and Christina Aguilera.) 'But [Max's] influences are random. Like, if you would take the riff out of a P!nk or an NSYNC song, it's like a Black Sabbath riff.' Somajo links pop's current 'hard-rock-riff-on-synth' sound back to Martin, who 'did it first'.[29]

Since '. . . Baby One More Time', Martin has gone on to pen some of the biggest chart-toppers of the past two decades, scoring an astonishing twenty-one number ones on the *Billboard* charts with such household names as NSYNC, Taylor Swift, Katy Perry and the Weeknd. Of Britney, Martin remains an unabashed fan, telling *The Guardian* that the singer is a 'genius' and that he is a great admirer of her underrated creativity. In the rare interview, Martin described how Britney contributed her own input to all the hits they made together, saying, 'We had conversations with her about what she wanted to do and what she wanted to say.' Spears' abilities are often publicly overlooked, he added, as 'everyone she has ever worked with praises her work behind the scenes'.[30] Those feelings are echoed by Julia Michaels, who joined forces with Spears on her 2016 studio album, *Glory*. In a 2017 *Fader* article, Michaels attested:

> I don't think people realise how involved she is in the studio. Pop instincts are so ingrained in her brain that you play a guitar and she will sing the most incredible melody. She'll have a concept ready; she'll have lyrics ready. I don't think people give her enough credit.[31]

Indeed, Britney's contribution to the artistic creation of her music is often sadly ignored, despite arguably being a key reason that songs like '. . . Baby One More Time' have become timeless classics. As Weiss has contended, 'Max Martin is a genius. He's brilliant. He tailor-made those records for her. But she would never have had the career without her vision. She has this innate ability to move the media.' The chemistry between Spears and Martin was inherent in their working partnership, each complementing the other. 'It's kind of a perfect marriage of song and artist and songwriter,' chart analyst Chris Molanphy asserts. 'If Max Martin is John Hughes, he found his Molly Ringwald – his muse-vehicle for his particular brand of writing. You can't picture it being sung by anybody else.'[32]

Regardless of accolades from colleagues, Britney has been labelled a 'manufactured pop star' since the moment she emerged on the global scene, with certain commentators dismissing her as the 'product of a Swedish songwriting factory' who has had 'no real hand in either her music or her persona'.[33] Yet those who know the singer disagree. 'The public perception is that this is all created, that the record company created this – the artist, the music, the image,' decried music journalist Joe Levy. 'I have to tell you, if the record company could have created more than one Britney Spears, they would have done it – and they tried!'[34]

PIECE 4

The Magic of '. . . Baby One More Time'

The pink pom-poms. The tied-up shirt. The 'oh, BAY-BAY, BAY-BAY'. The video for Britney Spears' first single, '. . . Baby One More Time', struck a chord with an array of people as it cinematically combined the perennial feelings of adolescent obsession with the low-slung trouser look of an entire generation. Like the strange alchemy that happens when chocolate and peanut butter come together to make something surprisingly delicious, it was the amalgamation of multiple disparate elements, blending together in symphonic harmony, that made the video for '. . . Baby One More Time' an international hit, premiering on TV screens on 26 November 1998.

1. DIRECTOR

British-born Nigel Dick was a veteran of the music business in 1998 when Britney Spears came into his life. Having directed a plethora of iconic videos for some of the biggest acts in the world (including the original star-studded bonanza of Band Aid's 'Do They Know It's Christmas?', Guns N' Roses' 'Welcome to the Jungle', and 'Wonderwall' by Oasis), Dick was already familiar with the pop arena pre-Spears. His video for 'As Long as You Love Me' by the Backstreet Boys had helped launch the group to mega stardom, taking their single from an album track to a signature song and bagging them the 1997 MTV Europe Select Award for Fan-Voted Favourite Video. Upon first hearing '. . . Baby One More Time', Dick thought the song was 'really, really good', but few of his colleagues initially saw much value in this new discovery from the heartland. 'She's an unknown girl. She's sixteen years old. It's candyfloss pop,' Dick recalled people telling him at the time.[35]

2. CONCEPT

The original idea Dick had for the video of '. . . Baby One More Time' was for an animated Spears to be in outer space and then land on Mars. However, teenage Spears did not like this concept, telling label bosses that it was 'horrible' and 'cheesy' with Power Ranger overtones. Britney's main beef was that she worried kids her own age would not be able to relate to the storyline Dick had come up with. In a 1999 *Rolling Stone* interview, Spears recounted seeing the original treatment for her song: 'I said, "This is not right. If you want me to reach four-year-olds, then okay, but, if you want me to reach my age group . . ." So I had this idea where we're in school and bored out of our minds and we have Catholic uniforms on. I said, "Why don't we have knee-highs and tie the shirts up to give it a little attitude?"'[36] She asked her label if she could speak directly to Dick and pitch her thoughts for the perfect video, one centred on high-school girls daydreaming about guys. In a later interview about the making of the video, Dick said:

> She came up with the basic part of the idea, she had a comment about the wardrobe. Apart from that, everything else was up to me. She did have a reasonable amount of input and that's good because I was a grown man, you know? I wasn't a teenage girl. And I'd never been to a school with girls in it. I had no knowledge of what it was like to be in a school with girls and boys. So it was a good idea to listen to what she had to say.[37]

Dick admitted having to 'swallow his pride' about taking directions from a teenager. In an early 'making-of' video, Britney describes the inspiration and storyline for '. . . Baby One More Time':

> The concept was kind of my idea and it takes place at a school. The kids can't wait to get out of school, you know? Then we all get out and we just like have a bunch of fun. And it's talking about a guy I wish I [hadn't] broken up with – me wishing that we were back together. So yeah, that's basically it. And we're just like a bunch of dancing kids having a lot of fun at school and doing whatever. It's so cool.[38]

While her own days as a Louisiana high schooler surely helped shape Britney's vision for the video, her *Mickey Mouse Club* experience also had a hand in the format, specifically a dance number from the show's seventh season. Performed to Aretha Franklin's 'Think', the three-minute routine was a precursor of the finished product that would become Britney's first international smash. On the *Micky Mouse Club*, it was Christina Aguilera who danced the lead, with Britney serving as one of four backing dancers. All five girls wore Catholic school uniforms, though no tummies or knees were exposed; full coverage was provided by grey, opaque tights and long-sleeved, buttoned-up white blouses. It was all uncompromised modesty. Yet the Janet Jackson-esque military-precision dance moves provided an appetiser for the future pop princess. *Mickey Mouse Club* choreographer Myles Thoroughgood was not surprised when he saw the singer's first video or heard stories about her initial chutzpah. 'You've got to remember that part of Britney's education with us was to always ask herself: "How can I relate what I'm doing to the audience?" She was conditioned to think creatively. She took that lesson away and translated it into her own career,' he recounts. 'People forget that Britney was trained to think that way and, when she feels confident within her group or with someone, she absolutely asks questions and speaks up.'[39]

Dick was immediately impressed with Spears, telling an interviewer in 2018 that 'there was no real drama' when shooting the video. 'As far as I knew, she was just a schoolgirl from the south,' Dick continued, '[but] she was very relaxed in front of the camera. She was very, very drilled with her dance routine . . . I've yet to work with somebody who puts in as much preparation, and was as eager to rehearse, as she was.'[40]

In contrast, a short video of Spears captured during the same period features a giddy, overwhelmed teen, clearly wanting to please. 'Okay, this is my first video I ever shot,' Spears says into the camera:

> And, um, it was really, really hectic and nerve-racking. I was really nervous about how the end results were going to turn out. I remember the first day I was on the set, there were all these people running around. I was like, 'Oh, my goodness.' I wanted everything to be really, really cool because I knew the song was really cool. I knew all the footage that we had was good. To my surprise, everything turned out really, really cool.[41]

3. LOCATION

Britney was inspired by the 1978 musical classic *Grease*, in which young adults spontaneously burst into song and dance, expressing their woes of summer lovin' past in the hallways of their school. Venice High – the actual backdrop of the much-loved film – was picked as the location for Britney's video in its entirety. The phenomena of '. . . Baby One More Time' builds on the institution's already-established mythology in popular culture. From its inception, the school seemed primed to house what would become the quintessential California dream. When Venice Union Polytechnic High School was founded in 1911, it was originally two blocks from the beach, with classes taking place in old lagoon bathhouses. A 2-mile move inland to a 29-acre campus and a rechristening to the snappier title of

'Venice High' came a decade later. Britney and other Rydell High fans will be well versed in the opening scenes of *Grease*, during which the Pink Ladies and the T-Birds walk up to the manicured façade of their school. Greeting them is actress Myrna Loy – or a sculptural rendering of her, at least. Created when she was an unknown teen, Loy posed as the full-length figure of 'inspiration' for part of a group of pieces that Venice High sculpture teacher Harry Fielding Winebrenner was creating. Loy's face looks hopefully towards the sky, with one arm extended towards the heavens and one arm flung behind her. She went on to become one of the highest-paid actresses of her day, starring alongside classic Hollywood greats like Clark Gable and Jean Harlow. Loy earned the nickname 'The Queen of Hollywood' for her work in film; however, her humanitarian contributions made her equally deserving of such a regal title. Loy openly lobbied for ending discrimination in Tinseltown, famously asking an MGM studio executive in 1934, 'Why does every black person in the movies have to play a servant?' before suggesting, 'How about a black person walking up the steps of a courthouse carrying a briefcase?'[42] When the Second World War broke out, Loy toured to raise money for the effort and visited wounded soldiers. Her open disgust towards the Nazis landed her on Hitler's blacklist.

Loy and *Grease* are not the only pre-'. . . Baby One More Time' Venice High boasts, though. Notable alumni include professional skateboarder and documentary filmmaker Stacy Peralta and Gen-X actor du jour Crispin Glover. The campus has also been used as the set for *A Nightmare on Elm Street*, *American History X* and yet another teen cult classic, 1989's *Heathers*. Before Britney even set foot on the school's manicured lawns for the three-day shoot of the video that would make her a star, Venice High already had the perfect pedigree for a hit.

4. WARDROBE

The navel-revealing tops worn by Spears and her dancing schoolfriends caused a massive stir when the video debuted. One interview claimed that Dick said Spears was 'fully conscious of the "forbidden fruit" aspect' of her wardrobe imagery, knowing it would 'grab the attention of her contemporaries, and older guys would dig it as well. She was thinking of maximum exposure.'[43] A more likely scenario is that Dick was once again going with what the target market would want – in this case, his star. Indeed, the now-iconic look was not Dick's first choice; he wanted the teen clad in jeans and T-shirts:

> I don't have kids, so my understanding of what teenagers wore was limited to driving home from the office and seeing kids standing by a bus stop. Certainly, my initial reaction was, 'Are you sure we should be going down this route with this young lady?' And the people who were in control, the record label and whatnot, said, 'Yes, this is the route we want to take.' I was kind of aware that some people might feel that that was exploitative. And, as it turned out, I got a huge amount of grief about it once the video came out.[44]

Britney, however, was intent on having a look that reflected the idea she had in her head; she wanted the uniform. In a 1998 interview with *People* magazine, Spears confided that the original outfits looked 'kind of dorky', which is what led the teen to make the decision to tie up the shirts and 'look cute'.[45]

Britney did not seem to understand what the controversy was about. 'There are so many other teenagers out there that dress more provocatively than I do and no one says anything about them,' the star said in a 2001 article.[46] She also added an important piece of context to her visual choices: 'I'm wearing a sports bra under [the shirt]. All I did was tie up my shirt. I didn't *do* anything. Sure, I'm wearing thigh-highs, but kids wear these – it's the style. Have you seen MTV? All those girls in thongs?'[47]

Vanessa Grigoriadis – the journalist who wrote the scathing 2008 *Rolling Stone* exposé 'The Tragedy of Britney Spears' – questioned how much Britney was actually aware of and how much was an act. 'This has always been the question with Britney: does she *know* what she's doing?,' wrote Grigoriadis, adding that Britney's wardrobe was 'very much on the edge of what was acceptable then'.[48] Many people did not find it 'acceptable' at all, including an organisation that Britney would become well acquainted with – the American Family Association (AFA). Headquartered in Tupelo, Mississippi (a town made famous for being the birthplace of Elvis Presley), the AFA are a fundamentalist religious-right Christian organisation. The group called for a boycott of both Spears' debut album and tour after seeing the video for '. . . Baby One More Time', describing it as a 'paedophile's dream disguised as pop art'.[49]

Despite the misgivings, one of the reasons '. . . Baby One More Time' works so well is that Spears styled the video to her sensibilities and those of her peers, not to what adults thought a teen would find cool. The *Lolita*-like adult projection of the various signs and symbols within the video – the uniforms, the pom-poms in the hair – only come with the knowledge of age, education and experience. These visuals may be packed with meaning to an older viewer because of their own associations, but not because of what is inherently in the video. Is a thirteen-year-old even going to know what or who *Lolita* is? They will more likely pick up on the power of a slightly older girl slamming a locker with authority or crushing on a boy. There is an indisputable accessibility to '. . . Baby One More Time' that is relatable to a teen audience in a way that few contemporary videos were, especially in the late 1990s when million-dollar budgets for videos were not unheard of. Just as the video's story would be both familiar and aspirational to kids watching, the ability to look like the performers in the video was also completely attainable as every piece of kit worn by the dancers was purchased from big-box low-cost retailer KMART. Nothing bought for the shoot cost more than $17, making the 'Britney look' well within everyone's reach. This further strengthened the normality and relatability of Spears in a way that her contemporaries had not yet mastered, helping her to build a devoted fanbase from the very start.

5. LOVE INTEREST

'. . . Baby One More Time' has been described as a video of a girl daydreaming about 'hot guys'. This is fairly accurate, though the addition of gymnastics, sassy dance moves and cavorting around on a basketball court would need to be included for further accuracy. Maybe it's the Venice High/*Grease* connection or maybe its Britney's high ponytails, but there is a sweet, unspoiled Sandy-esque innocence about Spears throughout the video of love gone awry. The focus of her lust is only featured in one shot, sitting on the bleachers of the indoor basketball court. The singular reference point amid a sea of boys, girls, backflips and convertible cars is a great euphemism for the emotional and hormonal roller coaster of teenagedom. But the glimpse of the love interest may have been fleeting for another reason: the role was originally supposed to go to someone else – Reg Jones, Britney's high-school beau.

Jones had followed Spears from Louisiana to New York as the singer prepared to film '. . . Baby One More Time'. Things were going so well with Britney that Jive Records decided to send her out as the opening act for NSYNC's tour once her video had wrapped. The shows would reunite Britney with two of her *Mickey Mouse Club* friends, JC Chasez and Justin Timberlake. This did not go down well with Jones, causing him and Spears to have a massive fight two days before they were set to go to Los Angeles to shoot the video. Britney told her hometown boyfriend that she was excited to be 'with Justin again', leading Reg to accuse Britney of having more than platonic intentions towards the boy bander.[50] As a result, Britney fired Reg from the video and sent him back to Kentwood. However, there was now a problem: Britney needed someone to play the all-important 'hot guy' for her to crush on in the video. Help came from her family. Cousin Chad was a model for Abercrombie & Fitch – tanned, ripped and all-American good-looking. In '. . . Baby One More Time', his blond hair contrasts perfectly against the black tank top he dons in the crucial close-up shot.

6. ICONIC STATUS

When '. . . Baby One More Time' was released, the main vehicle in the US for flogging artists and videos to 13–18-year-olds was the weekday MTV fodder *Total Request Live* (*TRL*). The show featured a top-ten countdown, as voted for by viewers via phone or online. During the last two years of the '90s and into the early 2000s, the mainstays of the show fell into three main categories: boy bands (like the Backstreet Boys and NSYNC); the emerging genre of 'rage rock' (headed up by artists Korn and Limp Bizkit, with hip-hop bad boy Eminem making occasional appearances); and, lastly, female pop singers. When Britney emerged on the scene, however, it was the male-heavy music of the first two categories that ruled *TRL*. Though '. . . Baby One More Time' came out at the end of November 1998, it did not get to number one on *TRL* until March the following year and was almost always third place on the coveted chart throughout its run on the show, losing out to behemoths the Backstreet Boys and NSYNC. Britney seemingly could never topple the boys she was surrounded by.

However, Spears would eventually triumph over all her male counterparts. When *TRL* ended its decade-long run in 2008, it was Britney's '. . . Baby One More Time' that was crowned Most Iconic Video Ever.[51]

Britney was, in many ways, an unexpected pick as *TRL*'s victor, given that the testosterone emanating from the show was so heavy it was like watching a televised fraternity party (complete with tattoos, dog-barking applause and sculpted facial hair). Yes, sure, there were *some* girls – Britney, Christina Aguilera and maybe even Mandy Moore would pop up once in a while – but it was predominantly a boy-heavy extravaganza. The girls were almost an afterthought.

What made the show's success even more stunning was the fact that its popularity came right after a surge of strong female artists had taken the world by storm – the likes of Alanis Morissette and Garbage. Yet, in *TRL*'s 'bro'dom, women all but vanished. Ultimately, this oversight makes Britney's win that much sweeter: she got the last laugh for women everywhere.

PIECE 5

Breastgate

When Britney Spears' debut single first hit airwaves in October 1998, the singer was just sixteen years old. The accompanying publicity showcased an attractive young woman, as fresh and likeable as any kid in any American town. This image allowed Britney to straddle several marketable demographics. For teenage girls, she was one of them – a relatable entity who you could invite over for a sleepover and confide your crushes to. The UK cover for her . . . *Baby One More Time* album could not have offered a safer oasis for mums and dads drowning in a sea of scary 'parental advisory' stickers. The image is Britney posed in a white top, hands in a prayer position, looking tan, blonde and friendly – the perfect babysitter for your tween. The pristine white background and swirling girly font complete the picture of clean, prudent fare.

Fast-forward a year to the video for Britney's third single, 'You Drive Me Crazy', and there is a visual difference – if one is looking for it. The green crop top Britney is wearing is well filled this time, with ample cleavage on display. While the video for '. . . Baby One More Time', with its school uniforms, knotted blouses and sports bras, had hints of burgeoning sexuality, it was dominated by an alluring naiveté. 'You Drive Me Crazy' flipped that ratio on its head. There are still glimpses of innocent Britney in the video, but it is the emboldened, carnal creature lurking beneath her sweet southern surface that dominates the screen. The hip-thrusting dance moves, pouting lips and jiggling breasts seem worlds away from the daydreaming high schooler the world had first met just a year prior.

Speculation mounted as to whether Britney had undergone breast augmentation, even though she was still below the legal minimum age required to undertake such a procedure. Around the same time as her seemingly larger chest made its debut, Britney also suffered a knee injury, requiring her to undergo minor surgery to remove a 1-inch piece of cartilage from her leg. Britney's keyboard player Dan Kenney recalled how he 'started hearing rumors that Miss Spears didn't really have a knee injury, but actually had breast augmentation surgery', citing a suggestion that the cosmetic procedure was spun into a knee injury to avoid being made public. 'However,' Kenney added, 'shortly after hearing that rumor, I saw her in an MTV interview while on crutches. So I didn't really know what to believe.'[52]

Reg Jones, Spears' ex-boyfriend from high school, claimed that Britney had been longing for breast implants for some time. 'She started talking about getting a boob job when she was sixteen . . . She believed that she would be a more popular performer if she had the smoking hot body . . . I wasn't in the operating room myself, of course, but she did it, I know she did it.' Meanwhile, Justin Timberlake, who was dating Britney during the controversy, deflected the matter by saying, 'I don't know about her breasts; I was always too busy looking at her fantastic butt.'[53]

Fans who had bought into the wholesome 'good girl' image perpetuated by the start of the . . . *Baby One More Time* album campaign were perturbed by the idea that their simulacrum of purity could possibly be tarnished by such a tawdry act as breast enlargement. In the 2021 documentary *Framing Britney Spears*, a voice, played over some B-roll footage, captures such feelings, proclaiming, 'I know she is aiming for the little kids market. She needs to back off, she needs to put a pair of blue jeans on and just sing.'[54] This is an emotion that was mirrored on the cover of the 14 February 2000 edition of *People* magazine, which featured Spears alongside the headline 'Too Sexy Too Soon?'[55] This contrast illustrates one of the main tenets of Britney: her brand and massive popularity – at least initially – were based on a tension between idealised girl-next-door chastity and in-heat sex kitten.

In 1999, Britney attempted to clear up any doubt, telling *TV Guide* that her increase in cup size was due to Mother Nature's cosmic, not cosmetic, intervention. 'When I first signed with the record label, we took a lot of photos and those were the pictures that got used . . . I weighed 105 pounds; I weigh 130 now. I went through a major growth spurt,' she claimed.[56] Science suggests that most girls reach their full height by the time they are fourteen or fifteen years old, with breasts continuing to grow and 'change in shape or contour up until age eighteen'.[57] This makes it possible – but unlikely – that Britney's sudden chest enhancement was due to a last-minute growth spurt only affecting her bosom. Either way, this pressure to maintain the delicate balance between ingénue and harlot was incredibly challenging under the microscopic scrutiny experienced by the singer.

What was most astounding about 'Breastgate' was the complete lack of discretion or dismay displayed as Britney's body was publicly dissected. It seemed perfectly expected and reasonable to grill a young pop performer – who was not old enough to legally drink alcohol or vote in the US – about her body. On television talk shows, in print media and on fan websites, it seemed forgotten that the focus of discussion was still a kid herself. One Google group from 1999 – under the title 'Britney Spears breast implants?' – has a range of unfounded comments, including: 'It was reported in my local paper today that she got em for her Rolling Stone cover shoot, so that explains her "sprained ankle/knee"'; 'There are doctors out there who clear some kids to have breast implants as early as age 13, it's gross, yes, but it's not uncommon.'[58]

Almost a decade later, the topic was still being discussed. A 2008 cover story in *Rolling Stone* cited confessions from a supposed 'source' close to Britney. This source contended that Lynne gave teenage Britney permission to get implants, stating that the mother/daughter duo made 'the assumption that the culture demanded it', though the magazine added a disclaimer stating, 'Britney has denied having implants.' In the same piece, the source went on to say, 'When Britney saw the papers, she was crying in the bathtub uncontrollably, asking, "Why is everyone being so mean to me?" . . . It was very hurtful for her to go through something so private so publicly.' The article then contradicted itself, suggesting that 'Britney regretted the implants, particularly because her chest was still growing and, when her natural breasts became larger, she had the implants removed'. If Britney denied having the procedure in the first place, why would she then have them removed? While it is diffi-cult in this particular piece to differentiate between what is true and what may not be entirely correct, the article did underscore one key issue that Britney has faced throughout her career: all of the uproar was not necessarily about her breasts, but about her identity. Choreographer Darrin Henson – who worked on several videos from Britney's first album, as well as Christina Aguilera's 'Genie in a Bottle' – suggested there was a lack of clarity between Britney's 'personas'. 'When other girls did their boobs, they were like, "Yeah, I did my boobs, move on," but Britney was brought up to lie about herself,' Henson asserted, adding, 'The girl doesn't know who she is.'[59]

A possible example of this can be seen in one very uncom-fortable and inexplicably inappropriate interview from 1999. Dutch journalist Ivo Niehe – a middle-aged, balding male – turns to the then-seventeen-year-old Britney and says, 'There's one subject we didn't discuss. Everyone's talking about it. Well, your breasts.' An audible gasp of horror combined with laugh-ter can be heard emanating from the studio audience. Britney responds in her typical classy manner, cutely crinkling her nose and saying, 'My breasts?' Niehe then follows up with, 'Okay, in general, what do you think about breast implants, just in general?' Britney answers, 'I think it's sad that people think I've done that, the press started that. If you want to do that, that's fine, but I personally wouldn't do that.'

In *Framing Britney Spears*, this exchange is highlighted as a pinnacle of the creepy and often vile treatment the still-teenage Spears was subjected to. The re-emergence of the clip in the documentary brought Niehe back into the public's awareness. Niehe gave an interview in response as he felt it was important to share his side of the now-infamous exchange. In a statement to Dutch news, Niehe contended that, before the camera was rolling, Britney's team mandated that the plastic surgery question be included in the interview. 'We agreed to give her a serious opportunity to react to all the commotion. What did she, as a seventeen-year-old American, think about plastic surgery? Britney was pleased to make extensive use of this,' Niehe stated. He then argued that this narrative 'naturally did not suit the documentary makers, so they only used the one question, which was asked with great irony as we did not want to talk about it anyway'.[60]

The *Framing Britney Spears* edit makes the talk-show host look like the poster boy for creepy sex pest instead of, as he claims, simply an interviewer doing what the singer and her management wanted. This obviously creates a nebulous stew of confusion. Is Britney the pawn or the one steering the conversation? Was it her management that arranged the entire interview, making Niehe the victim? Did the documentary makers edit the clip to fit their storyline, thereby completely changing the context of the original exchange? This one interview raises the question of identity for all involved: who is telling the truth; who is orchestrating what; who is deciding which story is being told?

The fixation on Britney's bosom has continued over the decades, with her alleged implants coming and going on a fairly regular basis, if some fans are to be believed. In 2018, one plastic surgery-focused website proclaimed 'oops, she probably did it again' after Spears posted a video on Instagram showing off her 'ample bosom and deep cleavage'.[61] But it seems that Britney would not be alone if she did seek breast augmentation in her mid-thirties. According to plastic surgeon Dr Terry Dubrow, the average age for a woman looking to get implants is thirty-four.[62] As of 2020, breast augmentation is still the most popular plastic surgery procedure around the world.[63]

More importantly, it is unclear why it matters to anyone but Britney whether or not she has had a boob job. Does it impact her music, her personality or her various enterprises? It could be seen that cosmetic surgery conflicts with the 'authentic' part of brand Britney and that her (possibly) fake boobs are a symbol of other ways in which she is not genuine. However, nothing is more real and relatable than a woman feeling insecure about her body.

Yet, like a turkey at Christmas, it has become accepted and expected to carve apart Britney's body for widespread consumption, her 'personal' anatomy long since sacrificed for a gluttonous public feast.

PIECE 6

Double-Denim Fantasy

At the start of 2001, Britney Spears and NSYNC's Justin Timberlake ruled the charts, reigning as the king and queen of teen pop. The American Music Awards were fast approaching and the 'it' couple wanted to make a major splash with their red-carpet looks. While on a trip to New Orleans, the duo came up with the idea of wearing head-to-toe denim. In a 2020 interview, costume designer Steven Gerstein, who was working with Timberlake's boy band at the time, recalled how the outfits took shape: 'It went from an idea to being made within days . . . I called people in New York and said, "Go buy fifty pairs of vintage Levi's."' The combination of the two stars made for tabloid catnip. 'The Britney/Justin connection added fuel to the fire, but it was really organic,' Gerstein confided. 'It was just two kids wanting to do something cool and being super cute matching. It was kind of like their prom.'

Spears' denim extravaganza comprised a floor-length strapless dress made from various shades of the fabric. The gown's tight bustier led to an almost fish-tailed, lighter-coloured skirt, with a repurposed, darker jean pocket placed at the unfinished hemline. The woman responsible for sewing the look together was Linda Stokes, a Los Angeles-based seamstress known for offering her services twenty-four hours a day. 'She was fantastic, the most humble and accommodating woman,' Gerstein said of Stokes. 'If you were to ask any stylist in LA from the late '90s to the mid-'00s if they know Linda Stokes, everyone has taken that drive [to her base in Woodland Hills] at three in the morning . . . If it wasn't for Linda Stokes, a lot of LA wouldn't have gotten dressed at the time.'[64]

Spears' accessories were equally resplendent in their perfect matchy-matchyness. A silver and diamond-studded belt was looped around her small waist, cunningly coordinated with her purse, which was also denim and featured a sparkly strap. Her glittering, oversized V-shaped choker and crystal bracelet completed an already memorable outfit. However, in a seemingly impossible feat, Timberlake's Canadian tuxedo was just as eye-catching as Britney's ensemble. His suit was a denim remake of the Costume National two-piece he had worn on the cover of NSYNC's 2001 album, *Celebrity*. The fit and style of his jacket resembled a hybrid blazer/sport coat, completely redefining the possibilities of denim's full remit. Another mash-up sat upon the singer's head in the form of a dark-blue fedora/cowboy hat. The cap was trimmed with a 'ribbon' made from the waistband of a pair of jeans, with the button at the front. The finishing touch was Timberlake's glittery pendant necklace – an exact twin in colour and style to the jewels bedecking his girlfriend.

In recent interviews, Timberlake has admitted he does not regret the double-denim glamour of 2001. When appearing as a guest on a podcast hosted by former NSYNC bandmate Lance Bass, Timberlake joked, 'I don't know, man, you could kinda rock that today.' He concluded the interview saying, 'Look, man, you do a lot of things when you're young and in love, man. That's what you do.'[65]

So what became of the two outfits once they had been photo-graphed for all the world to see, discuss and imitate?

Britney memorabilia is highly collectable – no shock there – so it is unsurprising that auctioneers Nate D. Sanders were able to sell the denim gown to an undisclosed buyer for $7,199 in 2013. Most clothing worn on red carpets is either returned to the designer or gifted to the celebrity wearing it (though it is unclear which of these scenarios happened with the American Music Awards look), so it is possible that the Spears estate gave Sanders the dress to sell in the first place.

Justin's suit has had a more nebulous journey. After the break-up of NSYNC, Gerstein recalled having lots of the band's discarded clothes still in storage at his house. 'I had that suit for the longest time in my garage,' he said of the iconic two-piece. He eventually sent all of the NSYNC goods back to management, who began archiving various items related to the band. 'It was bittersweet, a symbol that an era was ending,' commented a wistful Gerstein.[66]

Over the years, celebrities and mere humans alike have attempted to replicate 'denimgate', decking themselves out top to bottom in an homage to the unforgettable Spears/Timberlake moment. In 2014, Katy Perry wore a strapless denim dress to the VMAs and walked the carpet with American rapper Riff Raff, who wore a matching suit, while Victoria's Secret supermodel Devon Windsor and fiancé Johnny Dex recreated the popsters' look for Halloween in 2018. Indeed, 31 October is a popular day for the denim decadence to be revisited as the internet is filled with tutorials on how to capture the blue magic as a costume.

However, the true legacy of denimgate goes far beyond All Hallows' Eve; it can actually be seen at any high-street store all year round. Once a huge sartorial no-no, a rainbow of mix-and-match denim in varying shades of indigo (with some acid-wash thrown in) is now prominently displayed throughout most clothing outlets. The omnipresence of blue overkill is testament to the lasting impact that a power couple's outfit choices (worn for one night, over two decades ago) had on the way contemporary consumers dress today – even if shoppers have no idea of the provenance of their fashion decisions.

PIECE 7

What a Girl Wants

At 8 a.m. every weekday, the first bell rings at McComb's Parklane Academy – the private Christian school attended by Britney Spears as a child. Like all good Southern Baptist institutions of its ilk, the academy prides itself on instilling Christian and patriotic values into its students from the moment the academic day begins. First on Britney's morning agenda would have been Bible readings, followed by the pledge of allegiance and a singalong to the national anthem. Representatives from the True Love Waits movement were also a common sight on the campus. The movement, founded in 1992, had the 'primary goal' of convincing 'young people [to] commit to and sign' a pledge vowing a chaste existence until marriage. ('Believing that true love waits, I make a commitment to God, myself, my family, my friends, my future mate, and my future children to be sexually abstinent from this day until the day I enter a biblical marriage relationship.'[67]) Speaking about the school, a former classmate of Britney's, Kelly Burch, recalled, 'Christian moral values was a big thing there – not that that was a bad thing.'

This framework of good old-fashioned principles became a cornerstone of the early Britney publicity campaign. It was arguably an easy selling point for the young singer to take on board after being inducted into such a belief system on a regular basis during her school career. The first focus demographic Britney needed to conquer was young/tween girls, so the pristine image of an untarnished, hymen-intact idol was crucial for maximum marketing penetration. Record label Jive encouraged Spears to stress this message of purity repeatedly. In a 2000 interview, Britney stated that she had never been sexually active, didn't 'believe in smoking cigarettes' and thought that 'everyone should serve God'. As the interviewer pushed her to elaborate further, Spears answered, 'I am as interested in sex as any young woman is, but I am choosing to save myself.'[68]

Britney's virginity was especially of interest because her arrival on the pop-culture landscape came at the end of almost two decades of devastation caused by sexually transmitted HIV. Statistics estimate that the HIV crisis peaked in 1995 – just three years before Spears reached international acclaim.[69] What is the easiest way to protect your child from the 'scary ravages' broadcast by the media? Tell them to be abstinent. Spears provided the perfect panacea for the panic.

This push for American teens to keep their trousers up was further fuelled by politicos getting involved, chucking huge sums of money at the cause. The irony cannot be lost that it was Bill Clinton – the US president impeached because of a sex scandal – who brought forth the 1996 Personal Responsibility and Work Opportunity Act. Nicknamed the 'Workfare Act', the doctrine made 'the ethereal status of virginity the standard for American teenagers'.[70] It allowed for $437.5 million in federal and state funding to be funnelled into organisations willing to further the eight ideological tenets, one of which was 'a mutually faithful monogamous relationship in the context of marriage is the expected standard of sexual activity'. A study from 1999 found that '86 per cent of school districts with a sex ed policy required promotion of abstinence' and '51 per cent of districts required abstinence be taught as the preferred method of birth control'.[71] In this context, a chaste, unspoiled Britney reflected not just a product that parents felt they could 'safely' give their kids, but also an ideology that the kids themselves were actively – though perhaps subconsciously – encouraged to partake in.

For her fans, 'virginal' Britney represented the natural hormonal turmoil of adolescence mixed with the fear brought on by the AIDS crisis. She allowed girls to be at once provocative and pure. As one *New York Times* commentator put it: 'No wonder teenagers are drawn to Britney Spears, a proudly self-identifying virgin who practically pole-dances on prime-time TV then says she's waiting for true love . . . Spears saturates kids with sexuality; then, like their teachers, tells them to guard their chastity.' Britney's flawless persona, bright, bubbly charisma and unadulterated naiveté regarding all things 'birds and bees'-related became not just part of her brand, but actually an integral factor in her very authenticity, making Spears 'the most celebrated virgin since Joan of Arc'.[72] It was a vibe that was easy and encouraged as Clinton's successor, President George W. Bush, continued to pump dollars into the anti-sex movement, earmarking more than $33 million for abstinence-only education in 2002.[73] In a 2017 *Guardian* article, writer Amy Deneson described the time as a moment when 'virginity culture bloomed into . . . Britney Spears, abstinence-only education, and father–daughter Purityball portraits'.[74]

What started out as an exercise in selling more records and concert tickets – part of the predictable cycle of promoting an emerging artist – instead became the tale of a worldwide market pondering how a young woman could sing, look and dance provocatively without having had a sexual liaison of some variety. It was acceptable, expected and desirable to relentlessly question Spears on the state of her chastity. In *Framing Britney Spears*, a teen Britney is shown at a press conference repeating back the question she has just been asked for all to hear: 'Am I . . . a virgin? Yes, I am a virgin and I want to try to wait to have sex until I am married. I want to wait for that special someone. Thank you.'[75] She is smiling, giggling and accommodating, making it seem silly that this would even be of interest or speculated about – and rightly so. A 2015 study found that the average age of (penetrative, heterosexual) virginity loss for American men was 16.9 years old and the average age for American women was 17.2 – around the same age as Britney at the time of the interview.[76]

In 2000, an unnamed businessman contacted Jive offering £7.5 million in exchange for Britney's virtue. When reporting on the offer, *The Guardian* argued that the singer's 'sexual inexperience' was actually 'infinitely more titillating than the mani-cured, PR-generated excuse for sluttiness that she totes about in her videos', though the article simultaneously accused Britney of 'swirl[ing] her virginity about like a tasselled nipple'. The female journalist then went on to harpoon Spears – whom she referred to as being 'just-above-average prettiness' and 'collagen plump' – for her 'uniquely confused and confusing sexuality . . . so utterly intoxicating' to men. The piece concluded that Britney's virginity was 'worth millions more' than the 'paltry' offer, 'both to her and to her record company'. Inevitably, it was Britney herself, upon learning of the proposition, who provided the most appropriate comment, responding, 'It's a disgusting offer . . . He should go and have a cold shower and leave me alone. It's outrageous how a man like that can offer something which is totally unacceptable.'[77] In retrospect, it seems strange that her response was not echoed more widely; instead, it was Britney's audacity to titillate that got stuck in the craw of the media.

What was also disheartening was the way that former flame Justin Timberlake treated Spears after their well-publicised break-up. When Britney and Timberlake called their relation-ship off in 2002, headlines began postulating as to whether the couple had ever consummated their relationship. The pair had been together romantically for more than two years and had even co-habited at one point when they were not on tour. Now untethered from Spears, Timberlake spoke freely about the intimate details the two had shared. In a *20/20* interview with Barbara Walters, Timberlake burst out laughing when asked by the reporter if Britney had 'kept her promise to wait until marriage'.[78] When the subject of his ex-girlfriend's purity was raised in another exchange between Timberlake and the press, he responded, 'She lost her virginity a while ago – and I should know.'[79] The singer was similarly boastful of his 'conquest' when appearing as a guest on a New York radio show. In answer to the direct question, 'Did you fuck Britney Spears?', Timberlake proudly guffawed, 'Okay, I did it.'[80]

Betrayed by one of the few people she probably felt she could trust, Britney then began the process of trying to explain away her contravention of the pledge she had become so closely associated with. She took to the media to tell her side of the story, claiming to have only slept with one person who she 'thought was the one'.[81] Nevertheless, she admitted that she 'was wrong' and did not think that Timberlake was 'gonna go on Barbara Walters' and 'sell' her out. However, according to a 'friend' of the former NSYNC-er, Timberlake apparently did not 'sell' Britney out; her claims were simply 'wild accusation from someone who looks embarrassingly desperate'.[82] The smiling façade Britney had perfected in front of the prying paparazzi finally broke in Mexico when reporters met Spears and her entourage as they left an airport in Toluca. As questions about Timberlake began raining down on the singer, she flipped her middle finger at the entire scrum – an image that was captured and shared around the world. This only led to the further disintegration of the already-crumbling epitome of saintly Britney.

Pundits also came down hard on what they saw as a 'betrayal' of the chaste Britney they had bought into. Even the BBC was guilty of reporting the 'news' in a disparaging manner, claiming that Britney's 'innocent image has begun to wear thin'.[83] But it wasn't just the press and 'sources' who began to stick their knives into the once-untarnishable Spears. Music industry peers who had worked with the singer early in her career came forward with claims that the virgin image was simply part of a 'PR blitz'. Spears had been sexually active for a long time, they suggested, and had been intimate with Timberlake from 'the very beginning'. The *NME* article reporting these allegations also asserted that Spears actually lost 'it' at the age of fourteen to her high-school boyfriend, Reg Jones.[84] Later, in a 2008 *Rolling Stone* cover story, an unnamed 'friend' claimed that, though the singer portrayed the naïve babe in public in her early days, things were much different when Spears was off stage and away from the cameras. 'There were all these slick businessmen for Britney who let seedy people come around, offering her drinks and drugs, and she thought it was fun,' alleged the source. 'If Britney wanted to party to blow off stress, that's what her team wanted her to do.'[85]

Britney's mistakes were not missed by the next batch of freshly hatched talent coming after her on the music industry conveyer belt. Remaining pristine was at the forefront of all messaging. Take the 2008 MTV Video Music Awards (aka the VMAs). Freshly crowned *American Idol* winner Jordin Sparks took to the stage and used it as her personal pulpit. 'I just have one thing to say about promise rings,' Sparks began. 'Not everybody, guy or girl, wants to be a slut!' A line in the sand had been drawn between the tragedy of Britney's great meltdown – the tacit insinuation from Sparks being that Spears was said 'slut' – and the bright, clean upstarts.

Pop successors all bleated on about how important 'waiting' was to them, purposefully making a harsh contrast between themselves and Spears. In 2003, fellow blonde singer Jessica Simpson confessed that she was 'so lucky' to not have lost her virginity in 'the back of a Jeep or something'. The three Jonas Brothers, Demi Lovato and Hilary Duff all followed Simpson, telling anyone who would listen that they would not have sex until they were safely within the bounds of matrimony. Even Britney's fellow Disney protégées stepped up to align themselves with the Almighty. 'I'm going to keep my promise to myself, to my family and to God,' Selena Gomez told reporters in 2008 while she was starring in the channel's Emmy Award-winning television series *Wizards of Waverly Place*. That same year, fellow mouse-created star Miley Cyrus piped up on the topic, telling *People* magazine, 'Even at my age, a lot of girls are starting to fall . . . if [staying a virgin] is a commitment girls make, that's great.'[86] In a scarily similar arc, Cyrus would herself get lambasted five years later for performing provocatively with Robin Thicke at the 2013 VMAs and then appearing naked in her 'Wrecking Ball' video. Just as Britney had titillated and intrigued a little over a decade before, 'Wrecking Ball' obtained an incredible 19 million views within twenty-four hours of its release, becoming Cyrus's first US Hot 100 top ten and selling over 2 million copies.

Minor blips by celebrities like Cyrus simply prove that no one has really learned from what happened to Britney. In a 2013 interview, Joe Jonas discussed how his group's participation in the True Love Waits organisation became a focus of both media and fan obsession as the brothers became commercially successful. Jonas had 'taken' the abstinence pledge at age eleven and wore a purity ring to denote his commitment to saving himself until marriage. 'The topic that dominated news coverage of us for a long time was the whole promise-ring thing. We couldn't escape it,' said Jonas:

> I remember this interview with this guy whose entire agenda was to focus on the rings. He kept pushing the subject and, when we insisted that we didn't want to talk about it, he told us, 'I can write whatever I want,' which terrified us. That's the thing: we didn't know any better and we just wanted to make people happy . . . Like, why do you even care about my fifteen-year-old brother's sex life?

Fans began to copy what they thought their idols were doing – a phenomena that frustrated Jonas, who lost his virginity at the age of twenty. 'People were coming up to us, saying, "Thank you so much, I'm waiting because you guys are, too!" And we just thought, "No! That's not what we're about,"' Jonas recalled.[87]

The fascination with a group of males wanting to wait until marriage to have sex arose because it contravened the accepted societal mythology of boys wanting to 'sow their wild oats'. Women, meanwhile, are often divided by the Madonna–Whore Dichotomy – the perception that all women are either 'good', chaste, pure Madonnas or 'bad', promiscuous, seductive whores. Spears' ability to straddle both those classifications led to a unique kind of confusion, compulsion and controversy for audiences and journalists alike, shared by few, if any, of her contemporaries. Joe Jonas's ability to move beyond that moment in his career illustrates one of the great hypocrisies between the way men and women's sexual appetites and expectations are treated. It also vividly demonstrates how vicious the treatment of Spears was on this most personal of subjects.

The backlash of fear-stoked AIDS hysteria may have been one of the factors leading to the marketable wave of abstinence that first elevated and then crucified Britney. Yet this has not stopped Spears from generously contributing to several HIV charities, including the Elton John AIDS Foundation. Fittingly, one of the organisation's main goals is to eliminate stigma and discrimination. Britney herself has been a victim of both.

PIECE 8

Slave 4 Peta

In July 2001, Britney Spears recorded what would become one of her signature songs. Written by the brilliant production duo the Neptunes (Chad Hugo and Pharrell Williams), 'I'm a Slave 4 U' was the first single from Spears' third self-titled album and a sultry declaration of breaking free from her teen image. Though the song was originally intended for Janet Jackson's *All for You* LP, Spears made it completely her own and clearly related to the lyrics, which she said were 'about me just wanting to go out and forget who I am and dance and have a good time. That's kinda where I am right now. I love working, but, at the same time, I love having a good time.'[88] The track's grunting, panting and moaning vocalisations had reviewers drawing likenesses between 'I'm a Slave 4 U' and 1982's 'Nasty Girl' by Prince protégées Vanity 6 – an apt comparison since the latter's lyrics ('Think I'm a nasty girl? / Tonight I'm livin' in a fantasy') are a verbal illustration of the look and feel Spears was striking in her 2001 outing.[89] With Spears scheduled to premiere her newest work at September's VMAs in New York, there was no better opportunity to promote visibility and awareness of the singer's revamped aesthetic and musical style.

On the night of the big performance, the first camera shot is of a darkened, steamy stage. As the stuttering opening beats of 'I'm a Slave 4 U' begin emanating, a set of jungle wildlife, hanging vines, misty fog and writhing dancers in war paint and loincloths become visible on stage. Cameras then pan to Britney – her skin slick and shiny, her body packed into a green bikini with scarves hanging from the waist – posing inside a cage with a tiger. Upon emerging, Spears shimmies through the song, throwing in plenty of belly-dancing-inspired moves taught to her by Puerto Rican choreographer and ex-wife of Prince, Mayte Garcia. Britney looks powerful and in control, despite the track's lyrics proclaiming the opposite message. This idea of strength and dominance is further underscored when, just over halfway through the performance, Britney picks up a live albino Burmese python named Banana and spends almost a full minute gyrating around the stage with the animal wrapped around her shoulders. It is a literal show of physical brawn and bravery displayed by Spears for the whole world to see.

Though over in less than five minutes, the impact of Britney's routine was massive. The production was so well received that the snake got its own Tumblr account and Madame Tussauds immortalised the singer's VMAs look as a waxwork for one of their museums.

Not everyone was celebrating Britney's triumph, though. Officials at People for the Ethical Treatment of Animals (PETA) did not see it as an iconic event in pop history. The organisation had already contacted the Spears camp before the VMAs asking them to 'refrain from using live cheetahs during the debut performance', which the original version of the act had envisioned. Dan Mathews, then-PETA director of campaigns, personally wrote a letter to Britney:

> We greatly appreciate the fashion statement you so often make by wearing animal-friendly pleather. We're writing today in the hope that you'll open your heart to the plight of captive 'wild' animals caged and forced to tolerate bright lights, crowds and frightening levels of noise. Please consider that cheetahs are shy, solitary animals who, in their natural habitat, would have a home range of up to 1,500 square kilometres. To display them in cages in front of thousands of people with loud music would be cruel.

This specific request was clearly taken on board as cheetahs were absent from the MTV extravaganza. However, PETA did not want *any* animals featured, with spokeswoman Jenny Wood saying, 'We did hear from [Britney's] people and she's most likely not going to have cheetahs on stage . . . But she may have other animals and we're trying to convince them not to have any animals at all.'[90] The campaigners were reportedly especially 'outraged' by the snake being a key element in the show.[91]

Britney was not the first pop icon to come under fire from PETA, though. Janet Jackson had previously attracted the organisation's attention when they became aware that she wanted to use an animal as part of her live tour performance of 'Black Cat'. 'When Janet Jackson was planning to use a black panther onstage during her concert tour, we sent her information about inhumane training of wild cats and pointed out that the noise and the lights would be very stressful to live animals,' Wood recalled. The group were successful in their appeal to Jackson, who 'agreed not to have live animals on stage'.[92]

Like Jackson, Britney responded by telling PETA she would 'drop the act' that included animals.[93] Spears even went one step further and agreed to star in the activists' best-known campaign: the long-running 'I'd rather go naked than wear fur' series, which featured celebrities posing in 'various states of undress'.[94] By 2001, the cause had already called upon pop culture's elite, ranging from *Baywatch* babe Pamela Anderson to punk-rock icons the Go-Go's and even basketball bad boy Dennis Rodman, so Britney (who had already fronted numerous sponsorships and advertisements herself) seemed like the ideal cover girl.

However, all the good will forged after the VMAs seemed to be forgotten by 2008 when Spears released her sixth studio album, *Circus*. PETA took issue not only with the name of the LP, but also with the music video for the title track, which once again featured animals – this time, lions and elephants. PETA director Debbie Leahy was not impressed, saying in a statement, 'Britney may think her life is a circus, but, for the animals who are whipped, chained and beaten to perform under the real big top, the cruelty is very real . . . She may be headed for a comeback, but, when it comes to animals, she still can't get her act together.'[95]

Since then, controversy between PETA and Spears has settled down. With Britney under a conservatorship, it has been rare – if not impossible – for her to make any statements directly to the press or any other organisation. However, in 2020, the issue of using live animals in Britney performances was brought back into the spotlight by the Netflix show *Tiger King*. A true-crime documentary series, *Tiger King* is centred around a zoo run by the eccentric Joseph Allen Maldonado-Passage, known professionally as Joe Exotic. Much of the story revolves around conflict between Exotic and other big-cat owners and conservationists, specifically Carole Baskin, CEO of Big Cat Rescue. *Tiger King* became an immediate cultural phenomenon upon its release, with more than 34.3 million people watching the show within the first ten days of it being available.

In what may be one of the weirdest sociological Venn diagrams of the past decade, an intersecting group of die-hard Britney fans and *Tiger King* viewers spotted a familiar face among Exotic's colleagues: Bhagavan 'Doc' Antle. Eagle-eyed observers recognised Antle from an appearance he had made almost twenty years before – as the tiger handler in the cage with Spears at the start of her 'I'm a Slave 4 U' VMAs performance. At the time, he was a reputable animal expert and had been brought in to advise on films such as *Dr Dolittle* and *Ace Ventura: Pet Detective*, making him a trusted figure in the entertainment industry, regardless of PETA's objections.

The *Tiger King*/Spears interrelation, though tenuous, is hard not to love. Antle is barely visible during the 2001 performance – yes, he is present on stage, but he is also dressed entirely in black so as not to be memorable. Even after repeated viewings of the Britney clip, one is hard-pressed to reach an immediate 'IT'S A MATCH!' moment, making it that much more of a head-scratcher as to how discerning fans spotted the animal trainer. What is undeniable is that it was the presence of Britney's co-star Banana the python that set the performance apart and made it an instant classic. Without Banana, 'I'm a Slave 4 U' would have just been another superficial MTV number – fun to watch, but almost instantly forgotten. Banana made Britney seem tough, sassy and exotic, providing another dimension to not only the song itself, but also the Britney persona. If PETA had won and the show had been Banana-less, it is doubtful that 'I'm a Slave 4 U' would have had such a profound impact on Britney's career or enjoyed such extended staying power as a seminal pop event.

PIECE 9

Not Quite John Hughes

Flipping through channels and stumbling upon the 1987 Andrew McCarthy film *Mannequin* at first feels like hitting the lazy-day jackpot. For those unfamiliar with this late-twentieth-century period piece, the plot revolves around a department store window dresser who falls in love with a mannequin that comes to life. Of course, she only becomes animated when alone with the hapless McCarthy. Just seeing the title of the film amid the list of other viewing options provides the same momentary feeling of nostalgic comfort found when hearing a song from your prom. Yet to revisit a film from childhood is a dangerous opiate to tamper with. What was once wildly funny, well scripted and inexplicably relatable to a fourteen-year-old moviegoer is now appallingly lame, confusing and corny to a more cultured adult palate. *Mannequin* demands the viewer to accept and even cheer for McCarthy's desire to get horizontal with a plastic dummy as, of course, a 'perfect woman is one who only comes to life when given permission to do so'.[96] Like high-school crushes, some things are better left in the past.

Therefore, one might be wary that Britney's main foray into big-screen glory could fall into this no-go abyss, with even the most hardcore Spears fans possibly pausing before diving back into 2002's *Crossroads* (especially as both films happen to star Kim Cattrall). For the uninitiated: the movie revolves around three childhood friends reuniting after high-school graduation and taking an unplanned road trip to California – obviously with a hot, hunky, misunderstood tattooed musician driving them in a classic convertible car. Life lessons are learned, searching conversations are had, and it all wraps up in a big rock concert at the end.

But, beyond the glittery make-up, low-rise jeans and midriff-baring free-for-all, *Crossroads* tackles more taboo topics in its 94-minute runtime than most television dramas cover during an entire series. There is date rape, parental abandonment, child abuse and body image, not to mention some race and class issues thrown in for good measure, rounding out the list of struggles commonly faced by teen girls. Of course, the cast all look gorgeous in their turn-of-the-millennium outfits as they discuss and confront said issues. However, the fact that these topics are even on the table in such a no-nonsense, up-front, non-apologetic way raises *Crossroads* far above the average 'chick flick' that it could easily have ended up being.

When *Crossroads* was released, there was still a heavy stench in the air from Mariah Carey's *Glitter*, which had come out the year before. The film had cost $22 million to make, but tanked at the box office, taking in just $5 million during its theatrical run. Carey blamed the 9/11 terrorist attack for this horrible performance, rather than poor acting or a bad storyline – two elements that many critics pointed to as *possibly* being the bigger issues with the movie.

Crossroads, in comparison, got a measly budget of $12 million (at a time when the average film cost around $55 million to make) and was on a three-month shooting schedule. The finished product was tested on young female audiences who 'scored the film off the charts', reacting with numbers that distributor Paramount had 'never seen before'.[97] This could be partially attributed to the women behind the camera: director Tamara Davis and screenwriter Shonda Rhimes. Davis was already a powerhouse in her own right when she joined the *Crossroads* project, having made a name for herself in the music video world working with bands like Sonic Youth and Black Flag. Rhimes, meanwhile, would go on to become one of Hollywood's most sought-after television talents, most revered for her international hit show *Grey's Anatomy*. The combination of the two women worked: *Crossroads* made $14 million during its opening weekend, going on to bring in a total of $61 million globally. The film certainly resonated with the intended audience – but not the reviewers.

Critics universally panned the film, failing to see beyond the female-led cast, slumber-party aesthetic and admittedly sugar-coated themes of friendship and first love. This movie was not made by, for or about adult men; it was centred around teenage girls – a fact that seemed lost on almost every authority who saw the film. 'A movie so pathetically lame that hopefully even Spears' most ardent young fans will give this stinker a big thumbs down,' said the *New York Post*.[98] 'Go see *Crossroads* if you want to hear Britney sing or see her wear next-to-nothing. But, otherwise, avoid this train wreck at all costs,' echoed the *Baltimore Sun*.[99] 'Everything she (Spears) does seems diluted and second-hand and is never transformed into something original or indelibly self-expressive,' stabbed the *New Yorker*.[100] Only Roger Ebert, in his albeit overall negative review, seemed to grasp *Crossroads* at all, stating, 'I went to *Crossroads* expecting a glitzy bimbofest and got the bimbos but not the fest. Britney Spears' feature debut is curiously low-key and even sad.'[101]

Crossroads is far from perfect. It does not reach the glorified heights of the John Hughes gold standard of teen fare seen in the exhalated trifecta of *Pretty in Pink*, *The Breakfast Club* and *Sixteen Candles*, though even these beloved films have received more recent criticism for some of the unsavoury themes used for comedic effect. (Indeed, Hughes' muse, Molly Ringwald, has openly discussed her discomfort when watching the movies with her daughter.) Similarly, *Crossroads* has its issues. There are bad tattoos. There is blatant product placement. There are many unexplained situations. How do they finance the entire trip? How does Britney go from singing in her undies in her bedroom to busting out an entire choreographed routine on stage at a karaoke competition to raise money? How come everyone always looks so cute and refreshed on this trip even though they are sharing rooms, carting themselves across the country and living on crisps? Like an out-of-place note at a jazz concert, these things must be overlooked and filtered out to appreciate the highs of female bonding and empowerment that are implicitly at the core of this film, as well as the message that a woman can be smart, beautiful and have her own mind. The main protagonist, Britney, chooses herself over a boy or her father's expectations – a rare conclusion, especially in the teen genre.

So, if your lazy remote-flicking leads you to happen upon *Crossroads*, don't be surprised if the film actually stands up to the passage of time and an adult perspective. If anything, even the most ardent Britney hater might begrudgingly respect that, of all the possible scripts Spears could have taken at the time, she went for one that had bite and brought to light some of the darkest parts of being a girl. Sure, there is plenty of fluff and puff, but there is also plenty of sadness and depth that feels unexpected in a teen movie starring the world's biggest pop star.

The same cannot be said for *Mannequin*.

PIECE 10

Britney v. Christina

From the start of her professional career, Christina Aguilera quickly became known for her astounding vocal range – a trait that became obvious the moment she auditioned for the *Mickey Mouse Club*. As her solo aspirations began to take off in early adulthood, Aguilera was given songs that showcased her talent, with high crescendos and demanding Mariah Carey-esque bridges that most other performers would find impossible to pull off. In contrast, many of Britney Spears' cuts sounded like autotune had been generously applied to the final mix. Since being introduced to the marketplace in 1997, autotune has been used by music producers 'to tighten up slight pitch imperfections in a pre-recorded track' and 'fix' a poor vocal performance.[102] The use of autotune on a Spears track, some critics argued, positioned the singer as being less gifted and less authentic than Aguilera. In this equation, Christina was better; Britney, on the other hand, needed studio magic to make her sound palatable. Indeed, Aguilera, who wanted to be considered for her natural abilities, tried to separate her brand from Britney's as much as possible. In 2012, the singer found herself working with '. . . Baby One More Time' creator Max Martin. 'Max is legendary in the business,' Aguilera commented. 'He's known about me, but we haven't crossed paths.' She continued, 'When I came in, you heard his name with Backstreet Boys, NSYNC, Britney Spears – those records were the kind I wanted to stray apart from.'[103]

Yet, despite how much she tried to distance herself from Spears, the two were always intertwined, with Britney usually coming out on top. Though 'being real' has historically been valued as a positive characteristic, it proved not to matter in the case of Aguilera. Sales figures, YouTube views, music streams and media coverage have all been dominated by Spears – a slap in the face for the purported 'actual' talent.

Christina's debut album – the self-titled *Christina Aguilera* – was released just seven months after Spears' . . . *Baby One More Time*. The cover is a close-up of a blonde, pouty Aguilera in a white lace shirt. While the artwork on Spears' first record is toothache-worthy in its sweetness, Aguilera's stare down the camera is comparatively more challenging than seductive or welcoming. Though she may have been trying to portray herself as a more contemporary, well-rounded vocalist, everything had changed in the short timeframe between Britney's debut appearing in the pop charts and Aguilera's own release. Spears had heralded a new dawn of young, female, commercially relevant, money-making singers. Everyone who came after her, even Christina, could only try – and fail – to catch up. With Spears having successfully cornered the girl-next-door market in 1999, Aguilera had to differentiate herself another way – by being the risqué foil to Spears' apparent innocence.

The 'naughty' Christina – or 'Xtina', as she christened herself for her second release, *Stripped* – was not fond of clothes. The album's cover features a topless Aguilera, long blonde hair barely covering her breasts and tight-fitting trousers barely covering her pubic region. The music video for lead track 'Dirrty' was controversial when it dropped as it featured the singer wearing a bikini and leather chaps, with heavily kohled eyes, long black hair extensions, a nose piercing and a lip ring completing the look. It is unclear now why this video was so shocking or how it positioned Aguilera as more provocative than Spears. Britney had already emerged as not that innocent with 'I'm a Slave 4 U', but critics had heralded that track a triumph, with the *NME* even going so far as to proclaim, 'The song is funk the way God intended – hypnotic, insistent, mysterious, suggestive . . . If Prince was a nineteen-year-old former Disney Club host and virgin, he'd be proud to create such a record.'

'Dirrty' came out in 2002 – a full year after Britney had performed 'I'm a Slave 4 U' at the VMAs and almost two years after she had stripped to a nude ensemble at the same awards show during a medley of the Rolling Stones' 'Satisfaction' and 'Oops! . . . I Did It Again'. Perhaps Christina's 'face hardware', dark underlayer of hair and collaboration with hip-hop royalty Redman were all too much for the sensibilities of the chart audience, who were still reeling in the wake of Britney's transformation from schoolgirl to sexy vamp. Unlike Spears' virgin/seductress duality, Aguilera was unambiguous; her song lyrics, appearance and videos were unapologetically bad-ass.

Though she may be almost naked, Aguilera radiates power throughout the 'Dirrty' video. The clip kicks off with the singer sat astride a motorcycle before going into a ring to box another contender. These scenes are intercut with shots of Xtina singing to the camera in front of a crowd of sweaty, shirtless men. The message is that Christina is equal to – if not better than – the males; she is the one in control.

But not everyone saw Xtina's new image this way. *Time* magazine lambasted Aguilera, declaring that she looked as though 'she had arrived direct from an intergalactic hooker convention'.[104] In an article titled 'Who's Trashier? Christina Aguilera vs Britney Spears In Their Prime', writer Brit Tobi further analyses Aguilera's radical makeover between her first LP and *Stripped*: 'It all started with her baring it all for the album [cover], but then Xtina amped it up several notches in her music videos and appearances . . . Christina's hair and spray tan could have won her a walk-on performance on *Jersey Shore*!' The piece goes on to use each girl's origins as another point of opposition: 'With roots firmly planted in the deep south, Britney has often been slapped with the label of "dumb, girl-next-door" type due to her girlish southern belle style.'[105] A 1999 article in *The Guardian* also made this point, contending that Aguilera's image was 'naughtier' than 'Britney's corn-fed, Midwest, wholesome look'. The narrative being created was that New York-born Christina, with her Ecuadorian father, had a more diverse – read: 'Dirrty' – upbringing than Bible Belt-reared Spears.

The supposed 'feud' between the two singers really began after Spears and Justin Timberlake separated in 2002. Not long after the break-up, Aguilera joined forces with the newly single Justin for a co-headlining concert series coined the Justified & Stripped Tour. This caused dismay among some Britney fans, who saw it as yet another point of contention between the two female artists. (The idea of a love triangle between the three stars actually dated back to their Mouseketeer days, with Christina herself telling *Late Late Show* host James Corden that, even as kids, 'Timberlake had swag'.[106]) The pair spending time together on tour fuelled rumours of a short-lived fling after Timberlake's relationship with Spears ended, adding yet another notch to Aguilera's 'bad girl' reputation.

Companies took advantage of the seeming rift between the young women. In 2000, cola brand Pepsi signed Spears, proclaiming that 'youthful, inventive, optimistic and fun-loving' Britney was 'on the cutting edge of contemporary popular entertainment' and was thus 'the ultimate fit with the Pepsi brand'.[107] It was a 'relationship' that Pepsi's senior vice president of strategy and marketing claimed would 'resonate in every corner of the market'. Though the exact details were not shared publicly, it was speculated that Pepsi paid at least $50 million to seal the deal with Spears.

However, it was Aguilera who came out on top when she partnered with Coke a year later for a 2001 campaign. After the premiere of Spears' Pepsi ads, it also emerged in the press that the singer had 'demanded her tour dressing room be stocked with Coke', displaying a lack of allegiance to the very brand she was advertising.[108] This was a massive win for Aguilera. Indeed, Coke spokesman Mart Martin made sure to highlight this as another point of authenticity for Christina over Pepsi-paid, Coke-swilling Britney. Christina, he espoused, was 'a genuine talent' *and* 'a lifelong Coca-Cola drinker'. Then, taking another swipe at autotuned Spears, he continued, 'Coke has always been about being real and we believe Christina's real, too.'[109]

However, it wasn't a fight over Timberlake or soft drinks that fully ignited the feud between Britney and Christina; it was actually MTV's editing. In the now-infamous 2003 VMAs performance, a blonde Britney graces the stage, dressed in a white wedding gown, singing the Madonna classic 'Like a Virgin'. A raven-tressed Aguilera, also in frothy nuptial attire, joins Spears for the next part of the song. It's significant that dark-haired Aguilera is placed *after* Britney, literally playing second fiddle to her fair-haired counterpart. A tuxedo-wearing Madonna arrives soon after, accompanying the duo on the rest of the track. The song then morphs into Madge's newest single, 'Hollywood', and the three performers execute a choreographed dance routine together. When the tune reaches a crescendo, Madonna turns to Spears and lays a lingering smooch on the young star's lips. The camera then cuts away to capture audience member Timberlake's annoyed reaction to the unexpected act, thus missing the moment when Aguilera and Madonna also kiss. Aguilera later revealed that this made her feel disrespected and pushed aside since it was deemed more important to focus on Britney – be that her actual kiss or its impact on her ex-boyfriend – than to showcase Aguilera.

It is worth noting, however, that neither Britney nor Christina was originally in the frame for the Madge smooch; it was meant to be Jennifer Lopez. Only when Jenny from the Block passed on the appearance did the two pop princesses step in. The kiss was a watershed moment in many ways: besides Madonna passing the torch (via her tongue) to the younger performers, it also opened the door for same-sex relationships and romantic interactions to be shown more widely in mainstream popular culture. 'The kiss wasn't about just Xtina or just Britney or Madonna – it was about a single, fiery, significant moment, what it meant for queer visibility and the ways in which it changed media,' wrote Jill Gutowitz on the intomore.com website. She continued:

> Sure, it was meant to be gratuitous and provocative and, yes, lesbianism shouldn't be used to cater to the male gaze, nor should it be seen as shocking or an aberration, but it was also *awesome* for queer women to watch . . . fifteen years ago, queer visibility in TV wasn't just scant, it was nearly invisible . . . So, when Britney, Madonna and Christina collided on stage, on *live* TV – it was memorable. And it was *hot*. Problematic undertones aside, it actually blazed the trail for future sexy gay TV moments.[110]

Despite the shared exposure, Aguilera would go on to criticise Spears' actions leading up to the VMAs, saying that Britney had exhibited 'strange behaviour' during their rehearsals for the gala. 'Every time I tried to start a conversation with her – well, let's just say she seemed nervous the whole time, someone who desperately needs guidance,' Christina claimed.[111] In a rare public reaction, Britney responded to Aguilera's assertions with the comment, 'A lost girl? I think it's probably the other way around. I can't believe she said that about me.'[112]

The formerly simmering battle royale between the two powerhouses had now reached boiling point. In a 2004 *Us Weekly* interview, Aguilera voiced her disgust at Spears having purchased her own diamond upon getting engaged to Kevin Federline: 'I can't believe that girl bought her own engagement ring! I've seen it up close. It looks like she got it on QVC.' Further shade was later thrown by Xtina when she said of Spears' headline-grabbing antics, 'She's not trailer trash, but she sure acts that way.'[113]

However, the dispute seems to have been left in the '00s. When asked more recently about the feud, Aguilera commented, 'We were very close and our paths have always crossed and, interestingly, they will continue to cross.' This was certainly the case in 2012 when it was announced that Spears would be a judge on Simon Cowell's US talent competition *The X Factor*. Britney's debut was scheduled to run just two days after the start of Aguilera's third season judging rival series *The Voice*. The old comparisons were soon resurrected – this time, by the media and the producers of the respective shows. When *The Voice* executives became aware of the date of Spears' premiere, they announced that they would be running a special edition of their Aguilera-starring show in the same time slot as Cowell's series launch of Britney. Taking full advantage of the historic feud, Cowell slammed *The Voice* and

Aguilera with a statement suggesting that 'Christina – who has been a bit of a rival – isn't allowing Britney to have a night of her own'.[114] (Despite his apparent advocacy for Spears, Cowell later publicly criticised her performance on *The X Factor*, claiming that he 'booked someone who couldn't talk, which is a bit of a problem when you want someone to judge'.[115]) Aguilera, however, did not fall for Cowell's bait, but instead responded with support and grace towards the arrival of Spears on the reality television scene. She referred to Spears as 'a pro' who would 'give great advice' to aspiring entertainers, adding, 'I don't know the formats of other shows, I only know the show that I'm on, but I welcome these very talented women.' Though Cowell and company seemed keen to rekindle old clashes, Christina appeared to have turned a page. 'I'm not down with [pitting women against women] at this point of my life,' she said. 'I have no patience for it, so I'm like, "The more the merrier." It's a fun thing to be a part of and I think she'll have fun with it.'[116]

This olive-branch offering from Aguilera was extended again during a 2018 appearance on the American talk show *Jimmy Kimmel Live*. Aguilera told the host how she felt social media had provided celebrities with more power to communicate between themselves instead of relying on the press and media. 'When I was coming up, it was very obvious, you know? Me and Britney were definitely – there was the Britney/Christina considered rivalry thing,' Aguilera confided. 'Back in the day, whenever people were comparing me to other artists, I would have just loved to squash it before having an interview,' Aguilera continued. 'You do an interview and, back then, it was just like the media was the storyteller for you, rather than being like, "This is what it is, here's a picture of us right now hanging out in our pyjamas eating popcorn," or whatever.' She concluded the interview by saying, 'If we had social media back then, we would have probably done a song together and just squashed it.'[117]

The tragedy of the Britney-versus-Christina controversy was not only the personal strife it brought to two young women who could have been each other's best support system, but also how female rivalry was played out in the media for a generation of girls to witness. It became part of the pop narrative to tear down your contemporaries, not raise them up – once again at odds with the 'girl power' motto stamped on T-shirts and pencil cases at the time. While Britney and Christina themselves have moved on, there is still a public fascination with a rift that may have been a media creation in the first place; a rupture that never actually existed until the press saw an opportunity to sell papers and products while exploiting the insecurities of their newest pop stars.

PIECE 11

A Word from Our Sponsor

From early advertisements for cameras and trainers to more recent (and often blatant) product placement in her music videos, Britney Spears has been the queen of sponsorships and endorsement deals since she first rose to global fame. The late '90s and early '00s saw Spears representing a myriad of different products: some were a match made in tween demographic heaven; others were a stretch for even the most devoted fan to get behind. A sample of Britney-backed goods from the turn of the century acts as a time capsule for how the singer was marketed – and often exploited – across various commercial platforms.

YEAR: 1999
BRAND: Polaroid
PRODUCT: i-Zone
BRITNEY'S ROLE: Spokesperson

For the uninitiated, the i-Zone was the last hit product made by Polaroid before the camera corporation went bankrupt. The size of a large Toblerone chocolate bar, the i-Zone instantly printed out tiny 1.5-inch-long pictures, each with a sticker adhesive on the back, making them perfect to plaster on school lockers. Britney was the perfect spokesperson for the product as it was aimed at tweens and teens. The print ads featured a fresh-faced Spears, clothed in a pink long-sleeved top and trousers, taking a selfie and flashing a massive grin. The accompanying copy proclaimed, 'The real Britney in five photos or less.' The small type read: 'Tell us where you'd put a Polaroid i-Zone instant mini-photo sticker of Britney Spears and you could win a trip to meet Britney before her concert in West Palm Beach on September 10.' Copies of this commercial, once appearing in magazines across the US, can now be found online for purchase. For the completist Britney fan, a 'RARE AUTHENTIC PROMO POSTER' of this late-'90s relic has a going rate of $250 on eBay at the time of writing.

YEAR: 1999
BRAND: Skechers
PRODUCT: Skechers Energy
BRITNEY'S ROLE: Spokesperson

Britney was the face of this massively chunky trainer that helped launch the Skechers brand. Spears continued to work with the shoe company until 2002 when things hit a turbulent patch. A deal to collaborate on a Britney-branded roller skate, Skechers 4 Wheelers, did not meet up to the singer's expectations, leading her to eventually sue the company for $1.5 million. All must have been forgotten by 2019, though, as the footwear behemoths put out a commemorative Skechers Energy in three new colourways to celebrate twenty years of their launch with the pop princess.

YEAR: 2000
BRAND: Clairol
PRODUCT: Herbal Essence
BRITNEY'S ROLE: Hair washer

Before Britney signed up to be the new – and youngest ever – face of Clairol's Herbal Essence, the shampoo had been aimed primarily at the thirty-to-forty-something age group, with *Seinfeld* star Julia Louis-Dreyfus and *Will & Grace*'s Debra Messing fronting previous campaigns. Though the exclusive CD with an unreleased Britney track and interview may now be a collectible, arguably the best part of the sponsorship deal was the jingle, which had Britney crooning to the tonsorially curious about her 'urge to . . . 'errrrrbal.'

YEAR: 2000
BRAND: Got Milk?
PRODUCT: Milk
BRITNEY'S ROLE: Milk chugger

Started in 1995 as a bid to encourage milk consumption, the highly successful Got Milk? campaign was a rite of passage for celebrities in the '00s, signalling official A-list status. Everyone from *Friends* stars Jennifer Aniston and Lisa Kudrow (1995) to Aerosmith rocker Steve Tyler (2006) posed with a milk moustache for the Milk Processor Education Program ads. Britney was the 100th celebrity to represent the cause, gracing the organisation with two different looks for her turn as frontwoman in 2000. One ad shows a 1950s-styled Britney, complete with ballet flats, pedal pushers and a knotted shirt. The other image is rocker Britney, sporting low-cut leather-studded trousers and a midriff-bearing top. A cute little girl stands next to her in a golden ballerina outfit, suggesting a before-and-after motif. The accompanying verbiage encouraged viewers to 'grow up' – a directive to small children everywhere to gulp cow juice religiously if they wanted to go from enchanting kid to hard-core pop star.

YEAR: 2000
BRAND: Shades of Britney
PRODUCT: Sunglasses
BRITNEY'S ROLE: Namesake

For a moment at the start of the new millennium, Britney had her own sunglasses line brilliantly called 'Shades of Britney'. While the name alone should be enough to resurrect this brand, the lightly tinted purple lenses may give you pause before seeking them out on Etsy for sun protection. It is unclear what the singer's exact role was with Shades of Britney, besides giving them a kick-ass moniker.

A WORD FROM OUR SPONSOR

YEAR: 2002
BRAND: PlayStation
PRODUCT: *Britney's Dance Beat*
BRITNEY'S ROLE: Muse

At first glance, *Britney's Dance Beat* PlayStation game appears to be a Spears spin on the global phenomenon of 1998's *Dance Dance Revolution* – a game in which players tried to keep up with the on-screen choreography. The actual description does not provide any further illumination, simply stating, 'Singer Britney Spears is looking for backup dancers for her next world tour and she wants you to audition. Show Britney your hottest moves by keeping to the beat of her most popular songs, including "Oops! . . . I Did It Again" and "I'm a Slave 4 U".' Though the game required no actual busting of moves, it has scored a respectable 4.5 out of 5 stars on Amazon, where the avid Britney fan can now pick up a pre-loved copy for less than a fiver.

YEAR: 2003
BRAND: Sbarro
PRODUCT: LidRock
BRITNEY'S ROLE: Music provider

This brilliant yet mostly forgotten Britney campaign was a deal with Italian fast-food chain Sbarro. To promote *In the Zone*, two different Britney CDs were tucked inside the lids of large paper cups available exclusively at Sbarro eateries just before the full album was released. The company producing this innovative mash-up of rock and refreshment was called LidRock and saw the idea as offering great value to all stakeholders. Like other once-disposable Britney items, an unused LidRock (with paper Pepsi cup still attached) now has a starting price of $22.99 on auction sites – significantly higher than its original $2.99 price point (which also included a drink).

PIECE 12

Like a Prayer

Britney Spears was born and raised in an area of the US often referred to as the 'Bible Belt' – a term purportedly first used in 1924 by journalist H. L. Mencken in an article for the *Chicago Daily Tribune*. With the region's attendance at Christian churches considerably surpassing the national average, the Bible Belt has historically comprised a high percentage of residents who describe themselves as having 'conservative Protestant values'.[118] As a child, Spears was christened a Southern Baptist – the largest Protestant denomination in the US and a church that tends to be much more right-leaning in its beliefs than the general American public. In a recent poll, 66 per cent of Southern Baptists thought that abortion should be illegal in most or all cases, 61 per cent believed that the Bible should be taken literally, and 63 per cent said that 'homosexuality should be discouraged by society'.[119] These paradigms must have been drilled into the young Britney as key doctrines to live by. They also helped to create the first version of Spears that the public met – the innocent, sweet-natured Christian girl with good old-fashioned southern values.

However, fame brought new experiences and new people into Britney's orbit; it also led to feelings of isolation and loneliness when the overly avid fans and hordes of photographers made her a prisoner in her own home or hotel. Looking for answers, Spears reportedly turned to Neale Donald Walsch's best-selling *Conversations with God* for guidance. *Book 1* of the ten-edition series spent 137 weeks on the *New York Times* best-seller list after its 1995 release, making it almost as omnipresent as the Heavenly Father himself. In an interview with Larry King in 2000, Walsch revealed that inspiration for the tomes came during a particularly difficult time in his life. Feeling hopeless, he wrote a letter to God asking why things were so hard for him. The author claimed that, after rounding off his laundry list of complaints, he heard a voice over his shoulder ask, 'Do you really want an answer to all these questions or are you just venting?'[120] When he turned to see who had spoken, he found that he was alone. Immediately, Walsch claimed, answers to all of his queries began to fill his head. He decided to write them down and his notes eventually became the first book of the series.

Britney, like many other Americans, bought Walsch's works and saw them as a guide, even copying and memorising passages that connected with her. She was looking for answers of her own and was also known to see astrologists and psychics as part of her quest for personal enlightenment. Spears' Southern Baptist upbringing had not prepared her for the roller coaster of fame, adulation and pressure on which she now found herself and she soon began to doubt her faith. However, 'the more she openly questioned spirituality and religion, the more mixed messages and confusion she found'. She was particularly interested in figuring out why she had been chosen to be a star, allegedly asking those around her, 'Why is this happening to me? There must be a reason? What does it all mean?'[121] Britney wanted comfort and reassurance, looking for greater understanding in everything and everyone around her. In the 2013 documentary *I Am Britney Jean*, Spears confided, 'I believe there's definitely other forces out there other than angels, guardians, protectors. I definitely believe in heaven. I know there is a place beyond our wildest dreams.'[122]

There was one entity Britney found solace in, though: her childhood idol Madonna. In the absence of a clear path forward, the Material Girl perfectly filled Britney's devotional void. In postmodern capitalistic economies, this has become a normalised and accepted mode of worship, not just something particular to Spears. Daniel Boorstin perfectly summarised this phenomenon in his 1962 book, *The Image: A Guide to Pseudo-Events in America*, arguing how 'we still try to make our celebrities stand in for the heroes we no longer have or for those who have been pushed out of our view'. This was the exact situation a lost Spears found herself in. 'We imitate them as if they were cast in the mould of greatness. Yet the celebrity is usually nothing greater than a more-publicised version of us. In imitating him, in trying to dress like him, talk like him, look like him, we are simply imitating ourselves.'[123] Madonna became this almost more-than-human example for Spears as the young performer looked for meaning.

From her pre-performance soundtrack to the religion she followed, Britney became a Madonna devotee. An hour before showtime, she would put on either 1998's *Ray of Light* or 2000's *Music*. The Madonna albums could be heard blasting from her dressing room, with Britney's favourite track rumoured to be 'What It Feels Like for a Girl'. In a direct imitation of Madonna (as seen in the 1991 fly-on-the-wall documentary *Truth or Dare*), Britney would gather her entire posse of dancers, assistants and assorted crew members in a circle, say a prayer and give a last-minute pep talk before they took to the stage.

The two singers eventually met at a Madonna concert in Philadelphia. Before coming face to face with her idol, Britney talked with Lola, Madonna's eldest daughter. Spears recalled the interaction as an example of history repeating: while she was worshipping Madge, Lola was looking up to Britney. In a 2001 interview, Spears said that the child admitted to having all of Britney's 'Barbies' – a reference to the twenty-eight Britney dolls manufactured by Play Along Toys. Lola then asked Spears if she wanted to meet her mum. At that point, Britney felt the same nervous giddiness most people would have upon being confronted with their heroine. 'When I meet people, I am usually, you know, "Hi, what's up?"' Spears commented. 'But I was so nervous meeting her. I'm like, "OH MY GOD. I don't know what to say." So I walked in and I was like, "I feel like I should hug you." Like, EW, why did I say that?'[124]

Madonna and Britney would unite again for the much-publicised three-way kiss with Christina Aguilera at the 2003 VMAs. It was an event that meant much more to Spears than simply capturing the reaction shot of ex-boyfriend Justin Timberlake or signalling for more equal LGBTQ+ representation across the media. For Britney, it was the start of a true relationship as equals with her ultimate paragon. After the VMAs, according to Vanessa Grigoriadis's 2008 *Rolling Stone* exposé, Britney decided that she and Madonna were 'soul mates'. When asked about the elder star, Britney effused, 'Maybe she was my husband in another life.' An ex-manager interviewed for the article concurred, recalling, 'Britney and Madonna became friends after the performance and she started to think she was Madonna. She said, "Madonna calls her own shots, I can do that." But Madonna doesn't need to be told what to do. Britney does.'[125]

It is not surprising that it is Madonna whom Spears credits with helping her through the darkest times. 'I guess she's really taught me to stay true to myself,' Britney revealed in a 2011 interview with *Harper's Bazaar*. 'That seems like a simple thing to say, but she taught me through action, not just by saying it. There are so many people around you that have opinions, but you just have to listen to your instincts.'[126] Madonna did seem to have a genuine understanding and sympathy towards Britney following the various scandals that played out so publicly for the young woman. In 2008's *For the Record* documentary, Madonna said of Britney, 'There's a certain fragility about her and vulnerability about her that makes me feel maternal towards her. And there are aspects about her that I recognise.' However, Ms Ciccone also clearly laid out the issues specific to Britney that differed from her own experience as a singer coming of age in front of the world:

> When I first started out in my career, I was very privileged in my own life to be able to go to New York, make mistakes and have scary situations happen; to meet, make wrong decisions, choose wrong people to do things with, you know what I mean? Without the whole world, you know, putting a magnifying glass on you. And she's never had that opportunity.

In the case of Britney, 'you make a mistake, the whole world is watching, they beat up on you. Or they're not even mistakes – sometimes it's just called growing up. And a lot of it has to do with the people you surround yourself with because you are your environment.'

At the time, Madonna's guidance for Britney was to 'first and foremost' focus on 'her own spiritual growth, her own self-examination, her own growth as a human being and her relationship with her children.' If all those were to align, Madge claimed, 'then everything else will radiate off of that successfully'.[127] To help Britney along, Madonna began sharing her newfound love for Kabbalah – a belief in Jewish mysticism. For the veteran star, it was 'a genuine way of reaching out to Britney'. One especially lavish gift Madonna gave Spears was a black trunk filled with books of the Zohar – texts 'described by believers as "works of unequalled wisdom and spiritual power"'. However, there was one problem: they were all written in Hebrew. This did not pose any issues for the young star, though, who asserted that the main point was not necessarily to read the words but to 'meditate on the mystical shapes and Aramaic text'. From this, Spears contended, all spiritual aides would be gained: 'The words become clear as you meditate.'

The trunk was very important to Spears as it was both a gift from her own effigy of success and an important ethereal guide. For a significant amount of time, Britney turned her back on the Southern Baptist faith and her conservative upbringing. On her website, Britney told fans that her new religion had removed negativity from her life and certain things 'that were guiding [her] down the wrong path'.[128] She even claimed that Kabbalah gave her answers in areas where friends, family and managers had failed. In an *Elle* magazine interview, Britney confided, 'Kabbalah has helped my soul. I was brought up a Baptist . . . everything's in codes. The thing that drew me to Kabbalah is it all comes from light. This sounds so weird, I know, but . . . it all stems from light.'[129] Britney's dedication went so far as to get 'Mem Hey Shin' tattooed on her neck, which, translated from Hebrew, means, 'The power of this name brings the energy of healing at the deepest and most profound level.'[130] Spears was also spotted donning the 'believer's badge' – a piece of red string around her wrist. At her wedding to Kevin Federline in 2004, guests received a Kabbalah token as a gift from the bride.

However, Kabbalah did not satisfy Britney's long-term quest for meaning. Britney eventually had the trunk and all her other formerly precious Jewish implements removed from her house. 'She's tired of the way [Kabbalah leaders] kept hassling her for money,' a source told today.com. Britney never publicly acknowledged that it was the organisation's hunt for cash, rather than her own disinterest, that led to her abandoning the faith; if true, it must have been disheartening for the singer to once again find herself exploited for money and fame, even within the context of spiritual enlightenment. After the birth of Sean Preston, Spears wrote on her website, 'I no longer study Kabbalah . . . my baby is my religion.'[131]

Britney's break with Kabbalah reflects a larger trend happening across the US. In 2021, a Gallup survey revealed that the percentage of Americans who think of themselves as members of 'a church, synagogue or mosque' fell 'below 50 per cent'. This marks the lowest number of formal religious participants since the question was first posed to the general public in 1937. At that time, membership to a church was an astounding 73 per cent. The dramatic decline may be a result of younger Americans perceiving religious membership 'as a relic of an older generation'; however, if this trend continues, predictions are that the US 'will not have one dominant religion' in thirty years' time.[132]

Another hypothesis to explain the decreasing number of affiliates could be the changing perception of what traditional faith means. For people who grew up as digital natives, there is a value placed on personal ownership of a narrative, which has spawned a desire and a perceived ability to 'curate' pick-and-mix spirituality based on individual wants, needs and experiences. While this bespoke attitude towards faith may seem appropriate for the newer generations, the lack of a widely shared belief system has created a void that technology has looked to fill. The time a person spends engaging with digital media and virtual socialising 'has not only replaced, but arguably usurped old practices and beliefs'.[133]

For Britney, the search for significance and direction may continue because of her need to find a shared someone or something to look up to. Academics agree. 'The vacuum [of religion] can't just remain a vacuum,' academic Shadi Hamid has argued in a *Washington Post* interview. 'Americans are believers in some sense and there has to be structures of belief and belonging. The question is: what takes the place of that religious affiliation?'[134]

While Britney continues to look for answers, others may find that the singer herself actually fills the same chasm that Madonna once did for her. Indeed, as Boorstin said, 'Having manufactured our celebrities, we are tempted to believe that they are not synthetic at all, that they are somehow still God-made heroes who now abound with a marvellous modern prodigality.'[135] If Lola did in fact have 'all' twenty-eight Britney 'Barbies', then Boorstin's predictions for the future, made over sixty years ago, have come to fruition more than once.

PIECE 13

Don't You Noel That You're 'Toxic'

It was a series of lucky accidents that landed 'Toxic' – one of Britney Spears' most iconic songs – a place on her fourth studio album, *In the Zone*. From superstar rejections to a star-crossed veterinarian, the origins of 'Toxic' are almost as crazy as the wild bathroom transformation of the male passenger in the song's music video.

Cathy Dennis was already a star in her own right by 2003. In 1986, at the age of seventeen, the singer-songwriter signed to music mogul Simon Fuller's new 19 Entertainment, simultaneously inking a deal with record label Polydor. (Fuller would go on to manage the Spice Girls and be the brains behind shows like *The X Factor* and *American Idol*.) By 1991, Dennis had a number-one song on the US *Billboard* Dance Club chart with her track 'All Night Long (Touch Me)'. It wasn't long until the talented artist moved on to penning tracks for other people, including

Kylie Minogue's 2001 worldwide hit 'Can't Get You Out of My Head', which Dennis co-wrote with Rob Davis. The song sat at number one in the UK for a month, reintroduced the US to the Australian pop singer and sold over 3 million copies globally.

In 2003, Dennis was drafted in to create 'Toxic', originally with Janet Jackson in mind. The song was put together during a week-long marathon session in Sweden with writers Christian Karlsson and Pontus Winnberg (aka production duo Blood-shy & Avant) and Henrik Jonback. However, Dennis couldn't make 'Toxic' the perfect fit for the youngest Jackson sibling in just seven days. 'I'd had a meeting with Janet . . . I thought I'd have a go at writing something that would work for her,' Dennis recalled. 'Eventually, on day seven, which was the day I was flying back to England, I had run out of time.'[136]

Having missed the Jackson deadline, the song was then offered to – and rejected by – the Minogue camp. 'It wasn't written with Britney in mind because we did actually send it to another artist who turned it down,' Dennis says. 'Then it went to Britney . . . I like to think that songs finish up where they're meant to be.'[137]

Britney described the meaning of the tune in 2003, telling MTV, 'It's basically about a girl addicted to a guy. I really like "Toxic". It's an upbeat song. It's different, that's why I like it so much. This villain girl, she'll do anything to get what she wants. She goes through different obstacles.'[138]

For over a decade, the inspiration for 'Toxic' was never contemplated, leaving Britney's analysis of an obsessed protagonist willing to stop at nothing to get her man the most convincing summary of the song's meaning. However, that changed in 2014 with the arrival of a new television show on Channel 4 in the UK: *The Supervet*. Centred around the work of veterinarian Noel Fitzpatrick and his staff as they help ailing pets using cutting-edge surgery and treatments, the series made Fitzpatrick an unexpected heartthrob and best-selling author.

Super fans of *Supervet* soon realised that there was a 'Toxic' connection, though, having discovered that Fitzpatrick and Dennis once dated. (The two met when the songwriter brought her paralysed Labrador, Charlie, in for help.) When the relationship ended in 2003, heartbreak was likely fresh on Dennis's mind during her songwriting trip to Sweden. So, if the legend is to be believed, perhaps the lyrics to 'Toxic' illustrate that the mild-mannered housewives' favourite who once jumped out of his car to save a swan stuck in traffic is not only a dab hand at administering restorative tonics to all creatures great and small, but also caddishly adept at dispensing poison paradise with just a taste of his lips.

PIECE 14

The Sweet Smell of Britney

Released to coincide with her second album by the same name, Debbie Gibson's Electric Youth was marketed as 'the perfume of the young generation of the early '90s'. Described as 'a fruity floral with a sensual base of musk, woods and amber', the fragrance came in an embarrassing bottle with an atomiser that was actually a pink spring stuck into a see-through container of liquid that looked like urine. Yet somehow, with its notes of 'grapefruit', 'citrus', 'watermelon and red berries', the elixir appealed to certain people who weren't even fans of Gibson's music at the time.

While Gibson's foray into the world of scent may have been part of a promotional campaign for her album, Britney Spears has taken fragrance production to a new level, creating an unstoppable, extremely lucrative business that has grown and expanded even as her album sales have decreased. In 2013, it was reported that a bottle of Britney fragrance is sold every fifteen seconds worldwide, while it is estimated that she makes an estimated £36 million annually from her perfumes alone. As of 2021, Spears has thirty-two different fragrances in her line. To put this in perspective, hugely well-established houses like Chanel do not have more than twenty scents at one time.

According to Karen Grant, vice president and global beauty analyst for market research company the NPD Group, Spears' first endeavour – 2004's Curious – became 'by far' the number-one scent, 'not just in the celebrity category, but across the entire fragrance industry'.[139] In its first year alone, Curious netted over $100 million in sales. By 2013, one news report stated that Curious had sold 500 million bottles in just five years.[140] In units, that's five times more than the 100 million albums Spears has sold in her twenty-plus-year career. Just as Gibson's Electric Youth had sparked a teenage interest in perfume decades before, Curious brought a young consumer to the fragrance industry, taking their initial step into the world of perfume. Spears has continued her global dominance in the scent business ever since. At one point, her website claimed that the star's fragrance line accounted for an estimated 34 per cent of all fragrance sales worldwide (though this number was eventually taken down).

Experts point to several aspects that have made Spears' enterprise such a runaway success. Not surprisingly, the actual aromas of the products are rated as being 'more expensive than they are' with 'a kind of Californian brightness, lightness to them' – the sort of 'authentic, ultra-feminine, youthful fragrances' that 'teenage girls in particular . . . are drawn towards'. The packaging is also viewed as 'in line with [Britney's] overall brand and appeal', adding to the general consumer experience.[141] Unlike many perfumes that are available at high-street stores, Curious has held its own against more extravagant brands, even being shortlisted a finalist in the 'Women's Luxury' category at the Fragrance Foundation Awards (the Oscars of perfume) alongside Dior's Pure Poison, Prada's Eau de Parfum and DKNY's Be Delicious – all of which cost at least twice as much.

Spears' personal, hands-on approach to her line has had a huge impact on its success. As *InStyle*'s Rachel Syme wrote in 2018, most celebrity scents are simply 'bad'. The accepted process in the creation of a personality-fronted fragrance is for a star to describe to their business team what they want in a scent. Several competing companies then bid to win the celebrity's contract and the star often 'won't even smell the formula until it's done'. Britney, however, has been involved in her namesake products from conception to completion, according to Ron Rolleston, the executive vice president of global fragrance marketing at Revlon: 'We sat down and talked about her likes and dislikes, colours, bottle shapes, favourite scents and art that she found inspiring. Britney's love of flowers and a sensuality in scents forms the DNA of many of her fragrances.'[142] Britney's own passion for her products injects an authenticity that is lacking in other celebrity-endorsed fragrances.

The connection between celebrity and scent is not a new one (even predating Electric Youth). In 1952, when asked what she wore to bed, Marilyn Monroe coyly replied, 'Five drops of Chanel No. 5 – nothing else.'[143] Around the same time, Joan Crawford began hailing the seductive properties of Estée Lauder's Youth Dew, claiming the potion helped her snare her fourth husband, Pepsi CEO Alfred Steele. Legend has it that, while swaying together, Steele whispered in Crawford's ear, 'I can't stop dancing with you. You smell so exquisite.'[144] Leaving an alluring bouquet in one's wake continued to be important to the leading ladies of the silver screen. Several years later, Hubert de Givenchy created the scent L'Interdit for his friend Audrey Hepburn. When Givenchy asked the actress if he could sell the fragrance to the public, she supposedly replied, '*Je vous l'interdis!*' ('I forbid you!'), though she went on to be the face of the perfume's ad campaign nevertheless.

Despite all these close associations with specific fragrances, the first celebrity to officially release their own perfume was Italian seductress Sophia Loren. Launched in 1981 by Coty, the Sophia scent had notes of white floral and rose intended to capture the unique class and sophisticated elegance of the revered actress. While Loren may have been the first celebrity with her own fragrance, it was Elizabeth Taylor who laid the groundwork for Britney's perfume empire. Beyond the world of scent, the two icons share personal narratives of survival. In business, a genuine passion for their eponymous products led both to international dominance. When asked about her philosophy, Taylor answered, 'So many people place their name on products that aren't intrinsic to their soul. I think that's a little sad. I have to care about everything I do.'[145] Her acumen paid off. Like Spears, Taylor's first scent, 1988's Passion, earned her global acclaim, bringing home a Fragrance Foundation Award. But it wasn't until three years later, with the launch of White Diamonds, that Taylor became synonymous with scent.

As with Britney, by the time Taylor's perfumes hit the market, fans around the globe were very familiar with her work, love life, triumphs and challenges. People wanted to capture some of that Taylor *je ne sais quoi* for themselves. 'Elizabeth was so known for beauty and style and glamour,' said Tim Mendelson, Elizabeth Taylor's chief of staff for more than twenty years. When women put her fragrance on, 'they want to feel like they have a little bit of Elizabeth'.[146] Taylor knew the power of her brand and played into it. 'I want every woman who wears a House of Taylor fragrance to know she's beautiful, desirable and loved,' she said when asked what a perfume should do for someone.[147] At a 1987 press conference to announce her debut scent, the icon floated into the room, resplendent in a luxurious fur scarf and hat, red lips and a dark, smoky eye – the very image of fabulous decadence. 'There was so much authenticity,' Mendelson said. 'She designed [the fragrances] for herself. Elizabeth, whenever she made something or put her name on something, it had to be real.' The campaign to promote White Diamonds set Elizabeth Arden back $20 million and included a tour with Taylor across North America, as well as taking out the entire back page of *Vogue* – a costly venture at the time. The television ads underscored Taylor's unreserved glamour, showing an array of seemingly unconnected black-and-white shots, ranging from galloping horses and men gambling to Taylor herself looking stunning in a crisp gown. The opulent world created via these various marketing channels worked: by 2018, White Diamonds had made more than $1.5 billion in its 25-year history, with four bottles of the scent being sold every minute.[148]

Taylor's enterprise set the scene for the 21st-century celebrity as a branded entity. Declining album sales in the early '00s saw musical artists having to shift from generating their income the traditional way – selling records, concert tickets and merchandise – to becoming a consumerable entity themselves, a brand that could be utilised across a wide array of products. Jennifer Lopez was one of the first of the new batch of stars to embark on a high-profile perfume launch, kickstarting the craze for famous-fronted fragrances. Two years later, when Britney premiered Curious, the trend began to boom. Since then, the likes of Beyoncé, Little Mix, 50 Cent and even former US president Donald J. Trump have brought their own signature swill to market. Yet, despite the A-list names, the longevity of most of these scents was poor: no one wanted to smell like their favourite celebrity for the long term. 'They usually went up like a rocket and did really well at launch, but they had a hard time sustaining customers,' says Don Loftus, president of Parlux, a fragrance company whose celebrity portfolio includes the likes of Paris Hilton, Rihanna, and Jay-Z.[149] The gold rush to add some extra coin to sagging bank accounts started to end around 2016 when industry experts saw a sharp decrease in demand for star-backed scent. However, what has given Spears her staying power is that her product is good, with 2006's Midnight Fantasy even receiving a 'four stars; excellent' review in the *New York Times* by Chandler Burr. But, like so many other articles about Britney, Burr could not help but take a jab at the singer's private life while bestowing his compliments, describing the scent as being 'both a perfect olfactory incarnation of Spears (on the screen, not behind the wheel of a car) and a chef-d'oeuvre of the new neon sweets/ultra-gourmand category'.[150]

Burr's comments encapsulate the irony of Spears' success. Journalists and reviewers alike seem disquieted that someone who chews gum, has a complicated love life and speaks plainly could take the world by storm. As Syme wrote of Britney for *InStyle*, 'She could seriously suggest that people buy her fragrance, but, at that very moment, she was struggling to be taken seriously herself. She was trying to launch a perfume business in the middle of a tabloid maelstrom.'[151] Yet this is the brilliant alchemy of Britney Spears: she allows the public to see her struggles in a way that her contemporaries do not – or she at least allows the public to *think* they are seeing her struggles. 'Her perfumes feel very authentic. Consumers feel like they are buying into her life,' Loftus comments. 'Every launch has felt like it was at the moment for her and reflective of where she was in her life. That's the number-one rule of anything, really – you have to believe it came from the house.' This is why the perfumes of other huge names have flopped miserably. 'With celebrity fragrances, when it's not integrated with the actual brand, it loses its lustre,' notes Sue Phillips, president and CEO of fragrance-branding company Scenterprises. '[Britney] is one of the few celebrities who actually enjoys fragrances and it shows – you can see it in her sales. If you look at people like Lady Gaga or Madonna, whose fragrances *should* have done well, they didn't do as well as Britney because they didn't care. Britney really cares about fragrance.'[152]

Despite all the kudos lavished on the Spears fragrance line, the one demographic that brand Britney seems unable to crack is the high-end fashionista – a market still too snobby to admit to owning, let alone wearing, any of the singer's perfumes. Syme's *InStyle* piece highlighted a 2005 *New York Times* article in which women 'bravely confessed' to wearing Britney's Curious, though making sure to clarify that 'they would never wear the perfume all by itself'. Seemingly the only 'acceptable' way to don the scent was to pair it with another, more expensive brand – a practice that one of the women profiled likened to wearing 'a $14.99 Zara shirt with a $900 Dolce & Gabbana skirt'. Yet, as Syme pointed out, this is exactly what 'Britney was trying to tell us . . . There is nothing wrong with loving a $14 shirt. The Mississippi native knew her value and potential from a very early age – long before there would be any money to her name.'[153]

The hypocrisy of the 'brave' women admitting to wearing Britney's scent points to the flawed doctrine inherent in capitalistic systems: status is often based on demonstrating wealth and apparent individuality, not on having genuine self-worth. Britney's aspirational rags-to-riches personal narrative could have been used to market her perfumes as an elixir for anyone wanting to conquer the world in a similar fashion, compelling people to marinate themselves in Curious in the hope of replicating some of Spears' incredible success. However, the accessible price point and easy availability of the Britney fragrances makes them unappealing to those who equate desirability with expense and exclusivity. Britney's perfumes allow anyone to smell and feel good – a commodity arguably more precious than any rarefied essence you can buy.

PIECE 15

A Chaotic Future

When the reality show *Britney and Kevin: Chaotic* aired in May 2005, Britney Spears was already a television veteran and an international household name. The five-part fly-on-the-wall series followed Spears and her then-boyfriend Kevin Federline for the first six months of their relationship, from the early days of their courtship to their unexpected wedding, all captured by the pair themselves on hand-held cameras – an approach that was pretty much unheard of back then. At the time, there was a successful format for documenting the 'everyday' life of the rich and famous on the small screen: each episode would neatly wrap up a traditional story arc of beginning, middle and end. MTV's *The Osbournes* had perfected this style in the early '00s, bringing Ozzy and his brood to an entirely new audience, while *Newlyweds*, starring Jessica Simpson and 98 Degrees boy-band beauty Nick Lachey, had made multi-media stars out of the married singers.

The difference between that MTV fodder and *Chaotic* was that Britney was already a global superstar when she picked up the camera and started filming herself and Kevin; she was looking for a way to tell her story from her point of view. *Chaotic* was an opportunity for Britney to break away from the virginal, 'good girl' image she had been forced to portray for so long and finally present herself as a young woman looking for love, acceptance and even sex. *Chaotic* was a means for Spears to take control.

Originally marketed as an updated take on Madonna's 1991 documentary-style film *Truth or Dare*, *Chaotic* was conceptualised as 'the ultimate backstage pass' to the European portion of Spears' 2004 Onyx Hotel Tour. It was shopped to networks with the Madge-esque premise for a cool $1 million per episode. However, initial plans were scrapped once Britney met Kevin and asked him to join her on the road. Shooting moved to much more realistic behind-the-scenes environments, including hotel rooms, tour buses and backstage waiting rooms. The prop of the camera allowed Britney to be more vulnerable and more herself in front of her new love interest. Spears later confessed that seeing her paramour through the lens gave her confidence to open up. 'I didn't know him that well and, when I got the camera out, it made me feel better,' she said. 'It's really weird because it was like all this tension at first. We were so nervous being together . . . When I had the camera in my hand, it made me feel more outspoken. I think it helped at first.'[154] This 'outspoken' version of Spears unveiled by the camera allowed both Kevin and the *Chaotic* audience to get to know who the singer really was beneath all the marketed, airbrushed gloss.

Within moments of the first episode, viewers are provided with a much different version of Britney than the one previously seen. The format was immediately offputting to many critics, who claimed that 'the show's extreme shooting style makes it especially hard to stare at what is — no more no less — a totem to the pop singer's narcissism'. Spears asks her entourage about sex, talks to Federline openly about their great romantic life, and films some hot and heavy make-out sessions. When confronted with Britney looking for love, connection and intimacy in a genuine manner, the same media outlets that had spent years speculating about her personal liaisons now mercilessly criticised her. 'Two years ago, Britney Spears was coyly singing the praises of her still intact hymen. Then came Justin Timberlake, who unsuspectingly opened Pandora's Box — or so *Britney and Kevin: Chaotic* would have us believe,' a *Slant* magazine post crowed.[155] 'She says she's tired of the tabloids explaining her, so, instead, here's the "real" story she gives us: that she's a pampered celebrity surrounded by sycophants whom she can't bear to film for longer than thirty seconds without whipping the camera around back to herself, the true star,' wrote *Entertainment Weekly*.[156]

The huge double standard that exists between what is 'appropriate' for male rock stars and their female counterparts is no more evident than in another *Entertainment Weekly* post. The writer labels Federline 'Britney's boy toy . . . a piece of meat and nothing more' and then slut-shames Spears for being 'way too personal' and 'too willing to show off her goodies in front of Kevin'.[157] Spears' position of power is also ridiculed, her desires and needs belittled: 'Woman summons unemployed, undershirt-wearing man to her European tour, woman bangs man three times in one day and gets a TV show to tell the world.'[158] Britney's interest in sex is not confusing given she was forced to publicly play the shy virgin for so long; however, the clash between chaste Britney and *Chaotic* Britney proved to be deeply unsettling for many.

Though there is no on-screen drug use in *Chaotic*, the presence of substances was inferred by the press, who described Spears as being in a 'pathetic, desperate state of drugged-up confusion for all the world to see', with a seemingly 'fragile, distorted head-space'. In one scene, Spears was said to be staring 'vacantly and glassy-eyed . . . in what clearly appears to be a coke-, ecstasy- or speed-induced haze'. A different clip showed Britney returning to her leitmotif about 'missing out on life' – a feeling Federline attributed to 'all the partying', which a reviewer claimed must be code for 'all the drugs we've been using'.[159] If the two were indulging, their alleged exploits simply illustrate the common-ality of such substances in the music scene, providing an even more realistic portrait of Spears at that moment in time. If they were in fact stone-cold sober, the accusatory assumption of illicit gear being present is even more disturbing.

Britney's brutal, no-holds-barred approach was not acknowl-edged by many. She was attacked from every angle for being unintelligent or not looking 'cover girl' perfect. Britney's face, body and fashion choices were derided in almost every review of the show. 'Britney has campaigned for Proactiv, but she's unlikely to do so again after the folks at the anti-acne cream's company take a look at what all that sweaty Federline sex has done to her face,' wrote *Slant* magazine.[160] 'Consumed by ambition yet can't sing a note. With her piggy eyes, stumpy little legs and bad skin, she's an unlikely sex symbol,' commented aerialtelly.com.[161] Her wardrobe choices were equally maligned, with any non-stage-ready costumes taken as a fall from grace and critical references made to her 'official redneck uniform of a wife beater, sweatpants and trucker hat'.[162]

The show was universally panned and marked as 'career suicide'.[163] *Slant* declared that it couldn't 'be good for Britney's career', adding:

> It took [Madonna] exactly twenty years to rule the world, get married, get divorced, get freaky, have a baby, bemoan her celebrity status and respond to her critics in her songs and videos, win a Grammy, get married again and burn out. Having done all that in five years, all that's left for Britney is to burn out too. With *Chaotic*, she seems to have lit the fire herself.[164]

Britney's attempt at showing a genuine 'piece' of herself – reflecting what many young women her age experience – was demeaned. However, in retrospect, *Chaotic* was a game-changer, a forbearer to the omnipresent oversharing that is now accepted, normalised and arguably encouraged across social media and TV. Performing sexual acts on camera has helped make stars out of cast members of *Love Island*; capturing drunk antics and alcohol-induced philosophising on MTV's *Jersey Shore* has created a global phenomenon. For Britney, the same conduct was ridiculed, even demonised as the actions of a horny woman out of control. 'In 2005, this behaviour was lambasted for an unimaginable narcissism that only a dangerously self-obsessed diva like Britney could have,' notes Ross McNeilage for *Vice*. 'Today, it's a bankable format that has earned YouTubers a fortune' while even 'your next-door neighbour is talking about their missing Hermes parcels on their Instagram Stories'.[165] Britney was ahead of her time with *Chaotic* yet has rarely received any recognition for allowing herself to be shown in such a raw and real state. Begrudgingly, one writer did commend Spears for her 'semi-heroic survival', adding that the singer's ability to avoid 'the fate of Amy Winehouse and Anna Nicole Smith is a tribute to the resilience of the human spirit and an often cruel and predatory public's remarkable ability to forgive, if not forget'.[166]

Chaotic was an uncurated Spears, the self-confessed shy star allowing herself to be viewed in unflattering and all too human situations. This was Britney showing herself to be what she actually is: 'Funny, filthy . . . your everyday girl.'[167] But no one really wanted that Britney. Instead of being applauded for her bravery and honesty, Spears was crucified for having the audacity to be shown as an imperfect woman who expresses – and acts on – her desires. In a 2013 interview, Britney told a reporter that *Chaotic* was 'probably the worst thing' she had done in her career and commented that she 'would never do something like that again'.[168] Why would she? Britney gave us the opportunity to truly see her and she was universally rejected. Without the fantasy created by carefully choreographed interviews, videos and performances, the 'real' Spears, the one the paps were all so desperate to capture, turned out to be not so different than us – a reality we found repulsive.

PIECE 16

The Body Britney

Britney Spears' physique defined popular culture during the '00s in much the same way that fusion cuisine, the birth of reality TV and the *Matrix* trilogy did: they all heralded new western fascinations that would outlive the decade in which they were first established. From her ultra-low-rise pants (which miraculously rarely showed any butt crack) to her insanely toned, crop-top-displayed abs, the body of Britney was held up as the epitome of female perfection – an ideal unattainable for any actual human woman besides Spears. As sociology professor Meredith Nash contends, 'For many fans, both male and female, Britney Spears is her body, an icon of feminine beauty and the normalised ideal of slenderness.'[169] This mantle was further underpinned by Spears repeatedly being voted the 'most beautiful' and 'sexiest' woman alive. In 2002, 'the hottest little dish out of Louisiana since catfish gumbo' was just twenty, but that did not stop men's magazine

Stuff from crowning her 'Sexiest Woman in the World'.[170] Two years later, she was awarded the same title – this time, by topping a readers' poll in lad rag *FHM*.

However, just one year on, the focus of Britney's body as desirable and aspirational shifted with the pregnancy of her first son, Sean Preston. As Britney began to experience the natural changes that occur with carrying a child, the public suddenly felt that she had 'let herself go'. Nash argues that Britney's 'undisciplined, "fat" and metaphorically "leaky" body' was viewed as 'the antithesis of her controlled, pre-pregnancy self', with the word 'leaky' being used to denote the various fluids that are part of the birthing and mothering process. 'Like many pregnant women, Spears' heavily pregnant body threatens to expel fluid at any moment, either when her "water breaks" or postpartum when she breastfeeds,' explains Nash. Yet these very real and unavoidable functions of humanity were incongruous with the tight, taut Britney who was being held up as a visual role model just months before.

Britney's gestational weight gain – imperative for a healthy baby – was attacked both during and after her pregnancy. Snaps of Spears frequenting fast food outlets and wearing a T-shirt bearing the slogan 'Chocolate Lover' framed the singer's extra pounds as glutinous instead of a necessity for her unborn child. 'Her changing bodily shape', Nash suggests, was attributed 'to "fatness" rather than pregnancy'. On the day of her first child's birth, a skit by TV host Conan O'Brien went a step further, with the comedian saying, 'It's been reported that, during her pregnancy, Britney Spears has put on 50 pounds while the average woman only puts on 30 pounds . . . Doctors are attributing the extra 20 pounds to her diet of jerky and Shasta.' Frenemy Christina Aguilera also repeated these ideas, echoing that post-pregnancy Britney had 'let herself go'. (The *Daily Star* even claimed that Christina sent Spears a 'corset and a diet book' in celebration of the new baby, though Aguilera later refuted this assertion.)

Images of Spears flaunting her baby belly in a pink bikini 'provoked a number of both positive and negative responses, many of which were from women', notes Nash. The comments ranged from the contemptuous ('I hope I look better than she does when I am [pregnant]') to the more thoughtful ('I know how much fun it is to pick on Britney, I've been doing it, too, but I'm with you – sure glad the press wasn't following me around documenting everything I drank and ate').[171] The dissection of Spears was accepted as her body was not viewed as her own; it was 'communal property and she was vandalising it'.[172] Just as her schoolgirl phase and steamy snake dance had been controversial, knocked-up Britney was yet another version of 'woman' that made people feel uncomfortable. As Nash points out, the dualism of being a sexy mother is impossible in western culture – and sexy was the bedrock of the Britney brand. Spears – the once-coveted object of longing – was redefining 'her social and bodily identity' from someone *suggestively* sexual to someone who had clearly had sex. It became even more layered when a 'prominently pregnant' Spears smiled from the cover of *Elle* magazine, shrouded in the gauzy glow provided by a muted camera lens. Swathed in light pink and looking nearly angelic,

Spears gave off an almost 'immaculate conception' vibe, further playing into her enduring duality of 'raw sexuality and innocence' – an idea that Spears herself perpetuated within the pages of the magazine, referring to 'motherhood' as 'the culmination of a woman's life'.

While the photospread told a story of the glory of approaching motherhood, *US Weekly* was quick to report in October 2005 that Britney was 'very unhappy with how she look[ed], hate[d] being fat and [felt] embarrassed'.[173] The same 'news' outlet was also quick to run images of Spears snapped make-up free, in stained clothes and with acne outbreaks visible in close-up shots of her face.[174] These pictures deviated from the pristine, effortless mode of motherhood presented by the media, placing Britney's 'messy' lifestyle and appearance as undesirable for a parent. Yet, once again, they provided an accurate representation of the normal challenges that come with balancing multiple responsibilities while expecting or raising a child. However, instead of being comforted that even Britney can get a zit or don dirty clothes, the public were repulsed by these very real aspects of Spears and spun them into 'cultural assumptions about her suitability for motherhood'. The pregnant version of Britney, Nash postulates, represented 'a simultaneous site of abjection and monstrosity, sexuality and spectacle'.

Spears was not immune to what Nash terms the 'Hollywood-isation of American culture' – part of which portrays the ideal mother as being able to effortlessly juggle all areas of her life, including (and perhaps most importantly) dropping any weight gained during pregnancy as soon as possible after giving birth.

Nash argues that Britney was cast as the opposite of this fantastical standard as she dared to gain weight while carrying her son, ate unhealthy food and wore clothes that did not conceal the approaching arrival.

The analysis of Britney's body did not let up once she had given birth to son Sean. Just weeks after the baby's arrival, depending on which source one consulted for information, Britney was either still holding on to the poundage gained during pregnancy or already looking remarkable. This positioned Spears as either a failure (for not instantly 'springing back' to her pre-baby weight) or a triumph (for once again attaining a slim figure). The *National Enquirer* trumpeted that Britney hadn't 'lost the pregnancy weight', but was 'desperate to get back in superstar shape and resume her career'. However, at the same time, *People* magazine proclaimed that Spears had lost almost all of her baby weight – an accomplishment that was to be celebrated. 'She looks fantastic again. She's got her figure back and being a mom obviously suits her. If it wasn't for her maternity bra, you'd never know she'd had a baby,' the article announced.[175] These highly contradicting 'reports' only highlight the importance placed on Britney's body above any other aspect of her person.

While pregnant with second son Jayden, Britney once again took to the pages of a high-fashion magazine to show off her impending arrival – this time, a glossy editorial for *Harper's Bazaar*. The shots in the spread reframed Britney in an unexpected manner: as a heavily pregnant seductress. In the first picture, a tanned, brunette Spears looks alluringly into the camera lens, wearing only a string bikini (which is noted as being from designer Calvin Klein, for those who were wondering) and a long white-mink coat. It's a photo one might expect from a publication like *Playboy*, except for the big baby bump that dominates the frame. Another image is of Britney sitting cross-legged in a chair – this time, totally naked (save for a magnificent 'crystal-decked necklace'), though her peeking gaze is sweet rather than suggestive. A third look shows Britney from the shoulders up, wearing a necklace and a mask that both resemble bondage gear. In the spread's accompanying interview, Spears herself seems befuddled by how she should be desirable while expecting, saying, 'I'm not supposed to be this huge pregnant superstar.'[176]

Spears was not alone in her feelings; no woman in entertainment is 'supposed to be' carrying extra inches for any reason. Indeed, the idea of 'bouncing back' to a pre-pregnancy weight and body is not only encouraged but actually praised as a great achievement. After having her first daughter, actress Blake Lively reportedly had to enlist two personal trainers and a nutritionist to help her drop weight quickly for a forthcoming role that demanded a pre-baby-appearing body. In *The Sun*, she discussed the radical and rapid transformation from postpartum body to toned physique, admitting, 'It's not normal to look like that eight months after having a kid.' Although her own rapid descent on the scale was for her job, Lively still maintained it was 'absolutely absurd' for women to pressure themselves into losing weight right after having a child.

This expectation to 'regain' what was 'lost' during pregnancy has now become normalised for even the average woman (who most likely does not have the trainers, nutritionists and nannies available to the rich and famous). Yet some celebrities have spoken out about the common, natural changes that have happened to them after childbirth. In 2008, Kate Winslet told the *Daily Mail*, 'I've had two kids. I'm thirty-three. I don't look in the mirror and go: "Oh, I look fantastic!" Of course I don't. Nobody is perfect. I just don't believe in perfection. But I do believe in saying: "This is who I am and look at me not being perfect."' She proceeded to mention her 'crumble[d] baby belly' and her breasts that 'are worse for wear after two kids'. Winslet openly addressed the differences in her pre- and post-pregnancy frame again after the birth of her third child in 2014. While talking about filming the movie *Divergent*, Winslet disclosed that her body was 'soft' and that getting into her costume 'was a little bit like squeezing a sausage into a thimble! I had just had a baby! It just doesn't feel right.'[177]

Though Winslet's attitudes are refreshing, Britney's brand demanded the svelte, ripped, pre-baby figure first viewed in 2001's 'I'm a Slave 4 U' era. Indeed, even before she had kids, Spears' efforts to maintain that look were arguably very unhealthy. Britney reportedly resorted to diet pills, constant exercise and an incredibly strict food plan to keep her unnaturally slim shape. At one point, she was said to be doing a minimum of '800–1,000 stomach crunches' a day, with another 800–1,000 added on if she had a show to prep for.[178] After Britney was slammed for her 'bloated' appearance at the 2007 VMAs, the singer was put on 'a rigid diet centred around a 1,200-calorie, three-meals-a-day regimen and regular exercise workouts all geared towards a goal weight of 110 pounds'.[179] At 5 foot 4 and twenty-five years old, a healthy weight for Spears at the time would have been anywhere from 108 to 132 pounds. The average American woman of the same age and height weighs significantly more, coming in at 167.6 pounds.[180] While Britney's target weight was just within the acceptable healthy range, it did not take into account the reality that most women never lose all of the weight gained while carrying a baby. A 2015 study published in *Obstetrics & Gynecology* found that 'most women who gained the recommended amount of weight during pregnancy remain 2–5 pounds above their pre-pregnancy weight a year after giving birth'. It also discovered that 'a sizable minority, 15–20 per cent of women, will hold onto 10 pounds or more' indefinitely.[181]

Being a normal woman was not an option available to Britney; if she 'held on' to any extra pregnancy pounds, she would be slammed for appearing unkept and straying from the perfectly manicured look required of her. If Spears were to undergo any sort of 'corrective' body modification, she would risk being shamed for resorting to such measures. According to various sources (though not confirmed by the Spears camp), Britney first had liposuction after the 2007 VMAs.[182] The surgery was a 'desperate bid to improve her appearance', according to the *Daily Mail*.[183] Not even two weeks later, gossip site LondonNet declared that Spears was 'addicted to plastic surgery', having deemed herself a 'fat pig'. The article went on to claim that Britney wanted to get 'multiple procedures, including a breast enlargement and liposuction'. As usual, an unnamed 'insider' interviewed for the piece asserted that Britney had 'already consulted with at least three surgeons about new breast implants, a nose job, liposuction on her chin and Botox for her face. She sees no reason to stop, she constantly talks about getting work done.' The story also cited an alleged report that 'Britney was planning on spending $100,000 on cosmetic surgery in an effort to regain her once famous toned physique'.[184]

The crux of it is, if Spears dares to deviate from anything but immaculate perfection, she is lambasted for 'looking like she's been living under a rock since 1998' and yet any intervention is almost equally derided. A 2013 piece on another gossip forum seemed to cackle at the 'news' that Spears was 'planning a full-body overhaul', including a 'strict' diet and exercise regime and 'extensive plastic surgery to her body and face'. The catalyst for the '$150,000 cosmetic surgery to-do list' was supposedly Britney's unhappiness upon seeing photos of herself 'with a very obvious triple chin', though the writer of the content took it upon himself to pontificate, 'Couldn't she just hire a bunch of hot guys to follow her around and give her [a] dirty look every time she picks up a piece of bread?'[185] The article is just one of many demonstrating the toxicity and negativity that undoubtedly contributed to Spears' well-publicised mental-health problems.

Britney's issues with her body represent a struggle that many, many women share: the conflict between self-acceptance and societal expectations. Yet, no matter what Spears does, she cannot win; everywhere she turns, the microscope of global opinion is always ready to magnify her insecurities.

PIECE 17

No 'Fixin' for Britney

Though it had been less than a year since the universal condem-
nation of her show with Kevin Federline, Britney Spears decided
to give the small screen another go in 2006. This time, she
would be following in the footsteps of fellow musical icons Cher,
Madonna and Jennifer Lopez by appearing in a cameo role on
sitcom *Will & Grace*. The show revolved around the friendship
between a gay man (Will) and his straight female friend (Grace).
It was a huge hit for network NBC during its eight-series run,
earning eighteen Primetime Emmy Awards and being credited
for improving public opinion of the LGBTQ+ community. During the show's final season, an early press release announced
Britney's cameo. Her role would simultaneously poke fun at
and pay homage to the singer's religious roots. The proposed
premise of the episode, titled 'Buy, Buy Baby', revolved around
OutTV – the place of work of Will's best friend, Jack (played by

Sean Hayes) – being bought by a Christian television network. Spears was set to play a talking head for the new enterprise, contributing to a cooking segment called 'Cruci-fixins'.

A whiff of the whimsical name caught the attention of former Britney antagonists the American Family Association – and they did not like it. Indeed, the show in question must have been a triple whammy of horror for the AFA: firstly, the inclusive themes of *Will & Grace* were entirely unacceptable to a notoriously anti-gay organisation; secondly, any idea of humour at the expense of the church was not going to fly; thirdly, the date that the episode was set to air – the night before Good Friday – was viewed as problematic. 'NBC is clearly mocking the Christian faith,' the group's founder, Don Wildmon, wrote on the AFA website. 'They clearly have hostility toward the Christian faith.' Having Britney primed to play that particular character must have added fuel to the AFA's wrath, too. Though the star had once been the poster girl for chastity and Christian values, she had since kissed another woman in public, experimented with non-Baptist ideas of spirituality, and dared to admit to having and *enjoying* sex – all huge no-nos under the group's strict code of values.

Wildmon began to rally his troops for a boycott of the network, asking members to get in touch with NBC and demand that the episode not be shown. NBC quickly responded to the AFA's allegations, claiming that 'some erroneous information was mistakenly included in a press release describing an upcoming episode of *Will & Grace*'. The network went on to say that the show had 'yet to be written' and that the idea was meant for another episode. Disappointedly, they went on to conclude that 'the reference to "Cruci-fixins" will not be in the show' and 'the storyline will not contain a Christian characterization at all'.[186] To further placate the AFA, the air date for the Spears appearance was moved forward from its original 13 April slot to 30 March – a comfortable two weeks before Good Friday. However, none of this was enough for the AFA, who said that NBC were trying to 'confuse' viewers and make the organisation look like liars. The group still claimed a victory for their cause, saying that it was because of their members' lobbying that the network was forced to rewrite the entire script.

The resulting episode, though not featuring any 'fixins', still sees Spears playing co-host to Hayes' Jack. Spears' character, Amber Louise, has been tapped by the network to do a (non-cooking) segment called 'Amber Louise's Musings'. Britney seems to enjoy hamming it up as the career-driven southern girl who is secretly a 'hardcore lesbian' (with a taste for 'leather play, butch black girls, skunkin', pullin' the blinds and poodleballin''). To underscore her point, Amber Louise tells Jack, 'Whatever you got, I'll eat it, snort it or ride it, baby.' Spears has great comic timing and her priceless facial expressions throughout the skit give maximum impact to her lines. However, watching the show more than fifteen years after it was first aired is startling: some of Spears' dialogue parallels the life she would soon be forced to live. At one point, Amber Louise tells Jack, 'I'm not who you think I am . . . go along with this and it will work for you.'[187] The line could be acknowledging the shy, funny girl beneath the public veneer created by the ambitious, hard-working Spears, but it also foreshadows Britney being made to 'go along' with her conservatorship in order to see her kids. Though the lines are said for laughs within the context of the show, it is somewhat ominous to hear her say those words now with the retrospective knowledge of how her life would unfold.

With the success of *Will & Grace* under her belt, Britney looked to make an appearance on another of her favourite shows: CBS's *How I Met Your Mother* (*HIMYM*). Centred around a group of close friends in their twenties, the premise of *HIMYM* was a man telling his kids how he met his wife/their mother. It was a critical time for the series, which was in its third season, as a recent strike by the Writer's Guild of America had created uncertainty over the future of many shows. Though *HIMYM* maintained a loyal following, it had yet to grow into the powerhouse it would later become; Britney, on the other hand, was one of the biggest stars in the world. However, she was such a fan of the sitcom that she asked her 'team' to contact the show's co-creators, Carter Bays and Craig Thomas, and alert them of her interest in making a guest appearance.

At first, the duo had mixed emotions about bringing Spears into the *HIMYM* mix. The show had long faced the 'challenge' of getting 'eyeballs on it', so the possible addition of Spears was incredibly appealing in terms of viewership. At the same time, though, some cast members, including star Neil Patrick Harris, were concerned that the introduction of too many big-name celebrities might be detrimental. 'Our show does not need stunt casting to succeed . . . we're all really proud of the content of the show,' Harris said.[188] Though the creative team had been thinking of casting Britney in the role of receptionist Abby, they took on board the concerns expressed and began working on another part for the singer. With Spears no longer in the frame for Abby, the part was then planned for *Clueless* star Alicia Silverstone. However, Silverstone feared being overshadowed by Spears and dropped out, making the part of Abby available to Britney once more.[189]

The premise of 'Ten Sessions' – the episode in which Abby makes her first appearance – revolves around one of the main characters, Ted, trying to get a naff butterfly tattoo removed. While he hopes to capture the heart of the dermatologist responsible for eradicating the offensive ink, it is the mousy receptionist, Abby, who actually falls for him. Throughout the show, Abby transforms herself in an attempt to snare Ted, going from wearing glasses and cardigans to having her long hair flowing and her cleavage on show. After all of the negative accusations slung at Spears for being unintelligent, especially on *Chaotic*, it was a brave move to let herself play someone who was a bit ditzy. Abby's 'plain Jane' appearance at the start of her cameo went against the glitzy, glamourous Britney paradigm, once again proving that Spears was not afraid to be portrayed in a less-than-perfect light.

The regular cast of *HIMYM* raved about Spears' performance and her off-the-cuff ad libs, saying that she 'already had her character down pat' when she arrived on set. 'She came up with stuff that had everyone laughing,' co-star Jason Segel said. 'She's definitely a comedian.'[190] Britney was so well received that she was asked back to reprise the role of Abby in a following episode. Bray credited Spears with putting *HIMYM* 'on the map' and making the show more popular. 'It can't be overstated,' he said in an interview, 'Britney Spears rescued us from ever being on the bubble again. Thanks, Britney!'[191]

However, not everyone was as enthusiastic about the singer's star turn. 'Viewership is not our game,' said Harris. 'It's the network and the studio's game, you know? It's the promotion department's game . . . I think we have a great show going and I hope it's not screwed up by the desire for 700,000 more viewers.' Spears' appearance did make a splash, bringing in over 1 million more viewers than the show usually pulled in. Across the entire nine-series run of *HIMYM*, 'Ten Sessions' was the most-watched episode ever in the highly coveted 18–49-year-old demographic.[192] It was an illustration of not only Britney's resilience to bounce back from anything, but also her ability to make fun of herself while appealing to a diverse audience. Moreover, both episodes showcased Spears' versatility and how underrated she was as an actress. Whether Harris believed it or not, in the case of *HIMYM*, Britney may indeed have saved the day.

PIECE 18

Extra, Extra, This Just In

In a *Dateline* interview from 2006, reporter Matt Lauer asks Britney Spears, 'What do you think it will take for the paparazzi to leave you alone?' The singer replies, 'I don't know. I don't know.' Lauer continues, 'Is that one of your biggest wishes?' Spears tearfully responds, 'Yeah.'[193] It is a hard scene to watch. When the show aired, Spears recalled that she 'couldn't ever leave the house' without being followed by 'twenty cars' – a rabid mob desperate to get a shot of the star.[194] Even the general public were not below attempting to snap a pic of Spears, regardless of the circumstances. On an outing with Sean to the Malibu Country Mart, Britney fled inside the restaurant to seek relief from the swarm of paparazzi that had tailed her Mini Cooper. Exhausted and overwhelmed, she leant her head against the baby she was holding in her lap, only to find the staff at the eatery surrounding her and taking pictures of their own. There was no refuge for

Britney. Haunting images captured through the glass windows by the photographers standing outside show Britney cradling Sean in her arms, tears streaming down her face, looking utterly distraught and alone.

During the mid-'00s, an entire industry was created around taking pictures of Spears. Paparazzi agencies have estimated that Britney 'comprised up to 20 per cent of their coverage', with a 'multi-billion-dollar new-media economy' built upon images of the star.[195] It has also been calculated that simply putting Spears on the cover of a tabloid resulted in a 33 per cent uptick in sales, making it unsurprising that the singer was featured on the front of *People, Us Weekly, In Touch, Life & Style, OK!* and *Star* a total of 175 times over the 78-week period between January 2006 and July 2007. As writer Richard Cohen pointed out in the *Washington Post*, 'Most political leaders only dream of this much coverage.'[196] An Associated Press memo leaked in 2008 included the announcement that 'everything that happens to Britney is news'; indeed, the outlet had already planned the star's obituary so as not to be late printing it should the unthinkable happen. Even the most mundane activities like going to Starbucks or making a quick trip to the pet store would see up to 100 reporters, editors and photographers chasing Spears, all trying to get that elusive shot that bloggers and celebrity gossip sites desperately needed. 'She is by far the top person I have written about on my website ever,' claimed Perez Hilton, while Harvey Levin, founder of TMZ, also recognised the importance of Spears for his livelihood, commenting, 'We serialise Britney Spears. She's our President Bush.'[197]

Two outlets in particular did very well off of the public's insatiable appetite for all things Britney. In 2007, Britney-related content made up 10–15 per cent of Splash News's business, including one snap of the singer in a hot tub that bagged the company a cool $200,000. Competitor X17 earned 30 per cent of their overall income from Spears content, snagging $500,000 for the image that went around the world of Britney's bald head.[198]

Some of the people responsible for taking photos of Spears now claim that she manipulated the situation for her own gain just as much as they did. A handful of paps even contend that Spears enjoyed being the subject of such attention. It has been more than a decade since Los Angeles-based Rick Mendoza took his first picture of Britney. Since then, he has worked for TMZ and Hollywood TV. He thinks that, without the media spotlight on her personal struggles, Britney would not have had the follow-up success that she saw with her 2008 LP, *Circus*:

> She used us just as much as we used her. She knew the value of paparazzi . . . She stayed in the public eye for what? Two, three, four years. Guess what happened after that duration of time had elapsed? Boom! She releases *Circus*. It sells double platinum, she goes on a worldwide tour and she keeps the kids. Why didn't she shave her head at home? Because she wanted publicity. Was it really the paparazzi? She was already going through situations before the paparazzi.[199]

A 2008 *Rolling Stone* exposé on Spears suggested that Britney started 'to really enjoy her paparazzi chases' and would allegedly race 'around the city for two or three hours a day, aimlessly leading paps to various locations where she could interact with them just a little bit and then jump back into her car'. 'Britney is the most dangerous detail in Hollywood,' said TMZ bigwig Levin, describing the Spears 'chase' as 'a game of Frogger, with everyone jostling to be the first car behind Britney, the better to shoot all over her when she stops'.[200]

Daniel Ramos remembers the early days of 'Brit watch' from his time as director of photography for *US Weekly* – a post he held between 2001 and 2011. In *Framing Britney Spears*, he says, 'In the beginning, when paparazzi were following Britney, you could tell she enjoyed it. She would give up the shots, waving. She was very friendly, a sweetheart of a girl. It was like she needed us and we needed her. We both needed each other. It was a great kind of relationship.'

'I never wanted to be considered paparazzi,' Ramos continues. 'I wanted to be a film-maker. But it sucks you right in. It's hard to get out of it once you start making the kind of money these guys are making.' To fill his magazine, Ramos at one point needed up to 140,000 images a week, requiring a budget of up to $8 million a year. 'Once she started having her kids with Kevin Federline, it exploded. Everyone wanted a piece of Britney. The tabloids were paying a lot of money.'[201] What specifically began to drive sales were the 'unposed photographs'; Ramos quickly saw a 'hunger' for these sorts of shots and a dramatic sales increase when such images were included in the magazine. 'We made them people, too,' Mendoza says of capturing celebrities doing everyday activities. '*I'll* show you when they're taking out their garbage. *I'll* show you when they're picking their nose. Do people want to see that? Obviously yes.'[202]

A picture of Britney could fetch up to $1 million yet the barriers to enter the paparazzi 'profession' were low, mainly requiring one to have a digital camera, a telephoto lens and the patience to sit outside the star's house. 'It was when she left Kevin Federline . . . all of us said, "MONEY." She was worldwide, globally wanted. It's a public figure, public domain. That's the law. I didn't come here to take photographs. I came here to make a lot of money and make history,' Mendoza asserts.[203]

Photographer Nick Stern acted as a consultant on *Framing Britney Spears*. Like Mendoza, he was once on Spears pap duties; however, unlike Mendoza, Stern could only deal with it for a week before he called it quits and does not have fond memories of his time on the Britney beat. 'It was a culture of male toxicity and bravado among the photographers and doing the craziest things was almost worn as a badge of honour,' he recalls. 'If you jumped a red light doing 80 and you came very close to an accident, well, that was, "Wow, dude. That was awesome!" So it wasn't an environment that was sympathetic.'[204]

On a BBC podcast, Stern recounted another incident when he was brought in as a witness to a trial in Los Angeles:

> There was actually an agency boss there saying that to prevent news photographers chasing Britney Spears would be an infraction of their First-Amendment rights and it was justified under the US Constitution that they should

be allowed to continue doing whatever they saw fit to get whatever pictures they felt were justifiable.[205]

Nothing was deemed too low for the paps to snap. On 30 January 2008, X17 reported that Britney had attempted suicide. Concern quickly consumed the photographers gathered outside the star's house – not for Britney's well-being, but for the health of their pay cheques. 'You don't want an ambulance to roll out with a body bag and miss that,' said a French photographer, while another reportedly moaned, 'Man, Britney can't die because then I don't get my money!'[206]

Such dehumanising views are vile, once again positioning Britney – dead or alive – as a product to be purchased. However, consumers demanded to know every detail of Britney's life; there would not have been a Spears media ecosystem without a customer ready and willing to hand over cash or click on a site to observe the latest trials and tribulations of Spears. A post on a celebrity gossip site from late 2008, after Britney's conservatorship had begun, bemoaned the more sedate version of Spears that had recently been seen – or not seen – in public, posting, 'Putting on pants, eschewing the nightclubs, winning MTV awards, actually recording music – who is this girl and what has she done with Britney Spears?' It's not surprising that they were 'starting to worry': a posed image of Spears holding a statuette from a televised awards ceremony was far less titillating – and therefore far less lucrative – than the previous pictures splayed across the media.[207]

While it is tempting to blame the press, there is a larger societal narrative at play that needs to be addressed and reconciled, starting with public attitudes towards privacy, moral values and fundamental rights. Yet, in a country that elected Reagan the actor and Trump the reality star to the highest office in the land, the importance placed on celebrity culture seems unlikely to abate any time soon.

PIECE 19

Hair Trade

Esther's Haircutting Studio in Tarzana, California, is a tiny, unassuming, tan building set far back off Ventura Boulevard. To this day, it still seems an unlikely place for Britney Spears to have chosen as the scene of the most scrutinised haircut of the twenty-first century.

Yet, ever since Spears took the clippers to her locks on 16 February 2007, Esther's has been trading off the back of the star's visit, with the establishment's websites, social media and reviews all featuring images of or references to the singer. Indeed, Esther's ingenuity on how to maximise Britney's visit began immediately after the salon's famous client left the premises that momentous evening.

Pictures of a basin filled with Britney's hair, freshly shorn from the star's head, popped up on auction site eBay within hours of Spears' new look making international headlines. Though bids reached over $1 million, Esther's was forced to remove the ad after a flood of copycats from across the globe posted similar fake offerings. Undaunted, Esther's created the enterprising website buybritneyhair.com to hawk the discarded mane – supposedly in the name of charity. Billed as the 'ultimate Britney Spears experience' and 'a piece of history that cannot be duplicated', the locks also came with the clippers Spears used for the DIY look, the can of Red Bull she was drinking while at the establishment, a blue lighter she left behind, and ownership of the website itself.[208]

All in, it was a bumper package of dubiously purloined ephemera – and an *actual* piece of Spears – grimly celebrating pop culture's most infamous head-shaving since Elvis joined the army.

PIECE 20

Britney Goes Guerrilla

It was 1 May 2007 and Britney Spears' sixth tour was about to kick off. The opening show was set to take place at the San Diego, California, branch of House of Blues – the first of five gigs to be played at the chain's various venues across the US. Britney had not graced a stage in three years.

Things did not get off to an auspicious start. On the way from Los Angeles to San Diego (a journey of approximately 120 miles that takes just over two hours), Britney's tour bus was pulled over by the California Highway Patrol. The police had received numerous calls from 911 reporting a large vehicle going at excessive speed down Interstate 5. Talking to officers in the car park of Squid Joe's diner (located about 30 miles north of San Diego), Britney's driver described how he, the singer and her party had been pursued by paparazzi from the moment they left the star's home. Excused with a warning, the group were sent on their way – only to arrive at the venue and encounter a brigade of fans lined up around the block.

With just a handful of dates in total, the shows were mainly a tool to prove that, despite a year of Britney tabloid fodder, the star was still standing. Billed as The M+M's Tour (one 'M' standing for 'Mother', the other for 'Miss', representing the newly divorced Spears), the gigs could not strictly be described as 'concerts' since there was not an instrument in sight. Though Britney donned a headset, it was a costume accoutrement only as the entire set was unapologetically pre-recorded and lip-synced, with the music pumped out of unseen speakers.

More befitting the mood of a debauched sorority dance party than a tightly choreographed comeback, The M+M's Tour can be framed in two very different ways. The first: as a massive triumph – of the old-school two-fingers-up punk-rock variety – with the svelte, sexy Britney showing all those haters who called her fat and over-the-hill that she could still sell out venues at the drop of a hat and shake her groove thing. The other: as a massive car crash with questionable outfit choices, *Coyote Ugly*-esque dance moves and an unsatisfactory price–performance ratio, comprising yet another tragic misstep for the hapless Spears.

Rumours had been swirling on the internet and on local radio stations that the artist behind the mysterious M+M's Tour marquee at the House of Blues in San Diego was none other than Miss Spears herself. Some fans had hedged their bets and bought the $35 tickets when they went on sale, while others were left to the mercy of on-the-night scalpers, who were flogging the coveted entry for up to $500 a piece outside the venue.

Some poor souls, like Mark Stocker, lost their gamble. 'I'm a huge fan; I love her trashy appeal,' he said. 'I got all the way to the metal detector and, when they scanned my ticket, they said, "Dude, your ticket is already used." I'm so bummed.'[209]

It was not until an hour after doors opened that the DJ spinning records confirmed the fans' suspicions: the pop princess was indeed the one behind the sold-out show.

Averaging just fourteen minutes total, the set was a five-song mega mix of past hits and fan favourites, starting with a languorous rendition of '. . . Baby One More Time' performed by Britney and four interchangeable blonde back-up dancers. Though known for her high-energy, precise choreography, the Britney presented in The M+M's Tour was sloppy and ragdoll-like, pulling shapes more familiar to a drunk bridesmaid on a hen night than to a highly trained professional with over a decade of experience. Her quad of ladies was equally listless, plodding about the stage during shortened versions of the star's familiar songs, with seemingly no destination in mind but the end of the set.

The intention behind the first costume Britney appeared in was to leave nothing to the imagination. Gone was the 'offensive' weight the tabloids had blasted Spears for gaining over the course of her two pregnancies. Instead, a sparkling silver bra, tiny micro-skirt and white go-go boots highlighted the hard work undertaken by the singer to return to an 'acceptable' appearance – a change in physique that did not go unnoticed by fans or the press. One female journalist proclaimed to have seen 'no evidence of the weight gain' that had landed Britney on 'celebrity tabloid covers' the previous year, although a male reviewer captiously noted, 'The only trace of flab was her stomach, which was a bit pudgy.' Renee Rosen, a teenage audience member, also praised the singer, professing, 'I'm breathless. I'm so excited right now. She looked so beautiful, so skinny.'[210]

After barely two minutes of '. . . Baby One more Time', Britney and her lingerie-wearing pals writhed around to an abbreviated version of 'I'm a Slave 4 U'. The lights then lowered, leaving Britney alone with a chair and a spotlight to wiggle and grind to 'Breathe on Me'. Next, a lucky dude was pulled from the audience as the blonde squad re-emerged for some playful booty-shaking with the chosen lad. Whizzing through a quick costume change, Britney reappeared wearing a very short white fur jacket, a minuscule denim skirt and a pink bikini top. The event then moved on to 'Do Somethin'' – a song from Britney's 2004 *Greatest Hits: My Prerogative* album – before closing the brief set with 'Toxic'. Instead of a dance extravaganza, the concluding routine resembled a high-school cheerleading routine gone awry crossed with a lackadaisical human-dressage romp.

The M+M's Tour was a master stroke in fuckoffery, though. Britney defied all the rules that typically constitute a 'perfect' pop artist. She took to the stage without a care for her dance moves, her singing, her outfits or her hair (although she did wear alternating blonde and brunette wigs to cover her recently shaved head). Britney was there simply because she could be. On the flip side, the horrendous mix, the outrageous price to see the stilted show, and the star's complete lack of effort to bring life to her well-loved songs can only really be classed as failures.

It may seem strange to compare Britney to Prince, but there are elements of the late artist at play in The M+M's Tour. Prince was renowned, especially in the early 2000s, for doing pop-up, surprise gigs under assumed names. Instead of performing a litany of top-forty hits, the Purple One would often just get up on stage at a tiny venue and jam for an hour, seemingly oblivious to the audience who were paying for the privilege of sharing the oxygen of his greatness. He was simply doing his own thing. The M+M's Tour showcased a similar ambition: Britney was breaking free from the perfectly styled image she had been groomed and marketed to uphold. She was just getting up and doing her own thing. With Britney embracing a vibe that was more Primark than Prada while clodhopping languidly across the stage with her fillies, The M+M's Tour could have been a revelatory point of reinvention for the star – a 2.0 version of Spears, now playing by her own rules. Instead, it was more like a discounted matinee at the Moulin Rouge.

But perhaps that was the point all along: call it misjudged, jumbled or a mess, The M+M's Tour was an untethered fourteen-minute glimpse at Britney herself, stripped of her stylists, choreographers and handlers. It was arguably the most authentic Britney has ever been on stage.

PIECE 21

Ready to Break

Britney Spears was one of the first female celebrities in the twenty-first century to be both created and dismantled by the pressure of fame in front of a global audience. She has had several very public mental-health crises, ranging from shaving her head to attacking a paparazzo with an umbrella. In almost all instances, her assailability was mocked and her pain became the butt of many jokes instead of being recognised as the desperate cry for help that it was. AllMusic's Steve Erlewine suggested that 'each new disaster' in Britney's so-called demise was responsible for 'stripping away any residual sexiness in her public image', while journalist Vanessa Grigoriadis described Britney's problems as 'the most public downfall of any star in history'.[211] Since then, Spears' folly has been noted by fellow female performers, including Taylor Swift, Katy Perry and Ariana Grande, whose every move is now carefully choreographed by a gang of PRs and handlers, not allowing for any 'off-brand' behaviour. In the 2008 MTV film *For the Record*, Spears ominously predicted her own future, saying, 'I just feel like you do something wrong and you learn from it, you move on, but it's like I'm having to pay for it for a really long time.'[212]

And pay she has. In the past decade, many articles have taken out-of-context quotes Spears has made about various aspects of her life and used them to create a narrative of illness that is not only unsubstantiated but also inaccurate. One example can be seen in an article from *The Independent*, posted in 2013. The blaring headline reads 'Britney Spears opens up on bipolar disorder: "I turn into a different person."' The piece goes on to quote the singer as saying, 'I have always been kind of shy since I was a little girl. It's who I am to be modest, so I really can't help it. I turn into this different person, seriously, bipolar disorder.'[213]

Spears did say these words, but not in this order or situation. The line was taken from a scene in the 2013 documentary *I Am Britney Jean* when Spears is talking about her personality and how she is fairly reserved by nature. Yet, when she performs, she has this other side of her that emerges:

> I've always been kind of shy since I was a little girl. It's just like me. It's who I am to be modest, so I can't really help it. It's almost kind of like it's my alter ego. When I get on stage, I turn into this different person, seriously, bipolar disorder.[214]

By removing the context in which these words were originally voiced and editing the way in which they are presented, *The Independent* completely changes the meaning of what Spears was saying. Other reports are guilty of equally shameful stretching of any truth. The *Standard*, for example, claimed that Britney was speaking to her British boyfriend in a British accent, meaning that she must be 'suffering from dissociative identity disorder, which leads the sufferers to take on various personalities to dissociate them from reality'. The article also added that 'friends of the singer' reported how 'Britney has been showing different personalities, including "the British girl", "the weepy girl", "the diva" and "the incoherent girl"'.[215] To the untrained, breaking into a poorly executed London trill sounds like normal behaviour for an American dating a Brit, while the other 'personalities' do not seem peculiar for someone who has a demanding and stressful job.

Another piece, this time in *The Guardian*, ran under the banner 'Britney's tragic descent into mania is a journey I know all too well'. The article went on to describe Spears as '"gravely disabled", which is to say, in legal terms, that a mental disorder leaves her unable to provide for her own basic needs, such as food and shelter'.[216] Neither of these assertions, both appearing in reputable publications, has any clear source for such a diagnosis of Spears. The closest thing to a reliable outlet would be a statement Jamie Spears made about Britney just days after she was strapped to a gurney and carted away for her second trip to a mental facility. Mr Spears told Fox News that his daughter was 'a sick little girl', thus diminishing and infantilising Britney, portraying her as childlike and incapable of making her own decisions, and setting the stage in the public's mind for the conservatorship that would eventually be enforced on the singer.

These distortions of truth and nebulous statements were seen repeatedly when Britney was having her every move recorded by rabid paparazzi for the world to voyeuristically review. 'What's interesting to me is that most people think Britney finally hit rock bottom,' former fan-site webmaster Ruben Garay postulated. 'That couldn't be further from the truth. Unfortunately, it will only get worse because, up to this point, she has had her kids within her reach. The possibility of losing custody of her children will truly show us how bad things could get.'[217] Indeed, it was the idea of having no contact with her children, rather than any still-unspecified illness, that may have caused Spears' breakdown in 2008.

Britney Spears gave birth to her first child, Sean, on 14 September 2005. Just under a year later, her second son, Jayden, arrived on 12 September 2006. Within two months, Spears was filing for divorce from the children's father, Kevin Federline. Various magazines blamed Federline's partying as the root of the couple's problems. A *People* magazine cover story even claimed that Federline had gone to Las Vegas to celebrate the one-year anniversary of nightclub Tao, leaving Britney home by herself just three weeks after giving birth to Jayden.[218]

While two babies and a broken marriage was tough enough to manage, Spears also had the incessant glare of the world and a constant tail of photographers to contend with. Of the break-up, she later said:

> I was devastated . . . I did not know what to do with myself. I couldn't go anywhere . . . there were always thirty cars outside my house. So I am either a prisoner in my home or

I'm going to travel to Miami or New York and get out for like a week or two, then come back.

She admitted to being in a 'fragile' state at the time as she tried to juggle her own issues on top of 'breastfeeding one kid'.[219] A possibility that has not been discussed is that Britney was suffering from postpartum depression (PPD). Mentions of PPD, which affects more than one in ten women, are few and far between when analysing Spears' problems between late 2006 and early 2008.[220] PPD has often been stigmatised, with many women who suffer from it not seeking treatment – or not even being aware that there is a medical reason for what they are feeling. Britney had often talked about her dream of having a family and placed a huge value on becoming a parent. Couple these personal feelings of idealised motherhood with the constant scrutiny of the eyes of the world waiting for an imperfection and it seems impossible that Britney could have achieved any sort of stable, healthy mental state.

Occasionally, some celebrities have been forthright about their own struggles with PPD, openly discussing their trying postnatal experiences – many of which sound similar to what the media reported was happening to Britney after the birth of Jayden. In 2020, Reese Witherspoon shared that she has had multiple cases of PPD, confiding that she had 'to take pretty heavy medication' at one point as she 'wasn't thinking straight at all'. Fellow actress Brook Shields described the shame she felt over having PPD, revealing that she even had suicidal thoughts while in the grip of the condition. 'If I had been diagnosed with any other disease, I would have run to get help,' she now asserts. 'I would have worn it like a badge. I didn't at first – but finally I did fight. I survived.' Even Britney's own idol, Princess Diana of Wales, told Martin Bashir in the controversial 1995 *Panorama* interview that she, too, had grappled with PPD: 'I was unwell with postnatal depression, which no one ever discusses . . . and that in itself was a bit of a difficult time,' she said, continuing, 'You'd wake up in the morning feeling you didn't want to get out of bed, you felt misunderstood and just very, very low in yourself.'[221] Since Diana's on-air confession, things have improved slightly in terms of PPD being recognised, but not by much. Such a diagnosis seems to make for a much less splash-worthy front page than a glaring 'breakdown' headline, even though it is a fairly common issue for women. In addition to low mood, characteristics of PPD include a diminished ability to think clearly, concentrate or make decisions, as well as severe anxiety and panic attacks.[222] Symptoms can begin during pregnancy and last up to a year after giving birth; Britney showed many of the signs associated with the condition during that corresponding timeframe.

For the Record first aired in autumn 2008 – just months after Spears' public annihilation by media, press and public. In the film, she reflected on the recent past, giving perhaps the most understated interview ever, saying, 'I've been through a lot this year – well, actually, the past two or three years – and my trust has really been battered . . . I'm very weary of a lot of things, you know?'[223] It is hard to think of many – if any – other superstars who have been so highly exalted then so dramatically discredited. It is doubly difficult to reflect on this time in Spears' life through the lens of the potentially very valid reasons that may have caused her to stumble. In *The Battle for Britney*, Spears advocate Haley Herms succinctly flagged the crux of the situation: Britney's treatment was a case of absurd, blatant and unquestioned misogyny. For a female star to act this way (with or without medical reason) is unacceptable. Yet, as Herms perfectly summed up, 'If a man did what Britney did in 2007, everybody would be like, "Oh, bro, sorry you had a rough year."'[224]

PIECE 22

Leave Britney Alone!

In 2007, nineteen-year-old Cara Cunningham (better known by the stage name Chris Crocker) was a home-schooled gay teenager living in Tennessee. Crocker – who identifies as trans and is now referred to as 'they'/'their' – had recently started using YouTube and MySpace as outlets to talk about their sexuality and the importance of being 'real'. These videos soon hit a nerve with early adopters of both platforms and Crocker began to get noticed by fans and the press. In a May 2007 profile, the internet star was described as a 'new type of teenager', someone with the ability to transform their 'rural frustrations into national online fame, but who is still painfully disconnected'.[225]

Several months later, in reaction to the public ridicule Britney Spears received for her uninspired dancing and obvious lip-syncing during her 'comeback' VMAs performance, Crocker once again took to YouTube and dropped a video that changed everything. In the now-memorable clip, the teen is shown against a white-sheet backdrop, eyes encircled with thick strokes of black liner. Crocker breaks down in tears while defending Britney from her haters (including celebrity blogger Perez Hilton) and says to camera, 'If anything ever happens to her, I'm jumping off the nearest fucking building.' The title of this video was 'Leave Britney Alone'.[226]

The clip became an instant internet sensation, racking up more than 2 million views in just a day and securing Crocker multiple appearances across the US TV interview circuit. In several of these interviews, Crocker was asked to defend the authenticity of the emotion portrayed in the video. In response, the youngster adopted the same over-the-top persona used in 'Leave Britney Alone', playing the part of 'excited teenager thrilled to be in the spotlight', rather than the vulnerable adolescent beneath the televised veneer.

Besides watching the public breakdown of Spears from afar, Crocker was also trying to process some problems closer to home. After serving in Iraq, Crocker's mother had become addicted to crystal meth, leading to the family disowning her. Crocker has since recalled staying silent on these issues while making the media rounds:

> I've always looked up to Britney. And the other woman in my life who I looked up to – my mom – was falling apart. I didn't know how to explain that because I knew people wouldn't take me seriously. I knew it was too much to explain and it wasn't what people wanted to hear, so I gave them this character. It's the biggest thing in my life, being so wildly misunderstood.

Michael Strangelove, author of the 2010 book *Watching YouTube*, believes it was a unique combination of factors that led to Crocker's video becoming such a cultural phenomenon. 'It was unusual, it was early on, it was a part of the exploding gay pride culture,' says Strangelove. 'It was the right time and the right place and the right type of performance. Attach it to a popular celebrity and all the stars aligned.'[227]

Crocker became the archetypal YouTube celebrity by turning the camera inwards, achieving a level of fame usually obtained by featuring on a reality TV show. Through the magic of the internet, an entirely new path was opened up for the young star, with opportunities in music, acting and even porn suddenly presenting themselves. More importantly, Crocker proved that YouTube could be a viable platform for not just expressing yourself, but also connecting with a global audience in a new, previously unfathomable way.

In 2021, Crocker reflected on the impact of the media frenzy around the 2007 video. 'Maybe people reaching out to tell me, "Chris, you were right," would feel good if I knew that people could unpack that the reason no one took me serious was because I was a gender-bending teenager and the reaction to me was transphobic,' Crocker said.[228] The adolescent even received death threats and later confided that the majority of the bullying experienced after the video came from other members of the LGBTQ+ community, including being physically attacked on the street and in gay clubs. 'LGBT people were embarrassed of me because of the way the media made fun of me, which made them feel I gave them a bad name,'

Crocker has recalled, underscoring how different the world was in 2007. 'This was during a pre-*Drag Race* time before everyone and their mom was saying, "Yasss, queen!" It was a time of only embracing the *heteronormative* people in media.'[229]

Crocker, who now has over 1 million followers on Instagram, sold the infamous clip as a non-fungible token for $41,000 in 2021. They plan to use the funds to pay for their grandmother's care and their own gender transition surgery, with Crocker explaining, 'I would absolutely put that towards, like, me being able to become myself.' In August 2021, Crocker began hormone replacement therapy and announced that they will henceforth answer to the name of Cara.

Indeed, all Cara and Britney have ever wanted is the freedom to live their lives.

Miss American Dream:
Britney Spears aged
seventeen.

Britney (front, right) smiling alongside her fellow Mouseketeers, including Ryan Gosling, Christina Aguilera and Justin Timberlake.

Left: Ed McMahon, host of the show that gave Britney her first taste of stardom.

Right: Teenage Britney attending the 1999 Nickelodeon Kids' Choice Awards.

Left: Producer Max Martin has been creating hits with Britney since her debut.

Right: Britney lighting up the stage during her first UK tour in 2000.

Britney with pop 'rival' Christina Aguilera at the 2000 VMAs.

A date in double-denim:
Britney and Justin Timberlake
coordinating at the 2001
American Music Awards.

Britney stealing the show at the 2001 VMAs, with help from Banana the python.

A 2002 press conference for teen movie *Crossroads*, starring Britney in the lead role.

Britney sharing an on-stage kiss with Madonna during another iconic VMAs performance in 2003.

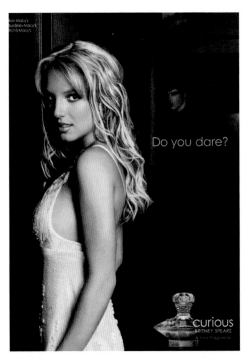

Promotional posters for the first two fragrances in Britney's now-multi-million-dollar perfume empire: Curious (2004) and Fantasy (2005).

Left: Britney and then-husband Kevin Federline photographed in 2005, shortly before the birth of their first child.

Below: Turning her hand to acting again, Britney made a two-episode cameo on *How I Met Your Mother* in 2006.

Britney arriving at family court in 2007, hounded by photographers
and reporters.

An ambulance transporting Britney to hospital in 2008, with the paparazzi
in hot pursuit.

Britney in 2012, appearing as a judge on the US version of *The X Factor*.

Businesswoman Britney launching her lingerie line in 2014.

A Las Vegas billboard advertising Britney's Piece of Me residency,
which ran for four hugely successful years.

Britney announcing her second Las Vegas residency, Domination,
prior to its sudden cancellation.

Put-on-a-show kind of girl: Britney performing in Las Vegas, 2016.

Above: Britney on stage during a medley of her hits at the 2016 *Billboard* Music Awards.

Right: A relentlessly busy Britney at the Jingle Ball in LA on 2 December 2016 (also the date of her thirty-fifth birthday).

Ardent fans can pay a visit to the Britney museum in the singer's hometown of Kentwood, Louisiana.

Supporters of the #FreeBritney movement have rallied around the pop star after details of her conservatorship came to light.

…Britney One More Time: the singer has attended the MTV VMAs on ten occasions over the course of her career. She made her debut at the event in 1999 (above, left), donned a full leather ensemble in 2002 (above, centre), received three awards in 2008 (above, right), was honoured as a 'vanguard' in 2011 (below, left), presented an award in 2015 (below, centre) and returned to perform at the show in 2016 (below, right).

Britney with her family, including father Jamie (left), who became his daughter's conservator in 2008.

Britney posing on the red carpet in 2019, having spent over a decade living under the conservatorship.

Princess of Pop: Britney Spears –
musician, performer and icon.

PIECE 23

Britney Births a Banger

Kevin Federline found out by text message that his wife of two years, Britney Spears, was filing for divorce, citing irreconcilable differences as her reason for dissolving the relationship. When he received the message, the aspiring rapper was doing interviews with Canadian TV channel MuchMusic as part of the promotional tour for his debut album, *Playing with Fire*. It has been suggested that, with Kevin sinking time and money into launching his own recording career and living the 'high life' afforded to him by his wife's wealth, Britney's old insecurities – loneliness and fear of abandonment – had begun to resurface. She wanted Federline to protest and fight for their relationship. However, if Britney was hoping that the threat of a split would be the catalyst for a change in Federline's behaviour, it had the opposite effect. According to a *Rolling Stone* article, instead of making a bid to stay with Spears, Federline went to a nightclub after receiving the news and scrawled on the wall, 'Today I'm a free man – fuck a wife, give me my kids, bitch!'

Britney's naiveté of the world, having grown up as a people pleaser guarded by handlers, left the star ill-equipped to face this new chapter in her life on her own. Indeed, one anecdote claims that she did not know how to use the internet until Paris Hilton taught her how to navigate Google. Her greatest hope was to be a mother and a wife; her greatest wish was to be normal and have a family. She had seemingly failed at both. Meanwhile, she had only recorded three songs in as many years.

Britney was now completely alone yet still surrounded by people. During her relationship with Kevin, Spears had fired long-term manager Larry Rudolph and fallen out with her parents. Soon after her separation, Britney started hanging out with heiress Hilton and actress Lindsay Lohan, club-hopping, drinking and partying. This new lifestyle could have been a young woman catching up on what she missed out on during her days of playing the chaste 'good girl' or it could have been Spears metaphorically pressing pause and putting her head in the sand.

It may have been jarring for those who bought into the pristine Spears to see her being escorted out of a nightclub, throwing up in public or acting unruly. As reported by *Rolling Stone*, Hilton's nickname for Britney was 'Animal' because she would act before thinking things through.[230] A poll by the Associated Press and America Online confirmed that the zealous reporting of her actions – from trading clothes with a stripper at a club to shaving her head – had massively decreased Britney's fanbase, though not the public's voracious obsession with knowing every intricacy about her life. It was within this stew of personal crisis, public obsession and career uncertainty that Britney made and dropped what is arguably her most creative and genre-splintering album to date: 2007's *Blackout*.

It is rare that the artistry or music of Britney is the first thing discussed or recognised when critics review the singer's work. Instead, it is almost always the tabloid tribulations that dominate any write-up; the actual songs are almost an afterthought once the regurgitation of Spears' perceived trespasses and failures is complete. *Blackout* proved to be no different. 'By contrast with poor old Britney, everything in Amy Winehouse's world is going just swimmingly,' wrote Alexis Petridis of *The Guardian* – a statement that is now tragic to read since Winehouse's passing.[231] Many of the other reviews led with similar media catnip, such as this artlessly presented piece in *Blender* magazine:

> Britney the pop singer has long been eclipsed by Britney the train wreck. Since her last studio album, she's become the star of an epic public meltdown, chronicled in tabloids and blogs: two marriages, one annulment, multiple rehab stints, a concussed live-television debacle, a failed custody battle and various misadventures in baby-dropping, head-shaving and crotch-exposing.[232]

Blackout may be the sum of these experiences, but, by reducing Britney to the scandal-sheet headlines, so many contemporary critics overlooked the on-point lyrics, innovative techniques and stylistic mash-ups that the album brought to the soundscape, creating the blueprint for countless artists who came after. In 2007, the top forty was filled with the grooving pop of Rihanna, Beyoncé and Kanye West, while Girls Aloud and the Sugababes brought technicolour bubblegum into the mix in the UK. Emo rock was also at its height, with Fall Out Boy and My Chemical Romance scoring high in the year-end charts. By comparison, *Blackout* was an alien entry that seemed to arrive from outer space.

The entire album shows a woman with agency. Credited as executive producer, Britney creates a dark yet hypnotic world, all killer no filler, comprising pop bangers and booty shakers alike. Two songs in particular depart from the usual Spears rule of not commenting on her personal trials. Opening track 'Gimme More' starts with the now-iconic declaration, 'It's Britney, bitch.' What began as a joke that producer Danja told Britney to say became an instantly quotable catchphrase. The disco-esque intro is accompanied by an almost demonic-sounding giggle – Britney insinuating that you can push her, but she won't break. However, the chorus seems to be asking how much the public really want to take from the singer, with references to cameras flashing and being watched preceding the crowd's repeated 'gimme, gimme more's. Spears' voiced is spliced and diced; any southern twang is gone, replaced throughout with a dark, robotic slink. 'The magic of *Blackout* was actually pretty simple,' Spears has recalled. 'It just wasn't so thought-out. I just did what I felt and it worked. Sometimes less is more, I guess.' This strategy worked. As one blogger put it, the album 'sounded like it came from the future – a dysto-pian and warped future, but nevertheless interesting'.[233]

The other telling tune, the haunting 'Piece of Me' (written and produced by 'Toxic' pop auteurs Bloodshy & Avant), plays like an autobiography, with Spears reeling off the realities of her life – from finding fame at seventeen and dealing with inva-sive paparazzi to becoming a mother and facing constant body criticism. The vocals have multiple layers of effects on them, making Britney seem disembodied from the experiences she is relating, adding to the impact of the words. As *Pitchfork* reviewer Tom Ewing astutely pointed out, 'Her typically clipped vocals make the line sound like, "You want a piece of meat,"' add-ing a secondary meaning to an already disturbing narrative.[234] However, 'Piece of Me' was an empowering anthem to some younger listeners, who viewed the track as a way of Spears fight-ing back against the vulture-like press and public. Este Haim, who plays bass and provides vocals for pop-rock band Haim, is an unabashed Spears fan. 'With "Piece of Me", it reminded me of Michael Jackson's "Leave Me Alone". She was throwing everything that people said about her back into people's faces and I loved that about her.' Bandmate Danielle agrees. 'Britney really did what she wanted with this record, which is so refresh-ing for that time coming off a bunch of records where she was prim and proper. This record came out and it felt like she was being herself and not letting anyone tell her what to do.'

Britney's name being on a unique-sounding album like *Blackout* allowed the LP to break rules and bring new influ-ences to the wider pop marketplace. In an article celebrating the ten-year anniversary of *Blackout*, Asma – another producer who has worked with the singer – underscored the importance of Spears stepping out and doing something unprecedented for a star of her stature: 'Some of the decisions made on that album were so visionary for pop music. It's not like nobody did that before, but Britney doing it was like, "Oh, shit."'[235]

The underestimation of Spears as an artist is a motif that has been repeated throughout the singer's life. The making of *Blackout* was no exception. 'Her public life might have been unmanageable, but, when it came to her work, Britney was the boss,' *Dazed* wrote in 2017:

> So, like an expert curator, she shaped and plotted the album with her deftness for pop music. Flooding the record with studio trickery and electronics . . . she picked producers who were plucking at genres and melding them together to create a Frankenstein musical behemoth threaded together by Britney's idiosyncratic vocal touches. As her A&R, Teresa LaBarbera Whites, said at the time, 'It's her magic that turns these songs into what they are.'[236]

Indeed, *Blackout* collaborators have corroborated Whites' assertion. Rapper, producer and songwriter T-Pain admitted that he'd expected Spears 'to be sitting on the couch eating Doritos or nachos or something' – but Britney surprised him:

> She came in there, shook my hand and went right into the booth. She was smiling the whole time. In an hour, we had a song. I sang it first and she sung over what I did . . . in key

and everything! Then did a whole 'nother song. She was about her business.

Songwriter Keri Hilson witnessed a similarly focused Spears, noting that she was amazed by the singer's work ethic. 'When we were arranging the vocals in the studio at her house,' Hilson said, 'she was about eight months pregnant and she was standing up in the vocal booth, just banging it out. Three weeks later, she had the baby.' Producer Pharrell Williams was also impressed by how Britney prioritised the making of *Blackout*, despite everything else that was going on in her life at the time. 'She's going through a lot that people don't recognise,' he recalled. 'You got to understand she was a child star and she's held on way longer than most people can. You got to understand the pressure . . . You're seeing a reality show that no one's producing, that no one's directing, and that's a problem.'[237] Julia Michaels, a writer on Spears' 2016 LP, *Glory*, shared similar praise of the singer, highlighting the fact that people view her as 'Britney Spears' – an 'incredible' dancer and performer – but often overlook her musical talent. 'I don't think they know that she can write. While we were working on *Glory*, literally everything she was saying sounded like the radio. We were like, "Yup. We're using that. Yup. That's done." It was incredible.'[238]

Though critics embraced *Blackout*, its title caused consternation; some thought it was a bit too closely referencing the hard-partying Spears portrayed in the press. This was not the intended meaning, however, according to Spears' label Jive. The name, they claimed, 'refers to blocking out negativity and embracing life fully'.[239] It still did not sit well with the press, though. In *The Guardian*, Petridis dubbed *Blackout* 'an unfortunate choice of title, given the nature of Spears' recent travails', while *Entertainment Weekly* commented that 'Spears has always been a performer who's valued image over creative output' when discussing the 'ominously titled *Blackout*'.[240]

The name of the LP was just one issue surrounding *Blackout*'s release. The original street date for the album was scheduled for 13 November 2007. However, Perez Hilton somehow got his paws on ten tracks and some unfinished demos and posted them on his popular website, forcing Britney's label to move the album's release forward to 30 October. Promotional efforts for *Blackout* were also minimal – a situation exacerbated by the universally panned performance of 'Gimme More' at the 2007 VMAs.

The cover artwork and pictures featured in the CD booklet were taken by Ellen von Unwerth, a German former fashion model. In a 2018 *Harper's Bazaar* interview, the photographer explained her feminist approach to taking pictures, saying, 'The women in my pictures are always strong, even if they are also sexy. My women always look self-assured. I try to make them look as beautiful as they can because every woman wants to feel beautiful, sexy and powerful. That's what I try to do.'[241] This motto comes across clearly in the snaps she captured of Spears for *Blackout*. Britney looks defiantly and directly down the barrel of the camera, donning a dark wig, white cowgirl hat, white gloves and a pink, sleeveless, sparkling dress. The back cover is similar, except Spears wears a blue dress. The design was not popular among reviewers, with some labelling the brightly coloured picture 'horrendous'.[242]

The images in the booklet were equally contentious, causing an uproar with the Catholic League, who accused Spears of 'mocking a Catholic sacrament'. The two black-and-white pictures in question feature Britney and a very handsome priest. In one, the singer is leaning against the side of a confessional while the priest looks on, seemingly knowing that a hot woman is on the other side of the partition. In the other, Spears is seated on the priest's lap. In both, Britney is wearing a crucifix and showing off a great pair of fishnet-stockinged legs.

The compositions drew comparisons with Madonna, especially the controversy surrounding the singer's 1989 'Like a Prayer' video. In under six minutes, Madonna was seen having sex with a saint, developing a stigmata and dancing around huge burning crosses. 'Madonna does it often, rolling around on disco balls with crosses,' said Kiera McCaffrey, the Catholic League's director of communication. 'These are powerful images . . . Is that the way a real entertainer wants people to talk about them? What would be great is if [Britney] got serious about her religious faith and, instead of mocking the confessional, maybe she could visit one for its intended purpose.'

Catholic League president Bill Donohue accused the insert of being part of a 'bottom-of-the-barrel' publicity stunt by Spears. He went on to defame the singer, saying that the shots were simply a 'cheap' way to 'get people to talk about Britney Spears' album without talking about her music':

All we see is how troubled this girl is now, especially with her family, losing her kids, with her career on a downward slide. And now she's put out this album and this is her tactic to promote it? She should be focusing on singing and dancing and trying to be an entertainer without mocking a Catholic sacrament.[243]

Yet it is Britney who gets the last laugh when it comes to *Blackout*. Upon reappraisal, the album is now considered a 'misunderstood punk masterpiece . . . one of the most innovative, influential pop albums of the past decade'.[244] It even earned a spot on *Rolling Stone*'s esteemed list of the '500 Greatest Albums of All Time', charting at number 441. During a period when Spears was the most hounded human in the world, probably feeling at her lowest, trusting no one, having her talent underrated on a global basis and facing accusations of being a bad mother, she created an unapologetic piece of art that broke all the rules and defied everyone's expectations. The result is a classic that really 'fucking bangs'.[245]

PIECE 24

Love for Sale

'Love is just like an unexplainable thing. And there's a saying that I have in my bathroom in Louisiana, it says, "Go
beyond reason to love for it's the only safety there is." And
it's true. You should always go beyond reason to love and
to be with the person that you want to be with and to be
cherished and to be treasured. I think it's why we're here
as people.'

– Britney Spears, *I Am Britney Jean*

Be it for financial gain, a grab at some refracted limelight or
simply 'bragging rights', Britney – the once-celebrated virgin –
was a highly desirable sexual conquest. Even a hint of a possible
liaison, real or fictitious, was enough to send tabloid tongues into
rabid overdrive. In his book, *The Unknown Keyboard Player*, Dan
Kenney, formerly part of Britney's backing band, discusses this

fascination with 'bedding' Britney. 'I was twenty-five years old when I landed the gig playing keyboards for Britney Spears,' writes Kenney, admitting that the question he still gets asked 'most frequently' is: 'Did you bang her?' Kenney goes on to note, 'It's only a male question. No woman ever, not even once, has asked me this. Only guys.'[246]

While any possible Britney hook-up was evaluated in minute detail, her former paramour Justin Timberlake worked his way through a long roster of flings and relationships – ranging from Spears' former party pal Lindsay Lohan to songstress Rihanna and actress Cameron Diaz – relatively unscathed. He faced no grilling about the intimate details of his liaisons nor did his partners ever run to the press for a cash windfall. In contrast, just claiming to have been with Britney – the biggest celebrity in the world – guaranteed a pay day of one kind or another.

NAME: Donald 'Reg' Jones
RELATIONSHIP: High-school boyfriend
WHAT HE GAINED: Money from selling Britney's
   personal letters

'It was fireworks right from the beginning right on to the end,' Britney's former beau Donald 'Reg' Jones recounts of the teenage relationship. The two first got together when Spears returned home to Louisiana after filming the *Mickey Mouse Club*. However, it was not long until Britney's career brought her to New York and Jones knew his days were numbered. One afternoon, while he was (fittingly) watching *Titanic*, Britney phoned him from Los Angeles to say that she had just beaten Leonardo DiCaprio at ping-pong. 'How do you compete with that?' says Jones.

Jones blames Britney's first assistant/tour manager Felicia 'Fe' Culotta for the break-up of his relationship with the young star, recalling that he and Culotta 'didn't get along' and that 'she did everything she could to either keep us apart or make sure people around Britney saw me as a negative influence on her'.[247]

After the relationship ended, Jones held on to some notes that Britney had sent him over the course of their time together. In 2021, Jones gave the ephemera to Julien's auction house in Beverly Hills to sell. The letters were valued at between £2,800 and £4,250. Two of the pieces date back to when Spears had just moved to the Big Apple as her recording career was taking off. 'What was wrong with you at lunch? You were mean,' one reads, while another is the dreaded break-up letter that ultimately finalised the end of the coupling. 'Look, I'm really sorry that it had to be this way, but I think we both knew this was coming,' says the handwritten message from Spears to Jones. 'I've had a great two years,' it continues. 'Who knows, two years from now or even ten, we might get back together if it's meant to be.'[248]

NAME: Columbus Short
RELATIONSHIP: On-the-road hook-up
WHAT HE GAINED: Money and 'bragging rights'
from selling his story

In 2003, Columbus Short was a married backing dancer expecting his first child. While on tour with Britney, a photograph of him kissing the singer was made public. 'The chemistry was magical . . . our feelings were so strong,' he recalls.[249] A year later, the recently single Short sold his story to tabloid magazine *The Star*, recounting his time spent with Spears. 'It's true, I slept with Britney,' Short says in the interview, though he adds that things never went beyond kissing and hugging as the two were never alone together.

However, Short records a more intimate encounter in his 2020 autobiography, *Short Stories*. In the book, the dancer claims to have consummated his relationship with Britney one crazy night in 2003, adding that the singular rendezvous was supposedly enough for Britney to answer that she wanted to marry him during a game of truth or dare on the road.

The liaison did not last long, though, as Short contends that Britney's parents were not supportive of the two dating. 'I was next to her while she was on the phone with them crying,' Short says, alleging that they then asked her, 'Why are you f**king that n****r?' He recounts that Britney 'looked at me so apologetically, knowing I'd heard it . . . I shook my head and didn't say anything because what was there to say?'[250]

NAME: Fred Durst
RELATIONSHIP: Rock-star nookie
WHAT HE GAINED: Publicity and dubious respect for
   'bagging' Britney

In February 2003, a hungover Fred Durst – frontman of rage-rock band Limp Bizkit – took to the airwaves with notorious shock jock Howard Stern and swore on the blue eyes of his son,

Dallas, that the rumours flying around fan forums and the tabloids were true: he was in a relationship with Britney Spears. Durst had already alluded to having the hots for Spears on the Limp Bizkit website, writing in a post, 'Anybody out there who has a serious problem with my feelings for Britney should just chill and worry about your own feelings for a minute. [She] just happens to be a person I [wouldn't] have thought could make me feel this way.' He then concluded with the surprisingly heartfelt line, 'I have never felt this way, so there.'[251]

Though the 'Nookie' singer claimed that the duo had been together for some time, it was only when Britney denied even knowing the rocker that he saw it fitting to go public. 'It's sad that he's decided to make up stories and the situation feels very junior high school,' a spokesperson for Spears said. Durst, however, argued that pictures of the two stars began popping up in the tabloids after they collaborated on some music. 'Kids start seeing these pictures and asking, "What's going on?" I had to defend myself to my fans . . . It blew up really big. I started to get upset,' Durst explained.[252]

Stern cross-examined Durst for the details of any intimacies; Durst told the DJ that Spears was not the 'sweet, innocent girl' she seemed to be and that he had seen the pop princess 'drink and smoke'.[253] Everything else about his time with the singer could be found in the lyrics of his new, unreleased song, which included the couplet 'Ain't it funny, scared to admit it / Very first night made the Limp dog hit it.'[254]

Years later, Durst reflected on his rumoured romance with Britney. 'I guess at the time it was taboo for a guy like me to be associated with a gal like her,' he reminisced with a laugh.[255]

NAME: Colin Farrell
RELATIONSHIP: Hollywood make-out
WHAT HE GAINED: A public brush-off from Britney

At the start of 2003, infamous Hollywood bad boy Colin Farrell was filming his newest movie *S.W.A.T.* when Britney happened to pop by the set. The two hit it off and soon surprised fans and the media by walking the red carpet together for the premiere of Farrell's flick *The Recruit*. Though snaps from the night show them looking very friendly, the actor insisted that they were not dating and that Spears was 'just a mate', repeatedly reiterating that they had only met days before. The duo was then spotted making out at an after party at Los Angeles hotspot Chateau Marmont. A member of the public captured the lip-lock and reportedly sold the image for 'a lot of money'. Several months later, when asked about the Irish heartthrob during an interview with *W* magazine, Britney confided that she had indeed kissed the actor, saying, 'He's the cutest, hottest thing in the world – wooh! . . . But it was nothing serious.'

Farrell felt dissed by what he saw as a very big, public brush-off and is said to have retaliated by sending Britney several unsolicited gifts: first, a top printed with the line 'I slept with Colin Farrell and all I got was this lousy T-shirt'; then a bumper sticker reading 'Honk if you've slept with Colin Farrell'. An unimpressed Britney was reported to have been 'furious' upon receipt.[256]

NAME: Isaac Cohen
RELATIONSHIP: Rebound fling
WHAT HE GAINED: Money from telling the tabloids
intimate details about Britney

It had only been a month since Britney had filed for divorce from husband Kevin Federline when she was set up on a blind date with model Isaac Cohen. The relationship only lasted seven weeks, after which Cohen sprinted to tabloid *News of the World* to sell all the salacious specifics.

'By the time I met Britney, she was burnt out,' Cohen stated. 'She knew she had been drinking and partying to try to banish the bad stuff from her life. Far from the trashy drunk, I saw a very shy, sweet girl who was just desperately sad about what had happened with her marriage.' Unsurprisingly, Cohen asserted that Britney 'was not over her marriage' and even recalled seeing the singer's wedding dress hanging in a glass box on the wall the first time he went to her house. 'As we made love that night, it was like Kevin was in bed beside us. She had not even begun to move on with her life,' Cohen alleged.

The model claimed to have provided Britney with support when her beloved aunt, Sandra Bridges Covington, passed away from cancer in 2007 – a loss that 'totally devastated' Spears. 'It was yet another blow . . . it was me she turned to for comfort and me who travelled to Louisiana [with Britney] for the funeral,' reported Cohen.[257] He also said that Britney was very self-conscious of her post-baby body: 'Like any woman who has had two children, she worried about her figure . . . she had such low self-esteem, she sometimes would not listen. She would say, "Am I fat? Am I fat?," then spend hours dancing around the house trying to burn off calories.'[258] The relationship did not reach even the two-month mark before Cohen supposedly rang Britney to call things off. According to an unnamed friend, it had all become 'a bit much for him . . . too much of a whirlwind'.[259]

NAME: Adnan Ghalib
RELATIONSHIP: Dating the enemy
WHAT HE GAINED: Money and momentary fame

Never doubt the power of a takeaway sandwich to get sparks flying – as was the case for British transplant Adnan Ghalib. In late 2007, the Birmingham-born snapper was just another pap following Britney around Los Angeles when he found himself among a scrum of photographers in sub chain Quiznos waiting for Britney to emerge from the fast-food restaurant's bathroom. Suddenly, the singer opened the door and beckoned him to join her. As soon as images of Ghalib entering the bog with Britney began circulating, Ghalib's wife filed for a legal separation. Instead of being heartbroken, Ghalib started crowing to his friends that he planned to marry and impregnate the star.

Not long after the tête-à-tête in the loo, the pap was papped again – this time, while driving down the Pacific Coast Highway, following Spears' car. Britney eventually pulled over and jumped in Ghalib's vehicle, kickstarting a fleeting relationship between the two shortly before Spears was taken to the hospital for the first time. As soon as she got out, the couple tried to take a getaway together, seemingly evading photographers as they criss-crossed through Palm Springs and over the US border into Mexico.

There was one company, however, that had the inside-track exclusive on every last-minute detail, accompanied by pictures of the new lovebirds. That company was Finalpixx – the photo agency Ghalib had started working for in 2007. 'She's never made the best choices in friends, even her relationships,' Ghalib said of Spears, clearly missing the irony.[260] 'She's easily influenced and that's where her bad choices come from.' Ghalib also claimed that the paps were a good presence in Britney's life, asserting, 'Maybe the only friends she's going to have that treat her with the respect she deserves are going to be the photographers that work her twenty-four hours a day. It's going to have to be us. I think we are her friends now.'[261]

When Finalpixx snapped an image of the couple at a Los Angeles drug store in mid-January 2008, rumours spread that Britney was shopping for a pregnancy test, though there was also the suggestion that the pictures had been staged for money. Alli Sims, Britney's former assistant, said that she believed Ghalib had 'bad intentions', while another source claimed that Spears' love interest knew that, 'if he had a child with her, he'd be made for life', adding that 'Adnan is a social climber who uses women to get what he wants'.[262] However, it was not until Britney was shown 'alleged proof' that Ghalib 'was tipping off' photo agency pals that she dumped him and had a restraining order taken out. She was said to be specifically worried that intimate images Ghalib had taken of her while they were together would be sold to the highest bidder. 'She is in a panic now as to how he might use everything he has learned against her,' said a friend.[263]

Within eight months, Britney's fears came true: Ghalib attempted to flog a supposed sex tape he had of himself and the singer. He spouted that he wouldn't 'discuss prices for hypothetical enquiries' as he was looking for 'a locked-in deal'.[264] Just days after attempting to pawn the sexy goods, Ghalib came back to the media professing that he had never claimed to own such a tape and that he was 'taking legal action' against those who said one existed.[265] The status or existence of the item is still unknown. In the early '00s, sex tapes had the power to make careers and broker deals worth millions of dollars. Indeed, both Paris Hilton and Kim Kardashian got their start in reality TV from their own intimate recordings being 'leaked' (though Hilton's video has since been reframed by some pundits as revenge porn). If such a film of Britney does exist, Ghalib may have seen it as a way to wring more money out of his time with Spears while simultaneously attempting to hold on to the spotlight himself for just a couple more seconds.

PIECE 25

If U Seek Britney

The year 2008 was jam-packed with historical celebrations and the emergence of culture changers. The summer Olympics took place in Beijing, China, and saw swimmer Michael Phelps crush the former record for most gold medals won by an individual at a single Games, bringing home eight of the glittering beauties for the US. In November, Barack Obama was elected president, becoming the first African American to do so. Spotify launched in Sweden that year, too; the platform would quickly go on to change the way fans consume and value music and artists. Bitcoin, the first decentralised digital currency, was also invented, signalling the dawn of a new approach to thinking about and using money.

Though all of these events were huge touchstones on an international level, they paled in comparison to a certain search term that generated more unique searches on Yahoo! than any other entity. The title of list-topper belonged to an individual who late-night TV host Jimmy Kimmel described as 'by far the most powerful celebrity on this planet'.[266] That person was Britney Spears.

In 2011, Google employee John Mueller shared a document showing that there were an astounding 593 different ways in which people typed Spears' name when doing an online search for her. In his explanation of the information, Mueller wrote:

> The data below shows some of the misspellings detected by our spelling correction system for the query ['Britney Spears'] and the count of how many different users spelled her name that way. Each of these variations was entered by at least two different unique users within a three-month period and was corrected to 'Britney Spears' by our spelling correction system (data for the correctly spelled query is shown for comparison).[267]

488941 britney spears	29 britent spears	9 brinttany spears	5 brney spears
40134 brittany spears	29 brittnany spears	9 britanay spears	5 broitney spears
36325 brittney spears	29 britttany spears	9 britinany spears	5 brotny spears
24342 britany spears	29 btiney spears	9 britn spears	5 bruteny spears
7331 britny spears	26 birttney spears	9 britnew spears	5 btiyney spears
6633 briteny spears	26 breitney spears	9 britneyn spears	5 btrittney spears
2696 britteny spears	26 brinity spears	9 britrney spears	5 gritney spears
1807 brimey spears	26 britenay spears	9 brtiny spears	5 spritney spears
1635 brittny spears	26 britneyt spears	9 brtittney spears	4 bittny spears
1479 brimtey spears	26 brittas spears	9 brtny spears	4 bnritney spears
1479 britanny spears	26 brittne spears	9 brytny spears	4 brandy spears
1338 britiny spears	26 btittany spears	9 rbitney spears	4 brbritney spears
1211 britnet spears	24 beitney spears	8 birtiny spears	4 breatiny spears
1096 britiney spears	24 birtony spears	8 bithney spears	4 brootney spears
991 britaney spears	24 brightney spears	8 brattany spears	4 bretiney spears
991 britnay spears	24 brintiny spears	8 breitny spears	4 brfitney spears
881 brithney spears	24 britanty spears	8 breteny spears	4 briattany spears
881 brtiney spears	24 britonny spears	8 brightny spears	4 briotony spears
664 birtney spears	24 britini spears	8 brimtay spears	4 briety spears

664 brimtney spears	24 britnwy spears	8 brimtey spears	4 briitny spears
664 briteney spears	24 brittni spears	8 briotney spears	4 briittany spears
601 bitney spears	24 brittnie spears	8 britanys spears	4 brinie spears
601 brinty spears	21 biritney spears	8 britley spears	4 brinteney spears
544 brittaney spears	21 birtany spears	8 britneyb spears	4 brinte spears
544 brittnay spears	21 bitony spears	8 britnrey spears	4 britaby spears
364 britey spears	21 bratney spears	8 britnty spears	4 britaey spears
364 brittiny spears	21 britani spears	8 brittner spears	4 britainey spears
329 brtney spers	21 britanie spears	8 brottany spears	4 britinie spears
269 bretney spears	21 britoany spears	7 baritney spears	4 britinney spears
269 britneys spears	21 brittay spears	7 birmtey spears	4 britmney spears
244 britne spears	21 brittinay spears	7 biteney spears	4 britnear spears
244 brytney spears	21 brtany spears	7 bitiny spears	4 britnel spears
220 breatney spears	21 brtiany spears	7 breateny spears	4 britneuy spears
220 britiany spears	19 birney spears	7 brianty spears	4 britnewy spears
199 britnney spears	19 brirtney spears	7 brimtye spears	4 britnmey spears
163 britnry spears	19 britnaey spears	7 britianny spears	4 brittaby spears
147 breatny spears	19 britnee spears	7 britly spears	4 brittery spears
147 brittiney spears	19 britony spears	7 britnej spears	4 britthey spears
147 britty spears	19 brittamty spears	7 britneyo spears	4 brittnaey spears
147 brotney spears	19 britttney spears	7 britniey spears	4 brittnat spears
147 brutney spears	17 birtny spears	7 britnnay spears	4 brittneny spears
133 britteney spears	17 brieny spears	7 brittian spears	4 brittnye spears
133 briyney spears	17 brintty spears	7 briyny spears	4 brittteny spears
121 bittany spears	17 brithy spears	7 brrittany spears	4 briutney spears
121 bridney spears	17 brittanie spears	7 brttiney spears	4 briyeny spears
121 britainy spears	15 brinney spears	7 btiteny spears	4 brnity spears
121 britmey spears	15 briten spears	7 btrittany spears	4 brrteny spears
109 brietney spears	15 briterney spears	6 beritny spears	4 brttiany spears
109 brithny spears	15 britheny spears	6 bhrithney spears	4 bryney spears
109 britni spears	15 britneny spears	6 birthney spears	4 brythney spears
109 brittant spears	15 brittamy spears	6 breathney spears	4 brytne spears
98 bittney spears	15 brittmey spears	6 breaty spears	4 brytni spears
98 brithey spears	15 brytnei spears	6 bretany spears	4 brytnie spears
98 brittiany spears	15 btirney spears	6 briatany spears	4 bvritney spears
98 btitney spears	15 rittney spears	6 brimt spears	4 dritney spears
89 brietny spers	14 brinet spears	6 britenney spears	4 priteny spears
89 brimety spears	14 britneyy spears	6 britian spears	3 beittamy spears
89 brimtny spears	14 britten spears	6 brititny spears	3 bichney spears
89 britnie spears	12 beritney spears	6 brititney spears	3 biritny spears
89 brittey spears	12 bretiny spears	6 britney spears	3 birnety spears

Source: Google, 2011

In 2012, it was revealed that Spears – with all variants of her name – had topped the list of global online dominance for seven of the twelve years documented, making her the 'most-searched celebrity since *basically the inception of the internet*', beating out the likes of Michael Jackson, One Direction, the Kardashians and Princess Diana.[268]

A decade later, the interest in Britney shows no sign of slowing down. A 2021 round-up of the hottest trending celebrities online still placed Spears in the top twenty, charting alongside relative newcomers Billie Eilish, Dua Lipa and Harry Styles.[269] It will be interesting to see whether any current Gen-Z celebrities, who have come of age in an entirely digital native economy, can command the same staying power as Spears in the years to come. Only time will tell.

Besides the tabloid obsession, it is Britney's devout fanbase, multiple business ventures and wide-ranging demographic appeal that have kept her relevant. If the newbies can learn from the framework Britney has created and exploit it to their benefit, they may be able to reach similar heights. Ultimately, though, while many others have tried to duplicate her success in the past, no one has ever realised the same level of profit, fame and longevity that seem to belong uniquely to Britney, Priteny, Rittney or Dritney . . .

PIECE 26

The Battle for Britney

A conservatorship is a legal guardianship usually put in place for those who cannot make their own decisions. It is typically used when an individual is unable to take care of themselves physically or mentally and is most often reserved for cases in which a person has dementia or another brain-functionality illness that could affect their financial decision-making capabilities. In 2008, after Britney Spears experienced several very public breakdowns, her father, Jamie, filed a petition to place her under a court-ordered arrangement of this nature. In the legal paperwork supporting the action, Britney's parents described her as 'an adult child in the throes of a mental-health crisis'.[270]

Originally approved following Britney's involuntarily stay in a psychiatric hospital, the conservatorship was only meant to be a temporary measure until Britney recovered. However, the arrangement was soon made permanent, designating Jamie as the singer's co-conservator alongside attorney Andrew Wallet. This put her estate, financial assets and some personal affairs – totalling more than $60 million – under the control of her father and his lawyer. As soon as she was released from the hospital, Spears protested against the arrangement. A recording shared by *Rolling Stone* of a call between Spears and a lawyer at the time captures the singer saying, 'I basically want my life back. I want to be able to drive my car. I want to be able to live in my house by myself. I want to be able to say who's going to be my body-guard.'[271] However, the conservatorship prohibited Britney from appointing her own lawyer to fight legal battles on her behalf.

In a voicemail left for her legal team in the early hours of 21 January 2009, the star claimed that the elder Spears had 'threatened' her 'several times' with the prospect of taking her children away. The aim of the call was to seek reassurance from the lawyers, with Britney asking them to 'guarantee that every-thing will be fine with the process of you guys taking care of everything – that things will stay the same as far as my custodial time'.[272] The transcripts of the message do not read like someone who would be unable to make her own decisions; they seem to be the legitimate concerns of a mother prioritising her kids above all else, even herself.

Jamie would not have been the obvious choice to act as guard-ian for his middle child. Growing up, Britney's father was an alcoholic, often absent from the family home. 'She felt like he was this scary guy who she didn't really know because he was never around,' commented a friend of Britney's about the rela-tionship between the two.[273] Though couched as concern for his daughter's mental and emotional wellbeing, the newly discovered interest in his offspring led a slew of Britney fans to wonder whether he was motivated by cash. 'Some people worry that Britney's family are using her for all the wrong reasons,' said Michelle Lee, editor of celebrity magazine *In Touch Weekly*.

Britney was – and still is – an indisputably huge business, having sold more than 83 million records worldwide and being the eighth best-selling female artist in American history. It is thus unsurprising that Britney has been the main breadwinner for the entire Spears family for decades. Britney is a branded industry unto herself, but this also means 'it is hard to see whether the people around her are there for the right reasons', Lee added.[274]

Among the 'people around her' was Lou Taylor, Britney's former business manager. Taylor initially came to the public's awareness in January 2008 when the singer was placed under her first 5150 psychiatric hold. At the time, her title was 'Britney Spears' family's spokesperson'. Taylor had already ingratiated herself into the clan as business manager for both Jamie and his youngest daughter, Jamie Lynn. According to Lynne Spears, it was Taylor who played an imperative part in placing Britney under the conservatorship. In her memoir, Britney's mother recalls how Taylor led the charge to formalise the legal arrangement:

> Quiet plans had been under way for six weeks for Jamie to petition the court for temporary conservatorship of Britney, but it seemed like an impossible dream at that point. In fact, Jamie was going to file for the conservatorship on 22 January, eight days beforehand, but he and his business manager, Lou, felt God leading them to wait, fast and pray.[275]

It seems Jamie is not the only one who may have profited from the situation with his daughter; Taylor's assets reportedly 'doubled once the conservatorship began'. However, Britney's standing as a gay icon and avid supporter of the queer community must not have sat well with Taylor, whose husband, Robert, remains a pastor at the evangelical, anti-LGBTQ+ Calvary Chapel. In an unvalidated email from Britney to her lawyer in 2007, the singer allegedly referred to Taylor as a 'crazy lady' and a 'stalker'.[276] It has since been claimed that Taylor also attempted (unsuccessfully) to place both Lindsay Lohan and Courtney Love under similar court-restricted arrangements when she worked with the two stars.

Yet, despite any nebulous influences, Britney did seem to take a massive turn for the better while under her father's watch. Within three months of the conservatorship being put into place, Britney's 'good behaviour' earned her expanded visitation rights with her sons.[277] Less than a year later, in December 2008, Britney's sixth studio album, *Circus*, debuted at number one on the *Billboard* charts. Things seemed to be on the upswing. However, this may have had more to do with Spears' survivor spirit than any other factor.

By 2019, over a decade since the implementation of the conservatorship, Britney had been incredibly busy, releasing four albums, performing a four-year residency in Las Vegas and adding a staggering twenty new fragrances to her wildly successful perfume empire. Yet, in January that year, Spears unexpectedly announced 'an indefinite work hiatus' and cancelled her second, newly scheduled Las Vegas residency, Britney: Domination. Shortly after, she checked into a mental-health centre, spurring her supporters to reignite their cause. While the official reason given for the change of plan was Britney wanting to focus on her family, specifically Jamie, who had been having ongoing health issues, there were also rumours that Spears needed the thirty-day hospital stay because the 'cocktail of meds she had been taking had become ineffective and left her unstable'. Britney later claimed that she was committed to the facility 'against her will' and 'forced' to take drugs.[278]

Britney's dedicated audience were once again starting to worry about their idol. However, it was a voicemail released by fan podcast *Britney's Gram* that really kicked things off. The audio show – centred around unpacking the meaning of Spears' Instagram posts – had become a community space for Britney devotees worldwide. In April 2019, an anonymous caller, claiming to be a former member of Spears' legal team, left a message on the podcast's hotline alleging that the star was being held against her will at a mental-health hospital and that it was Britney's refusal to take her medication that had led Jamie to cancel her Domination residency. 'I had chills down my spine just from the tone of his voice,' podcast host Tess Barker said of the message. The call solidified what many had thought for a long time, asserted *Britney's Gram* co-host Babs Gray: 'It was just the tipping point for those of us who were paying attention and had concerns about the conservatorship and the control over Britney. What the paralegal revealed just validated that something was really amiss and lit fire to the flame.'[279]

Incited by the call, Barker and Gray produced a special 'emergency' episode of their show to share the latest development in

Britney's situation, resulting in a live-streamed protest from outside City Hall, West Hollywood, on 22 April 2019. Fans felt that the voicemail had confirmed their worst fears: the singer was being stopped from making any decisions for herself. Advocates thrust 'Free Britney' signs in the air while repeatedly chanting 'Hands off Britney' and 'Justice for Britney'. In a scene that would be the first of many over the subsequent two years, the dozen-strong demonstrators were joined by an equal number of television crews covering the 'event' – a haunting replication of the unrelenting coverage Britney herself had endured a decade earlier.

The following month, Spears spoke to the judge in her conservatorship case for the first known time in more than two years, resulting in a court order for an expert 'to evaluate the singer's situation'.[280] Spears left the courthouse barefoot as fans outside chanted 'Free Britney' and waved signs of support. The movement soon gained traction, with campaigners drumming up over 125,000 signatures for their petition to end Britney's conservatorship and celebrities like Paris Hilton and Rose McGowan adopting the #FreeBritney hashtag. However, despite Spears' lawyers once again going to court in August 2020, the judge presiding over the case did not alter the conservatorship. This further enraged supporters, with the freebritney.net website reminding its readers that Britney 'is legally not her own person' and still 'needs permission from her conservators to leave her house or spend any of her own money'.[281]

According to Spears' friend and make-up artist Billy Brasfield, all Britney longs for in her life 'are the most normal things':

She wants to be able to drive her car when she wants to. In the conservatorship, she does not have that right. It's important to point out that there is an army of attorneys on the conservatorship side, working against Britney, that her money is paying for while she has a court-appointed attorney like a hooker on the street . . . There is a lot of money involved.[282]

Jamie Spears was unsurprisingly not enamoured with the efforts of the #FreeBritney movement. In August 2020, he denounced the advocates as 'a joke', saying, 'All these conspiracy theorists don't know anything. The world don't have a clue. It's up to the court of California to decide what's best for my daughter. It's no one else's business.' He also denied allegations that he was withholding money from Britney, commenting, 'I have to report every nickel and dime spent to the court every year. How the hell would I steal something?' He then went on to claim, 'People are being stalked and targeted with death threats. It's horrible. We don't want those kinds of fans.' He concluded the interview by professing, 'I love my daughter. I love all my kids. But this is our business. It's private.'[283]

Yet this 'love' for his offspring did not stop him going to court again in April 2021 looking for just shy of $2 million in legal fees and compensation to cover the time spent as his daughter's conservator between 1 November 2019 and 28 February 2021. (The court document had already recorded and approved payments for his time as conservator up to 31 October 2019.) In the filing, Jamie stated:

I am authorized and allowed to receive compensation through my personal services corporation Spears Management, Inc., for services performed as Conservator of the Estate of Britney Jean Spears, in the amount of $16,000 monthly plus $2,000 monthly for the cost of an office space in a secure location that is dedicated to Ms Spears' activities.[284]

Given Spears senior's continued defence of the conservatorship, the September 2021 announcement that he would be filing to terminate his daughter's mandate came as rather unexpected news. The court filing by his lawyers even acknowledged Britney's wish to reclaim her autonomy, noting:

She wants to be able to make decisions regarding her own medical care, deciding when, where and how often to get therapy. She wants to control the money she has made from her career and spend it without supervision or oversight. She wants to be able to get married and have a baby, if she so chooses. In short, she wants to live her life without the constraints of a conservator or court proceeding. As Mr Spears has said again and again, all he wants is what is best for his daughter. If Ms Spears believes that she can handle her own life, Mr Spears believes that she should get that chance.[285]

Three weeks after this filing, Jamie was suspended as Britney's conservator.

In the 2008 *For the Record* documentary, a beaten-down Britney tearfully confessed to feeling like a prisoner, completely powerless in a 'never-ending' situation. 'If I wasn't under the restraints I'm under, I'd feel so liberated,' she added, 'I always wanted to be free.'[286] Perhaps now, as she turns forty, her wish might finally come true.

PIECE 27

Jagged Little Thrill

Britney Spears has always embraced a cover song. Her 1999 . . . Baby One More Time Tour featured an extravaganza of vintage hits, ranging from the Sonny & Cher classic 'The Beat Goes On' to an '80s homage that included a Journey power ballad and tunes by two of Britney's idols, Janet Jackson and Madonna. However, the turn of the millennium saw the pop princess incorporating more rock into her repertoire, starting with a cover of the Rolling Stones' '(I Can't Get No) Satisfaction' on her second album, *Oops! . . . I Did It Again*. Her third studio release, the self-titled *Britney*, then went on to feature a recording of 'I Love Rock 'n' Roll' – a song made famous in 1981 by the iconic Joan Jett (whose own version was a cover of the Arrows' 1975 original).

By the time that 2009's The Circus Starring Britney Spears began touring coliseums and arenas, the practice of throwing a random tune by another artist into an evening's performance was nothing new for the seasoned professional. Yet there was something profound about Spears' inclusion and interpretation of one track in particular – a cover she performed during just a handful of dates across the Midwest. The breathtaking performance, which seems to have only been captured as crackly, low-resolution fan-filmed footage, showcases Britney at her rawest and arguably best. The sublime clip, clocking in at just three minutes and twenty-three seconds, is a video of Spears covering Alanis Morissette's breakthrough track from her 1995 album *Jagged Little Pill*, 'You Oughta Know'.

The song is an unapologetic, scathing litany of wrongs perpetrated by a former lover. In someone else's hands, it could have made for a bitter and unlikeable protagonist. Instead, the co-writing talents of Morissette and Glen Ballard provided power to the female voice. Upon its release, 'You Oughta Know' helped Morissette ascend to the status of Gen-X alt-rock goddess. At first glance, Morissette seems to be the antithesis of brand Britney and an unlikely choice for the pop star to cover. Morissette's appeal and glamour came from writing her own songs. They were relatable and captured experiences familiar to many people. With her long dark hair and soulful eyes, Morissette looked and dressed like your cool friend from college. In contrast, bouncy, blonde-haired Spears was all about the fun dance tunes – perfect for a cardio blast at the gym or a good boogie on a night out, but not necessarily what one would put on for a bout of serious introspection.

However, when you see Britney step up to the mic as the opening bars of the Alanis classic crash through the massive theatre, all of that is forgotten; the track belongs to Spears. Unlike many of her own songs that have been subjected to repeated accusations of lip-syncing or vocal 'help', it is instantly obvious that Spears is singing live, adding a gravelly Rod-Stewart-via-Stevie-Nicks-esque intonation. Wearing skin-tight low-rise trousers, a denim vest over a string bikini top and a pair of large black sunglasses, Spears tosses her hair extensions over her shoulders and starts singing the well-loved lyrics. Even though the camera is pointed at her back and her face is only occasionally visible, you can still feel all the disappointment and heartbreak she has experienced throughout her life. Her delivery is full of vitriol and anger. Unlike other Britney shows that depend on elaborate dance moves and lush stage sets, this it is just Spears standing at a mic, completely alone – and you cannot take your eyes off her.

In an interview a decade later, Morissette was asked what she thought about Spears performing her song in 2009. 'Awesome,' Alanis answered, 'I love Britney.'[287]

Though the cover was only included on her setlist six times, 'You Oughta Know' proved that Britney had the versatility to be a pop star *and* a rock star. It also illustrated that she does not need the (often literal) stage pyrotechnics to captivate an audience or hold their attention. She just needs the opportunity to do what she originally set out to do: sing.

PIECE 28

The People's Pop Princess

'It is a point to remember that, of all the ironies about Diana, perhaps the greatest was this: a girl given the name of the ancient goddess of hunting was, in the end, the most hunted person of the modern age.'

— Earl Spencer's eulogy at the funeral of
Diana, Princess of Wales, 1997

Britney Spears has long had an affinity for the British — and especially the royals. In a 2000 interview, Spears revealed her crush on the country's king-in-waiting. When asked about what she thought about Charles's eldest, Britney responded, 'Marry Prince William? I would love that. After all, who wouldn't want to be a princess? It's kind of hard to resist him as cute as he is.' In William, Britney saw someone who could identify with what she dealt with as a public figure (though she was not even two full years into her global rise to stardom at the time). 'I'm glad he seems like a normal guy and I can sympathise with him,' she continued. 'It's such a major production if I even want to go out, so I can only imagine what it's like for him. I think I would understand more than most people how hard it is.'[288] Sources near the royal reported that William was a 'fan' of Spears, prompting Britney's reps to reach out to palace officials to set up a rendezvous for the duo during Spears' next tour of the UK. In her memoir, Lynne Spears gushed about the possibility of a royal audience, writing, 'We were invited to meet him [William] in London . . . can you imagine being asked to go to Buckingham Palace?'[289]

'Rumours of a cyber romance' between Wills and Brit provided tabloid fodder for months, with Spears confiding that the two had become 'quite friendly' and were exchanging emails.[290] Sadly, the in-person meet-up was not to be. During a 2002 talk-show interview, Britney confessed that, although she had invited the prince to visit her and possibly grab a meal together, 'it didn't work out' in the end. Spears admitted that she had been 'blown off' and was unsure why.[291] Entertainment magazines later claimed it was a fox hunt that had diverted the young royal from meeting the American import, but there could have been other reasons, too. After a flurry of speculation, Buckingham Palace finally issued a statement of their own, saying that Prince William 'had received no correspondence with Britney Spears at all, either by letter or email'. According to some royal watchers, the nineteen-year-old heir saw the whole circus surrounding his possible liaison with Spears as a stunt and was said to have been 'upset at being exploited in such a manner'.[292]

The brush-offs did not affect Britney's fascination with the Windsors, though. Regal princess-esque glamour was the vibe for the 2014 launch of the Intimate Britney Spears Lingerie line. Held at London's Hotel Café Royal, the event featured waiters serving lavish cakes, macarons and 'tea in china cups, which reflected the collection's vintage theme'. The room was literally blooming with more than 1,000 flowers, including 500 of Britney's signature favourite – pale-pink roses. While making an appearance at what 'must have been the shortest press conference in history, lasting a mere two minutes', the singer revealed that she had shipped a care package of the undies to William's wife, Kate.[293] Spears then commented – in a British accent – that she 'would love to see Kate' in one of her designs. 'I'm going to send her one of every piece, so she'll have plenty to choose from.'[294]

However, Britney's interest in William predates both her unsolicited gifting and her teenage crush. The star's preoccupation is actually rooted in her long-term identification with the prince's mother, Diana, who was killed in a car accident in 1997 while trying to avoid paparazzi cameras in Paris. Spears clearly feels a strong connection between the treatment Princess Diana endured and the way her own personal dramas played out more than a decade later. The attributes both women share must at once comfort and terrify Britney.

In his 2009 *Vanity Fair* article 'Tragic Blondes: The Diana–Britney Connection', writer Steve Dennis compared the similarities between the two iconic figures. He highlighted how the young women were 'catapulted by populist taste; both were underdogs who achieved an against-all-odds fairy tale; both were huntresses, and prey, of the paparazzi; and both were dogged by scandal, creating "news" just by breathing'.[295] When the basic facts are placed side by side, Dennis's observations highlight some uncanny parallels:

MEDIA TITLE:
Diana: People's Princess
Britney: Pop Princess

FAMILY STATUS:
Diana/Britney: Divorced mother-of-two

QUEST IN LIFE:
Diana/Britney: True love and normalcy

BIGGEST HANG-UP:
Diana/Britney: Lack of self/low self-esteem

ON LOVE:
Diana: 'If you find someone you love, then hang on to that love.'
Britney: 'As much as you love is as much as you hurt.'

BIGGEST COMPLAINT:
Diana/Britney: Invasive paparazzi

BIGGEST FLIRTATION:
Diana/Britney: Invasive paparazzi

Source: Dennis, 2009

The commonalities shared by the late Diana and Britney conform to a specific archetype – one that includes other mythologised figures like Marilyn Monroe, Amy Winehouse and Janis Joplin. It's the narrative of a brilliant, complicated individual taken from life too soon, but it also exposes the media – and perhaps the public – as a complicit and arguably predatory force in that star's demise. In a piece for *Vox* in 2020, Constance Grady contended that this is the story of 'women whose combined innocence and sex appeal and star power makes the public worship them' and yet 'the idea that they might be using all that sex appeal and star power to make the public worship them on purpose, rather than out of sheer innocence', causes us to hound them. According to Grady, our obsession only has one end: the tragic demise 'of the women we love to death'.

For over a decade, Britney voraciously read anything she could get her hands on pertaining to Diana. Her reverence for the princess even stretched to the rider for her dressing room when on tour. During a 2011 appearance at the O2 Arena in London, the singer's requirements included 'fish and chips, McDonald's cheeseburgers without the buns and 100 prunes and figs', as well as a 'framed picture of Princess Diana'. Though clearly throwing dietary caution to the wind with the rest of her list, the final item was an insight into how much 'Britney adores the monarchy' and views Diana as, 'in many ways, her inspiration'.[296]

Britney finding such solace in Diana is understandable yet troubling. In many ways, Spears has been America's media equivalent of Diana. It does not matter what she does; her every move is recorded, shared, analysed and discarded as the rabid crowd waits for the next snippet to come to light. The appetite for celebrity gossip seems indomitable, with journalists, photographers and pretty much anyone equipped with a mobile phone stopping at nothing to get the scoop.

The 2020 investigation into how Martin Bashir persuaded Princess Diana to give a candid interview on the BBC show *Panorama* in 1995 illustrates the lengths to which even the most highly regarded news agencies will go in the name of securing an exclusive, lucrative story. A report on Bashir's actions states that the journalist 'lied and maintained the lie until he realised that it was no longer sustainable'.[297] The long-term impact of this one meeting was detrimental to Diana's well-being. Though strict royal rules prohibit him from publicly voicing his opinion, Prince William still made a fairly damning statement when the Bashir allegations were revealed, declaring that his mother 'was failed not just by a rogue reporter, but by leaders at the BBC who looked the other way rather than asking the tough questions'. Wills' younger brother, Prince Harry, went further, adding, 'Our mother lost her life because of this and nothing has changed. By protecting her legacy, we protect everyone and uphold the dignity with which she lived her life.'[298] Britney herself entered the fray, posting about the fallen princess on her Instagram:

> She never wanted to be the queen . . . she wanted to be the heart ❤❤❤ of the people !!!!!!!! She was more than class ♥ . . . she was sheer genius down to the way she spoke to the way she mothered her children 👤👤👤 The essence of being

completely oblivious to her own power !!!! 750 MILLION people watched her get married on TV 📺 !!!! She will always be remembered as one of the most remarkable women to date 👑👑👑 !!!!![299]

Britney has shared her own fears of meeting a similar fate to Diana. In a 2012 interview, Spears told *People* magazine that she could not leave her house without the paparazzi following her and that their ceaseless attention made her feel like she was in constant danger. 'Princess Diana got killed by one of these people. I'm not expecting people to pity me. I'm just telling the truth,' she confided.[300]

The tabloids argue that they are just giving the public what they want: a non-stop feed of celebrity gossip – the lewder, the better. Hundreds of thousands of dollars are spent by magazines like *People*, *Us Weekly*, the *National Enquirer* and *OK!* to fund such 'reporting'. A MarketWatch article succinctly encapsulated this duality, noting that, 'if indeed the paparazzi hound [Britney] into an early grave', like the deceased Diana, 'you can count on them to go on *Larry King Live* and express their distress and offer sympathy to the Spears clan . . . But they'll mostly just feel sorry for themselves – because they've killed the golden goose.'[301]

PIECE 29

Haunted Britney

Though fewer than 25 per cent of surveyed Brits say they are religious, almost 40 per cent believe a house can be haunted, 34 per cent think that ghosts are real, 28 per cent have felt the presence of a supernatural being and 9 per cent claim to have communicated with the other side.[302] In the US, the number of those who presume 'demons, aliens and ghosts' are actual beings is even higher, with a whopping 45 per cent of Americans convinced such entities exist (fun fact: Republicans polled slightly higher in these beliefs than Democrats).[303] Based on overall populace statistics, it is not surprising that Britney Spears may have had a 'spectral encounter' of her own.

As with many Britney stories, this anecdote comes via a friend – this time, make-up artist Julianne Kaye, who related the tale on the *We Need to Talk About Britney* podcast. In the early '00s, while dating Justin Timberlake, Britney bought 1895

Rising Glen Road – an 8,000-square-foot house set above Los Angeles' famed Sunset Strip. The pop-star power couple lived together in the five-bedroom, five-bathroom house throughout their relationship. The place was an opulent symbol of success, with views extending from West Hollywood all the way to the Pacific Ocean. Photos from the time captured the young lovebirds sitting on the front steps of the sumptuous pad, eating Mexican food, making googly eyes at each other and hamming it up for the camera. (Cans of Pepsi – Britney's sponsor of the day – were also casually placed in shot.) After the two broke up, Britney continued living there by herself, seemingly still happy in her gorgeous mansion. One day, however, she upped and left, immediately putting the house on the market and never returning. On the podcast, Kaye told host Jen Zaborowski exactly what had transpired to make Spears abandon her dream house for ever.

According to Kaye, Spears called the make-up artist one day in a panic. 'I had my friend do reiki healing on her . . . I guess she'd had a crazy partying weekend and needed to relax,' Kaye recounted to Zaborowski. After the healer left, Spears told Kaye that he had opened 'a spiritual portal or something', through which 'these bad spirits' had entered the house. 'They were trying to, like, push her down the stairs or something crazy.' Britney felt so uncomfortable that she decamped to the Hotel Casa del Mar in Santa Monica. Spears later confided to Kaye, 'I know you're gonna think I'm crazy. I'm not crazy. I know what I saw, I know what I felt.'[304] In retrospect, one specific detail of Spears' otherworldly encounter is the most chilling: the appearance of a 'very disturbed' man and woman who terrified Britney so much that she had to physically leave her beautiful residence.

The interview with Kaye was posted in 2021. By the time the anecdote aired, Spears had not lived in the supposedly haunted property for almost two decades, having sold the fully furnished Hollywood Hills abode in June 2003 to actress Brittany Murphy for $3.85 million. Murphy came to international fame at the age of seventeen in the '90s movie classic *Clueless*. She then starred in an array of hits before going on to act opposite rapper Eminem in his 2002 autobiographical film, *8 Mile*. Buying the house from Spears marked a high point in Murphy's life, proving she was a household name with an enviable address to go with it.

However, happiness was not to last long. On 20 December 2009, the actress was found on the floor of her bathroom. By the time Murphy arrived at Cedars-Sinai hospital, she had gone into cardiac arrest. She died two hours later, aged just thirty-two.

Not long after her passing, her husband, Simon Monjack, said that Murphy 'absolutely hated' Rising Glen and would often ask to go somewhere else instead of returning to their own home. Monjack claimed that his wife felt the place was unlucky and wanted to relocate to the East Coast where the two could pursue new opportunities.[305] Sadly, Monjack did not have the chance to move past his grief. On 23 May 2010, just five months after Murphy's passing, Monjack was found unconscious in the couple's master bedroom. By the time paramedics arrived, he was declared deceased.

Over a decade later, it is still unclear what killed Murphy and Monjack at 1895 Rising Glen Road. Suicide has been ruled out in both cases. Perhaps the 'disturbed' couple Spears encountered were the future ghosts of Murphy and Monjack? Or perhaps the 'crazy partying weekend' that went down before the incident supposedly occurred creates doubt towards the validity of Britney's story.

Under California law, a seller must disclose if anyone has died at a property within the preceding three years. Following the horrible tragedies of Murphy and Monjack, the house was marked by the media as 'cursed' and has been listed on the market ten different times. It was finally sold in December 2020 for $12.2 million after undergoing a major makeover that lasted three years. However, an interior-design facelift may not be enough to get rid of the bad vibes.

According to paranormal researcher John E. L. Tenney, speaking on *We Need to Talk About Britney*, ghosts are often tied to land, not to actual buildings, meaning that, no matter how fab the property looks, ghouls may still linger. Tenney also offered a theory that is popular with some of the more paranormally inclined. He hypothesised that time is not linear, so Britney could have been telling the truth: she could indeed have seen the ghosts of Murphy and Mojack from the future. For the more sceptical, however, Britney's vision was not a sign of her untapped clairvoyant ability, but rather the post-mortem effects of a raging weekend.

PIECE 30

The Museum of Britney

Named after settler Amos Kent, Britney Spears' hometown of Kentwood is officially part of the Deep South, located in the heart of the conservative Bible Belt of rural Louisiana near the Mississippi border. With this comes the expected landscape of rusting cars, double-wide mobile homes and discount stores.

Cultural mega hub New Orleans is a seventy-minute drive north on Interstate 55 – if one really keeps their foot on the gas – but may as well be in another galaxy. Kentwood is small, with a population of just over 2,200 people; its economy revolves around agriculture, earning it the title of 'Dairy Capital of the South'.[306] However, while the community used to have 200 thriving farms, a mix of factors (including modernisation and Walmart) have put almost all of them out of business, with only ten dairies still standing. The past two decades have seen the town in a downward spiral – windows broken, roofs crumbling and shops on the Main Street going bust. A brick archway at the entrance to the town has a 'Welcome to Kentwood' sign proudly hung, decorated with a yellow fleur de lis. Beneath the main sign, a swirly, bright-pink 'Home of Britney Spears' placard is an obvious and incongruous addition. With almost 30 per cent of all families in the town living below the poverty line and a median annual household income of just $17,297 (roughly £12,450), a homegrown star must seem like a miracle.

One place of interest that still receives footfall is the Kentwood Historical and Cultural Arts Museum. Originally opened in 1975 to pay respect to veterans of the Second World War, the converted funeral home entices people in by placing a life-size stand-up cut-out of Britney in its window, hinting at what treasures await within the walls of the depilated space. The juxtaposition of items within the museum is strange – a model battleship and snapshots of soldiers who served in the war are displayed alongside vintage Kentwood Dairy Festival crowns and cloaks – but also fitting for a proud southern community steeped in tradition. The newer additions to the collection are the Britney artefacts. In 2000, Britney's father loaned the museum a hodgepodge of personal effects, including 'platinum record plaques, framed magazine covers, family-framed photos, childhood dresses, MTV Awards, American Music Awards, a *CD:UK* trophy and awards from *Smash Hits* and *Hollywood Reporter*'.[307] Plush toys, dolls and the actual bed and bedspread that once belonged to Britney herself adorn another display, which the museum website proudly states 'is a spot-on recreation of Spears' childhood bedroom where fans can see where it all began'. The exhibit is the one room visitors cannot enter as it is housed behind a pane of glass. This makes for a ghoulish if accidental homage to the off-limits areas of Elvis's Graceland home in Memphis, Tennessee, where time seems to have stood still from the moment 'The King' left the building. For a donation of $3, fans can take a picture of the large, ornate feathered wings that Spears used in her 2011 Femme Fatale Tour, which she wore at the end of her show while 'flying' from the stage.

What sets the museum apart from a standard pop-royalty shrine is that much of the content has been contributed by fans. Spears' status as an aspirational and inspirational figure to multitudes of people across the globe has transformed the humble pale-yellow building into a place of almost sacred, transcendental pilgrimage, infused with meaning that goes way beyond Spears as a physical person. Two key displays demonstrate this arguably holy reverence fans hold for Spears.

The first – described by one visitor as the 'devotional focal point of the place' – is 'a light-up miniature replica of the stage used in a Spears HBO concert filmed during her Dream Within a Dream Tour of 2001–02'. It took over six months, working four hours a day, for fan-club member Randy Head, hailing from Salem, Oregon, to recreate the Barbie-sized grandstand. Head's version 'boasts 600 coloured lights and thousands of parts'.[308] A placard written by Head to accompany the diorama explains its inception further: 'I have seen a lot of drawings and paintings of Britney that have been done by other fans and I wanted to do something creative and special . . . I really had fun making it and having little Britney Spears concerts.'[309]

The second is an array of random merchandise and calendars that hang from adjacent walls; it appears to be a personal compilation as a printed banner above the various items proclaims that this 'Britney collection' belongs to Keith Collins-Hornchurch, London, United Kingdom – once a Spears superfan. 'You could not deny his love for Britney,' sister-in-law Nicola laughs during an interview, sat alongside husband Trevor, Keith's brother. The affection for Keith in her voice is still strong almost a decade after his death. 'He only lived around the corner from us,' Nicola says. 'We saw him quite often; Trevor and Keith didn't have their parents. We were a little unit, the three of us and our dog.'

Keith had been a long-time admirer of Spears. 'He loved the way she looked. He liked what personality he gleaned from performances and videos and interviews. I think he probably would have liked to be her boyfriend, but he'd have settled for anything,' Nicola grins. Keith's dedication meant catching as many of the singer's shows as possible during her UK tour in 2011. 'He was going to all the gigs around the country, staying at hotels and buying very expensive backstage passes in the hope that he might get to meet her,' Nicola continues. The two never connected, but Keith did catch a glimpse of another member of the Spears clan – Jamie. 'He was excited that he saw her dad once,' Nicola says, though she does not think Keith would be as ecstatic to run into the Spears patriarch now. 'I think, if he was around now, Keith would be devastated at the current situation with Britney. I think that would really upset him.'[310]

Sadly, just a year after experiencing this Spears high, Keith was diagnosed with brain cancer at the age of thirty-seven. It was discovered after he had a seizure in public and had to be rushed to hospital. The tumour made looking after Keith challenging at times. In 2012, the sick man decided to run away to LA to find Britney. Though Nicola and Trevor had been taking care of his passport to prevent such issues, Keith managed to get a replacement document and travel to Heathrow Airport before being stopped by police officers and returned safely to his family. 'He managed to get through airport security with pots and pans in a backpack and no hand luggage,' Nicola remembers. It was only when he 'kept trying to get on the wrong plane and then ended up trying to go through a security door' that Keith's mission to get to the West Coast was aborted. Nicola is convinced that, had Keith made it onto the right plane, she and Trevor 'wouldn't have ever seen him again'.[311] Nicola believes that the reason Keith was so determined to get to the Golden State was because it was where 'he thought everything was happening . . . that's where he might meet Britney'. Even as Keith's illness progressed, the singer was never far from his mind:

> I remember when he first began taking the steroids, he developed a very round face. He was upset because he thought, if he ever met Britney, she wouldn't look at him. It made him really sad. He eventually went on the internet and bought some weight-loss medication that Britney advertised. He hid that from us, but, because of the tumour, he would forget and take it in front of us. If Britney said buy something, he'd buy it.[312]

Keith never got to meet Britney, but he wanted to donate his treasures to a good home, so he mailed them to Kentwood himself – a final act of virtual pilgrimage. However, this, too, went awry due to his worsening health. 'He wanted to pack up the collection himself, but he had a seizure while he was in the post office in Hornchurch. Everything was left in the post office when he was taken to hospital,' Nicola recalls.[313] It fell to brother Trevor to finish the job and send the valuables to Louisiana. The museum dutifully delivered pictures of Keith's beloved items safely received.

For Keith, Britney may have represented freedom and possibility – the very things that the singer herself has been stripped of in her current situation. Towards the final years of his life, Keith was the one breaking free, trying new things and being adventurous. At Keith's funeral, many of his relatives were surprised by how much living he had packed into so few years. 'People were saying, "Oh, what a shame, he didn't do much" and what have you. But, actually, in those last few years, he managed to get around quite a bit. There was more to it than just the little boy who was deaf,' Trevor asserts. Nicola adds, 'He was kind of slow getting started with adult life. But there was no question about his abilities or his intellect. He just fell in love with Britney at an impressionable age and that grew. He loved Britney; he was devoted and faithful to her, even with all our teasing.'[314]

Nicola and Trevor set up the Keith Collins Fund in his name and have been told that Lynne and Jamie Lynn Spears have visited the exhibition in Kentwood and seen Keith's collection.

Brain tumours are the biggest cancer killer of children and adults under forty years old. For more information about raising awareness and funding life-saving research, please visit thebraintumourcharity.org.

PIECE 31

X-Posed

Britney Spears joined the second season of the US version of *The X Factor* as a judge in 2012. For her one-series stint in the role, she reportedly bagged a pay cheque of $15 million – the highest fee any personality had ever been paid to appear on the Simon Cowell talent show. But huge cash rewards were not enough to put a smile on Britney's face. At an event celebrating the newest panel of judges, Spears stood on stage alongside Cowell, teen star Demi Lovato and producer LA Reid. Cowell said a few words, hyping the forthcoming season, before handing the microphone to Spears. Britney looked nervous as she delivered a stilted, carefully worded speech. 'It's going to be so much fun and so different from anything I've ever done and I'm ready to find the true star,' she proclaimed, stating how 'excited' she was about the new opportunity.[315] However, Britney's hesitant voice, tense body language and downcast face read as anything but excited.

In light of Britney's 23 June 2021 conservatorship statement in which she described being put on lithium and other medications without her express permission, it is unclear what prescriptive regime, if any, the singer may have been on during her time on the reality programme. Regardless, the ruthless manner in which show creator Cowell and fill-in judge Louis Walsh demeaned Spears after the season's ratings did not beat time-slot opponent (and Christina Aguilera vehicle) *The Voice* were unprofessional at best and appallingly misogynistic at worst. Cowell was condescending towards Britney's tenure on the show, referring to it as a 'flop' and equating her presence to that of an underwhelming dinner-party guest, saying, 'You invite people for dinner and sometimes it's a fun night and other times it's not as fun as you hoped it would be.'[316]

Meanwhile, Walsh – one of the stalwart judges on the long-running UK version of *The X Factor* and the substitute judge for bronchitis-stricken Cowell during the show's auditions in Kansas City, Missouri – was even less diplomatic in his memories of Spears. The Irish music manager recalled Britney as being under the influence of various drugs and unable to sit straight in a chair for more than a few minutes without slumping onto the judges' table. 'They would literally have to stop the show and take her out because she was on so much medication and other stuff,' he alleged, adding, 'I felt sorry for her. Here she was – the biggest pop star on the planet – and she was just sitting there physically, but she wasn't there mentally. She had a lot of problems.' Yet Britney's health was not a consideration when so much money was at stake. 'She was getting millions of dollars to do it, so why the fuck wouldn't she sit there?' Walsh said.[317]

If Britney could be farmed out for profit, nothing else was relevant. 'She's not damaged goods,' then-manager Larry Rudolph reportedly assured Cowell. 'She can perform properly.' Radio personality Howard Stern predicted the opposite, telling the English mogul that Spears was 'a trainwreck'.

Reporter Tom Bower, who was sent to cover the first days of *X Factor* auditions, recalls his haunting first glimpse of the pop star. He encountered her leaning against a wall, 'pulling heavily' on Kool cigarettes, looking 'utterly miserable' as she was 'pushed onto a stage' and 'shiver[ing] nervously' as she 'forced smiles towards the bank of photographers, unaware that one snapper's lens was focused on her nails – heavily bitten and bloody'. Bower goes on to describe several situations in which Britney, as a judge, had to sit still and face a group of people for a long, uninterrupted period of time. She could 'hardly speak' and was noticeably awkward. The singer then told boss Cowell, 'I don't think I can do this. I can't do what the job requires,' while manager Rudolph explained that, 'for years, she only said politely "yes, sir" and "no, sir" and now she's gotta go onto the stage and explode'. Bower hypothesised that it wasn't an 'illness' that was plaguing Britney; it was years of being isolated from other people. Her stifling shyness and overwhelming fear were causing the paralysing anxiety.[318]

The star later revealed that, as a mother-of-two herself, she did not feel comfortable giving harsh critiques to children who were contestants on the show. The situation must have brought back memories from *Star Search* and the *Mickey Mouse Club* – both of which left searing first impressions of disappointment on young Britney. Commenting on her early days on the show and the challenge of facing her fans with feedback they may not want to hear, the singer told *Elle* magazine that she was initially 'having panic attack after panic attack' before realising that she could actually help the auditionees 'by being honest':

> Personally, I think that's the toughest part about being a judge on *The X Factor*. Most of them are still developing and it's hard to tell such young kids whether they have what it takes or not, so I try to be as protective as I can with their hopes and dreams.[319]

Britney did not reappear on the third and final season of the show. Rumours swirled that she had quit, been fired, or simply wanted to step away to focus on her music career. Many gossip columnists wrote that Cowell had thrown Spears a career lifeline when she needed it most, but she had squandered the opportunity for reinvention with her lacklustre judging.

It was hard not to see the full-circle parallels between Spears' beginnings on a televised talent show and her time on *The X Factor*. Where once an untarnished, eager child stood, a tired, anxious adult now took her place. And yet, despite the balance of power having shifted in the intervening twenty years, Britney Spears – with the eyes of primetime America fixed on her every move and utterance – was still very much the one being judged.

PIECE 32

Viva La Britney

In 2013, Britney Spears announced that she would be undertaking a residency in Las Vegas. Titled Britney: Piece of Me, the show was originally set to run for two years. The production was an instant hit, with the first fifty dates selling more tickets than any other Vegas show in history.[320] Britney's engagement was extended for a further two years, resulting in her performing a total of 248 shows by the time the residency ended in December 2017.[321] The venture was seen by many as a revitalisation of Britney's career, but, on a much larger scale, its success – and Britney's long-term presence in Sin City – brought a much-sought-after younger tourist demographic to the haven of indulgence. Las Vegas had been floundering for decades, viewed as a last-chance corral for artists in the golden years of their careers – the final stop before passing on to the entertainment glue factory in the sky. Britney singlehandedly proved that a Vegas residency could actually be a highly lucrative undertaking for more con-temporary artists, rebranding the desert oasis as a young, fun and hip destination – a status that the city had been trying to rekindle since its former glory days.

Not long after its founding by Mormons in 1905, Las Vegas gained a reputation for being *the* place to partake in risqué behaviour and debauched vices. In the 1930s, it became famous as the 'quickie divorce' capital of the world (when such a thing was unheard of). After acquiring its gaming licence in 1931, gambling also became a huge draw for visitors wanting to test their luck. To tempt their clientele to stay longer and spend more money, casino- and hotel-owners came up with the idea of booking appealing entertainers. A 25-year-old Wisconsin-born piano player named Władziu Valentino Liberace became the first performer to make a splash in the city, creating the blue-print for the long-term residency format. Liberace produced an immersive performance, going the extra mile with everything from his elaborate fur and rhinestone-encrusted costumes to the signature candelabra resting on his piano. Customers flocked to not only hear the pianist play, but also experience the clothes, the stage banter and the entire over-the-top extravaganza inher-ent in a Liberace show.

Las Vegas was also an integral ingredient in the enduring success of crooner Frank Sinatra. Sinatra first began performing there in 1951 while courting actress Ava Gardner. He became so popular that, by 1953, he was performing twice-nightly. Sinatra did this for forty-one years, making himself synonymous with the city. When Frank passed away in 1998, there was a clear sense of an era ending. The new way forward was uncertain, reliant on the ageing tourists who came to see Sinatra's fellow Vegas mainstays – the likes of Wayne Newton, Barry Manilow and Sheena Easton.

At the turn of the twenty-first century, things started to change. Artists who had seen more recent chart success began to take an interest in experimenting with a long-term stint. Celine Dion's 2003–07 A New Day residency at the Colosseum at Caesars Palace earned $385 million from 714 shows.[322] Elton John was not far behind the Canadian diva, staging his Red Piano shows from 2004 to 2009. He returned to Vegas in 2011 for his Million Dollar Piano residency at the Colosseum. The series made more than $131 million by the time it finished its run in 2018.

Celine and Sir Elton were great examples of how much money could be made by a superstar artist in Las Vegas. However, compared to either of those artists, Britney was in a much different place in her career when she started her time in Nevada. Though both stars were certainly still huge names when they undertook their shows, they were no longer chart-toppers. Celine catered to an older audience and had not had a top-ten single in several years, while John, despite being an international treasure with a wide appeal across many age groups, was performing a catalogue of hits that dated as far back as 1971. Britney, on the other hand, released her eighth studio album, *Britney Jean* (featuring the iconic 'Work Bitch', which reached number seven in the UK chart), the same year that she started her Vegas residency. By the time Britney left Vegas in 2017, she had also put out another full-length album, 2016's *Glory*, and had five singles chart on the *Billboard* Hot 100 – all while performing her shows.

Many holiday destinations have luxury hotels, great food and enjoyable entertainment; however, for those four years, only Las Vegas had Britney. For a younger clientele, Piece of Me was an opportunity to see the star they had grown up with while making the most of the other amenities Vegas had to offer. Britney introduced these new visitors to the city, hopefully enticing them to make return trips. She also flipped the wider perception of a Vegas residency on its head. Before Britney, an extended stay in Vegas signalled the fading days of a music career. Yet Spears showed what profitable financial opportunities the desert city could offer even contemporary artists. According to *Forbes*:

> With just one pop star, the connotation connected to having a Las Vegas residency has been completely changed and now it's a cool thing that all the biggest names in music want. They are able to see the value in signing on to do them and they no longer need to worry about what it will do to their image.[323]

The approximate amount of money Britney brought in is astonishing, offering a valid and very attractive reason for other acts to pounce on the idea of duplicating even a fraction of Spears' success. The original deal for the Piece of Me residency had Britney performing 100 shows for a fee of $310,000 per show. Throughout the run, most shows were sold out, despite the average ticket price hitting $151. After it was announced that the residency would be extended, the fee for each performance was increased to $475,000. By the time Britney completed her final

Vegas show at Planet Hollywood, ticket sales alone grossed a staggering $138 million. On top of this, concert-goers were having to pay for hotels, food, transportation and any gambling, drinking or extracurricular Vegas activities, making Britney an incredibly lucrative attraction for the city as a whole.

From the few interviews she gave over the course of the residency, Spears seemed to enjoy being in Vegas. During a chat on *Good Morning Britain*, Britney expressed her amazement at the stamina she once had. 'The way I used to travel all around the world and do a different show every night, I'm like, "How did I do it?!"' she remarked. 'But being based in Vegas and having one show that you just keep going back to, the consistency of that is really grounding and really cool.'

Critics who were fans of Britney seemed to agree that the Vegas run was a good move. 'Spears' residency was perhaps the smartest thing she ever did for her career when it comes to finances, rehabilitating her image and communicating with her longstanding fanbase,' wrote Ilana Kaplan in *The Independent*. Kaplan went on to give Piece of Me a sparkling review, saying of the 24-song show: 'The set encompassed every phase of her career, broken up into different acts to show her evolution from teen pop idol to a certified pop bad-ass. She looked immortal in her sparkly, barely-there bodysuits and thigh-high boots, dancing non-stop in between set change after set change.'[324]

It was only after Britney had gambled on Vegas that other mega artists dared to hedge their bets there, too, cashing in once Britney had paved the way. In 2015, Planet Hollywood – the home of Britney's Piece of Me – confirmed that they would also be hosting Jennifer Lopez's show, All I Have. Starting in 2016, each of Lopez's performances bagged her a cool $350,000. Not far behind J-Lo were the Backstreet Boys, who played nine Vegas shows in March 2017. The gigs were at 95 per cent capacity and made the forty-something 'Boys' $5.4 million. Never one to be excluded from any '00s nostalgia, Lady Gaga picked up the Vegas gauntlet when Britney left, announcing in December 2017 that she would be doing a two-year residency at Park MGM for a pay day of $100 million.

After such a huge smash, it seemed likely that Britney would come back and give another 'piece' of herself to Sin City once she had completed her European and North American Piece of Me Tour (based on the original residency). Further speculation arose when, in October 2018, Britney made a surprise appearance on the *Ellen* show. Wearing a curve-hugging wine-coloured dress and strutting onto the stage as 'Work Bitch' played, the singer told the pixie-haired host that she had an announcement to make. Britney went on to say that she couldn't actually reveal what the big news was until 18 October, which was six days away at the time. Ellen replied that everyone could find out what Britney had to share by tuning in to the television personality's YouTube channel on said date.

Good on her promise, Ellen's YouTube channel went live from outside the Park MGM, Las Vegas, on 12 October 2018. Strobe lighting, throngs of fans, thumping music and muscly men in shirts emblazoned with 'Britney' graced the screen for the first sixteen minutes of transmission, all waiting for word from the pop princess herself. Ellen's correspondent, Kalen Allen, hyped up the crowd and online audience, preparing viewers for whatever news awaited. A gum-chewing Mario Lopez ushered in a three-minute light show, accompanied by a high-energy Britney megamix.

Then, from below a platform, Britney appeared. Allen stumbled over her name, leaving Britney looking a bit uncomfortable as she waited for her cue to descend from the stage. Wearing a long-sleeved black dress with her blonde hair flowing long and loose, Spears walked gingerly down the staircase, aided by the 'Britney'-shirted men. Once on the ground, she approached some waiting fans who were waving Sharpies at her in the hope of receiving an autograph. The omnipresent 'Work Bitch' once again scored the moment. Security walked Britney to Allen, who gave the singer a kiss on the cheek. There was no sound to capture their exchange, but, from their body language, it seemed they were complimenting each other's ensembles. Britney then waved goodbye to him before walking away along a red carpet. Fans lined her pathway and signs announcing 'PARK MGM COMING 2019' came into shot, attached to the sides of the fencing barriers. Host Allen looked around uncomfortably as Spears climbed into a car waiting at the end of the carpet. The automobile pulled away and the star was gone, having been on camera for just two minutes. She had not publicly spoken a word or sang a note.

Three months later, on 4 January 2019, Britney announced on Twitter that she was cancelling Domination and going on an indefinite work hiatus. Spears has not performed since.

PIECE 33

A Mansion Full of Trophies

Over the course of her career, Britney Spears has been nominated for close to 1,000 different awards. She has won over 300 of these honours, giving her an impressive hit rate and a vast collection of trophies that is surely enough to fill a mansion on its own.

However, among the *Billboard* and Grammy accolades are some nefarious titles that may not have taken pride of place on her mantlepiece. Below are the highlights of the awards that Spears has amassed throughout her years in the spotlight, including some of the more questionable gongs.

The timing and type of each accolade provide telling insights into the evolving public view of the singer as she swayed from virginal schoolgirl to controlled money-making entity.

A MANSION FULL OF TROPHIES

YEAR	ORGANISATION	AWARD
1999	*Teen People* Awards	21 Hottest Stars Under 21
2000	*Teen People* Awards	25 Hottest Stars Under 25
2000	*Billboard* Music Awards	Biggest One-Week Sales of an Album Ever by a Female Artist: *Oops!* . . . *I Did It Again*
2000	Nickelodeon Kids' Choice Awards	Favourite Female Singer
2000	Guinness World Records	Best-Selling Album by a Teenage Solo Artist: . . . *Baby One More Time*
2000	Guinness World Records	Artist with Most Number-One Hits in the US
2001	*Teen People* Awards	25 Hottest Stars Under 25
2001	Guinness World Records	Fastest-Selling Album by a Teenage Solo Artist: *Oops!* . . . *I Did It Again*
2002	Barbie	Barbie Award *
2003	*Cosmopolitan* Awards	Fun, Fearless Female of the Year
2003	*Top of the Pops* Awards	Shameless Exhibitionist
2003	*Glamour* Awards	Woman of the Year
2003	*Spin* Awards	Worst Dressed
2003	*Spin* Awards	Worst Song: 'Me Against the Music' (feat. Madonna)
2003	Golden Raspberry Awards	Worst Actress (*Crossroads*)
2004	*Smash Hits* Poll Winners Party	Worst Dressed Star
2005	Grammy Awards	Best Dance Recording: 'Toxic'
2005	Golden Raspberry Awards	Worst Supporting Actress (*Fahrenheit 911*)
2005	*Spin* Awards	Worst Dressed
2006	*New York Dog* Awards	World's Worst Celebrity Dog Owner
2007	Z100 Awards	Most Overexposed Celebrity
2007	Teen Choice Awards	Choice OMG! Moment: Britney Spears Shaving Her Head
2008	*NME* Awards	Worst Album: *Blackout*
2008	*NME* Awards	Worst Style
2015	Best of Las Vegas Awards	Best Overall Show
2016	Best of Las Vegas Awards	Best Resident Performer

* *Even after copious research, what this award celebrates is unknown.*

PIECE 34

Over the Rainbow

The 29th GLAAD Media Awards in 2018 saw Britney Spears pick up another accolade to add to her long list of accomplishments; the singer was presented with the organisation's Vanguard Award. The honour is given to 'notables who have made a big difference in promoting equality and acceptance of LGBTQ+ people'.[325] Previous recipients of the award include Cher, Jennifer Lopez and Elizabeth Taylor.

Ricky Martin was picked to present Spears with the award. Like Britney, the babelicious 'King of Latin Pop' had faced his own challenges with the media, even suffering from PTSD after an especially invasive interview with American talking head Barbara Walters. Off the back of his global hit 'Livin' La Vida Loca', Martin was repeatedly grilled about his own sexuality until publicly coming out in 2010. After the awards show, Martin praised Spears via an Instagram post, saying of the star, 'She helps us accelerate acceptance.' Britney's speech at the show was a bit unspecific; it did not sound like a passionate rallying call for LGBTQ+ acceptance, but rather a bland sentiment for unity that could be applied to many situations:

> I feel like our society has always put such an emphasis on what's normal, and to be different is unusual or seen as strange. But to be accepted unconditionally – and to be able to express yourself as an individual through art – is such a blessing. Events like this, the one we are attending here tonight, show the world that we are not alone. We can all join hands together here and know that we are all beautiful. And we can lift each other up and show our gifts without hesitation.[326]

The GLAAD acknowledgement was not the first time Britney had been on the receiving end of gratitude for her LGBTQ+ allyship. In 2009, Spears was 'chosen by her gay fans' for the 'AlwaysNextForeverNow' award, which paid 'homage to role models within the lesbian, gay, bisexual and transgender community'. The ceremony was hosted by the world's most famous drag queen, RuPaul, and was then broadcast across the US on 'gay-themed' television station Logo.[327] This repeated narrative of Britney as a heroine in the 'community' is self-perpetuating; the continued positioning of the singer as a paragon of acceptance substantiates her status (despite her deeply religious upbringing making her an unlikely advocate for gay visibility). Indeed, in a 2013 interview, the star admitted that her prominence as an inspirational figure to queer audiences was seemingly accidental, saying, 'I think it was when I was on tour for my second album . . . I began to realise there were a lot of gay people coming to the shows and they were just having so much fun, laughing and really enjoying themselves.'[328] However, she has continued to build and engage with this contingent of fans, posting during Gay Pride 2020: 'Happy Pride Month!!!! I love my LGBTQ+ fans so much . . . You all bring me so much joy and I am proud to support you.'[329]

Britney's posts are working: a recent survey in California revealed that Spears has usurped Madonna and Cher as 'the greatest gay icon of all time'. The Equality Project's Joel Waddell commended Britney, saying, 'She is genuine in her affection for us and doesn't need to exploit us as a marketing tool like some other current Madonna-like icon.'[330] Such affirmations beg the question: what is it about Britney that speaks to this audience and has helped her ascend to such beloved heights?

It's hard to pinpoint exactly what traits need to combine to construct a 'gay icon', though there are common characteristics that often define the figures who have been granted such a mantle. There is usually a yin-and-yang narrative of hard times, substance abuse and picking the wrong romantic partners paired with an inextinguishable spark of hope and a refusal to go down without a fight. For the most part, these heroines are straight women with no clear ties to the LGBTQ+ community yet their celebrity standing has made their personal struggles public, creating points for identification among a wider audience. Often pointed to as the archetype for such a woman in the media eye is Dorothy herself – Judy Garland – who many view as the embodiment of such affection and iconic status. Garland's life and persona, both on and off stage, epitomised the challenges, triumphs and nadirs people associate with this type of canonised figure. A laundry list dissecting Garland's contrasting vulnerability and strength highlights the various attributes that made her so appealing to a gay audience. In an article for *The Independent*, Tim Waterstone, founder of Waterstones bookshops, called Garland 'mawkish, cliched, extravagantly manipulative of her audience' and yet 'so beautiful, with wide, wonderful eyes and a look of haunting yearning'. 'Her own life showed the struggle against loneliness, depression, destroyed relationships, drug dependency,' he added, but 'Judy Garland's people – often gay, typically outsiders, mostly alone – loved her as one'.[331] While Garland's tribulations frequently cast her as a tragic figure, it is those tribulations that have provided solace for many in the gay community who have likened her struggles to their own.

Professor Richard Dyer of King's College London argues that it was Garland's unique combination of accessibility – particularly in comparison to her untouchable screen-siren contemporaries like Elizabeth Taylor – coupled with personal hardship that created a relatable narrative for men who felt like outsiders. Judy was 'the image of family heterosexual normality', but 'it became clear after 1950 that she was not after all the ordinary girl she appeared to be'.

From this, Garland grew an entire mythology. The star's best-known song – *The Wizard of Oz*'s 'Over the Rainbow' – is rumoured to have been the inspiration behind the multicoloured symbol of the LGBTQ+ community, while the name

'Judy' has become a term of affection among queer circles. Even Garland's funeral was a must-attend event. On 27 January 1969, more than 20,000 New Yorkers swarmed the streets to see her white glass coffin pass by, making it the biggest public memorial the city had seen since fellow gay icon Rudolph Valentino's passing in 1927.

Several hours after Garland was laid to rest, a police raid on gay bar the Stonewall Inn led to riots and protests on the morning of 28 January. This prompted folklore that the two events were connected – a claim that has long been seen as controversial and was recently debunked. 'No one will ever know for sure which was the most important reason for what happened next,' wrote Charles Kaiser in his 1997 book, *The Gay Metropolis*. It could have been 'the freshness in their minds of Judy Garland's funeral', but it could also have been the example set by 'all the previous rebellions of the '60s – the civil rights revolution, the sexual revolution and the psychedelic revolution, each of which had punctured gaping holes in crumbling traditions of passivity, puritanism and bigotry'.[332]

Though Judy forged a path for other performers to tread, many of the voters who recently catapulted Britney to the 'gay icon' top spot were decades away from even being born when Garland passed. For those under fifty, especially those in their twenties and thirties, Spears was the first celebrity to publicly display her incredible highs and jaw-dropping lows – all played out in real time. An article from *Vice*, focusing on the appeal Britney holds for gay men, reads like a carbon copy of what the community found in Garland, noting that her allure 'rests in the way she brings together this sense of empowered sexuality with an essential vulnerability'. Jordan Miller, founder of Britney fan site Breathe Heavy, agrees, commenting, 'We watched a woman hit rock bottom . . . yet she never surrendered. Britney found the strength within to stand back up and continue sporting the role as a bombshell pop star.'[333] Indeed, Spears' resilience and ability to reinvent herself successfully no matter what comes her way – be that a shaved head, an altercation with the paps, a stay in a psychiatric unit or a tough conservatorship battle – offer a ray of hope to many. 'She is damaged and vulnerable to the point of pitiful and yet, evidently, she is indestructible,' writes Ben Appel in *HuffPost*. However, while he applauds Spears, acknowledging 'her unmistakable tenderness' and 'phoenix-out-of-the-fire comeback from a series of mental-health crises', he also dehumanises the star, calling her 'a doll' and likening him being a Britney aficionado to 'admitting that I'm a fan of Barbie'.[334]

Under the conservatorship, it has been nearly impossible to tell what Spears herself truly believes or thinks of anything. We do not even know if her social media is truly an outlet for expressing herself or just a carefully curated onslaught of posts created to titillate her devoted followers. Either way, the engagement between the Spears machine and her queer audience has continued, though it's unclear who is actually authoring what. In a 2017 campaign around Gay Pride Month, *Billboard* magazine asked various celebrities to write 'love letters' to the LGBTQ+ audience. Spears contributed a handwritten note, thanking the community for their inspiration and signing off the piece with 'I Love You'.[335] Britney has also consistently and visibly supported various queer causes, from appearing in a 2017 music video that talked about the freedom to love and the violence faced by the queer community in Brazil to signing an open letter opposing two anti-transgender bills in Texas. These gestures have not gone unnoticed by LGBTQ+ advocates. 'She is a force in the music world who has used her global platform to share messages of love and acceptance – something that the world needs today more than ever,' said Sarah Kate Ellis, president and CEO of GLAAD.[336]

However, unabashed love for Britney is not shared by all, as noted by *RuPaul's Drag Race* star Derrick Barry – the world's most famous Britney impersonator. 'People either love her or hate her,' says Barry of his inspiration. 'That's how you know you're doing something right.'[337] Criticism has been levelled at figures like Spears for having 'little or no connection to the LGBTQ+ community themselves, least of all their own identification with it', while it has been suggested that many admired divas have become gay icons by 'complete accident'.[338] Some even see Britney's zealous and public love for her gay following as staged – a marketing act conceived to create emotional ties between the singer and an audience willing to spend time, money and energy on the singer. Yet Britney's presentation in interviews and on social media when discussing her gay fans has been read as 'real talk' – a woman who, though world-famous, still speaks without pretention. For example, when asked about the origins of her 2013 single 'Work Bitch', Spears said:

> For me, the saying 'work, bitch' has been a term of endearment among my gay friends. Plus it's what we say in clubs

and in the dancing world all the time. My choreographers are gay and they inspire me so much. Plus I just love my gay fans, so it's something I really wanted to use.[339]

Spears sounded equally unsophisticated and possibly even condescending when she referred to the gay men at her shows as 'adorable and hilarious'. When confronted with the notion that such adjectives may have rubbed some fans up the wrong way, Spears replied, 'I would never say anything to be mean to them. I love my gay fans. Gay people are always usually my best friends in the whole world . . . I completely adore them.' Yet Spears has been somewhat reticent in clearly defining her own views on gay rights. In a 2013 interview, Britney was asked whether she would 'like to see her gay friends get married'. She responded with a hesitant 'yeah' and an ensuing silence. Not satisfied with this response, the interviewer emailed Britney after the chat asking her to 'elaborate' on the topic, posing the question: 'Do you believe gay people deserve equal rights?' The carefully worded reply read: 'Yeah. I think everyone should be treated equally.'[340]

For some, these plain-speaking, uncontroversial answers underscore Britney's authenticity – her simple manner illustrates her perceived sweetness. However, others believe that such responses are 'anything BUT naïve' and are 'clearly very cleverly calculating in every move'.[341] Georgia Goble, senior editor of Varsity Publications, reiterates this idea, writing that she 'can't help but think that profiting off a community whose struggles you do not share, while simultaneously benefiting from a mainstream who accepts you, is a rather problematic phenomenon, especially when there's a whole array of LGBTQ+ artists whose sexuality renders them niche and commercially unviable to the mainstream'. Goble concludes, 'It seems glaringly counterproductive that, at events designed to give precedence to the underrepresented voices of the gay community, the people we choose to put centre stage, in front of a crowd of thousands of people are . . . straight.'[342]

The debate about whether Britney is truly the gay ally 'she has made herself out to be' or simply a star who has 'latched onto the 'mosexuals for marketing purposes' has been raging for well over a decade.[343] Yet, regardless of any question marks over Britney's sincerity in supporting the gay community, fans still feel a kinship to the singer. Her initial success seemingly against all odds and her continued lack of outward pretension provide a narrative that endears Britney to many, thereby making it possible for any perceived trespasses or oversights to be readily forgiven and forgotten.

PIECE 35

Let the Show Begin

Being the opening act for Britney Spears has long been seen as the ideal way for an emerging artist to introduce themselves to the pop princess's legions of fans or for an established group to reach a younger, newer or more diverse audience. (Britney herself only once performed as a support act – back in 1998 for boy band NSYNC.) Looking over Britney's tour history, her opening acts changed regularly as her shows moved from one geographic area to another, providing a short window of opportunity for the 'support' to convert Britney admirers into followers of their own. However, being first to the stage ahead of music-industry royalty did not always guarantee career longevity. A round-up of some of the opening acts from Britney tours of old provides a walk down pop-music memory lane, noting the one-hit wonders and the 'where are they now?'s, as well as the early days of some now-renowned stars.

TOUR: . . . Baby One More Time Tour
YEAR: 1999
LOCATION: North America
ASSOCIATED ALBUM: . . . *Baby One More Time*
START DATE: 28 June 1999
END DATE: 15 September 1999
NUMBER OF SHOWS: 56
OPENING ACTS:

- **C-Note:** Backstreet Boys-lite group from Orlando, Florida.
- **Steps:** Holiday-camp British pop group exported from their homeland to the States in a bid to break the American teen marketplace. Didn't work.
- **Boyz N Girlz United:** Had mini-hit in 2000 with 'Messed Around', written by NSYNCer JC Chasez.
- **PYT:** All-girl group from Florida attempting to be the US answer to the Spice Girls. Also didn't work.
- **Michael Fredo**: Unremarkable pop singer/songwriter.
- **3rd Storee:** Slow-jam heavy group with a new-jack-swing vibe. Late-'90s answer to Boyz II Men.
- **Divine:** Disappointedly not the drag-queen muse of John Waters. In this case, an identikit R&B TLC knock-off.
- **Sky:** Canadian duo trying – and failing – to win the hearts of guilty Savage Garden apologists.
- **Joe McIntyre:** All grown up and dropping the 'y' from his first name, the former New Kid on the Block was striking out with his solo career.

TOUR: (You Drive Me) Crazy Tour
YEAR: 2000
LOCATION: North America
ASSOCIATED ALBUMS: . . . *Baby One More Time*;
Oops! . . . I Did It Again
START DATE: 8 March 2000
END DATE: 24 April 2000
NUMBER OF SHOWS: 25
OPENING ACTS:

- **LFO:** Abercrombie & Fitch-looking boy band with Sugar Ray-esque pop spiked with the slightest element of hip-hop and positively reeking of the year 2000. Not to be confused with the bass-heavy British techno pioneers of the same name.
- **Destiny's Child:** Then a foursome, the R&B girl group opened for Britney during her appearance in Hawaii.

TOUR: Oops! . . . I Did It Again World Tour
YEAR: 2000
LOCATIONS: North America; South America; Europe
ASSOCIATED ALBUM: *Oops! . . . I Did It Again*
START DATE: 20 June 2000
END DATE: 18 January 2001
NUMBER OF SHOWS: 88
OPENING ACTS:

- **No Authority:** Boy-band foursome signed to Michael Jackson's MJJ record label.

- **C-Note:** Backstreet Boys-lite group from Orlando, Florida. Made a return appearance after snagging the same spot on Spears' first headlining tour.
- **Take 5:** One more Orlando entry to the boy-band brigade from the hand of Lou Pearlman. This crew had a slightly funkier vibe than many of their well-preened peers, but no greater commercial success.
- **2gether:** Fictional band from an MTV movie and television series. Based on real-life boy bands like the Backstreet Boys and New Kids on the Block, but not as good.
- **A-Teens:** Comprising two boys and two girls, this Swedish group began life as an ABBA tribute band before going on to have decent worldwide success, selling 2 million records globally.
- **PYT:** Second appearance on a Spears tour for the all-girl group from Florida attempting to be the US answer to the Spice Girls. Still didn't work.
- **Sister2Sister:** Duo of Australian sisters who wrote their own songs and were VJs on MTV in their native land down under. Did what it said on the tin.
- **Nobody's Angel:** Another American attempt to duplicate the Spice Girls' success. The Angels were a multi-racial foursome serving up syrupy top-forty sounds.
- **Mikaila:** Oklahoma solo artist singing winsome songs of love.
- **Aaron Carter:** Younger brother to Backstreet Boy heartthrob Nick. During the Britney tour, he turned thirteen.

- **BBMak:** Disney-endorsed Liverpudlian threesome who sold 3 million albums in the early '00s before disappearing almost as quickly as they arrived.
- **Innosense:** American girl group that Britney had originally thought about joining before deciding to stick with being a solo act. Managed by Justin Timberlake's mother, Lynn Harless, and Backstreet Boys/NSYNC creator Lou Pearlman.
- **Josh Keaton:** Pop R&B crooner briefly signed to RCA records as a solo artist (to mass public indifference).

TOUR: Dream Within a Dream Tour
YEARS: 2001–02
LOCATIONS: North America; Asia
ASSOCIATED ALBUMS: *Britney*
START DATE: 1 November 2001
END DATE: 29 July 2002
NUMBER OF SHOWS: 69
OPENING ACT:

- **O-Town:** Formed on the reality TV show *Making the Band*, O-Town were the only opener for Britney during the entirety of the North American leg of her fourth tour. US top-ten singles: two. Marginally more successful in the UK.

TOUR: Onyx Hotel Tour
YEAR: 2004
LOCATIONS: Europe; North America
ASSOCIATED ALBUMS: *In the Zone*

START DATE: 2 March 2004
END DATE: 6 June 2004
NUMBER OF SHOWS: 54
OPENING ACTS:

- **Sky:** Return appearance on a Britney tour for the aforementioned duo.
- **Sweetnam:** Slightly older, slightly worse Canadian solo version of Hayley Williams from Paramore.
- **Wicked Wisdom:** Metal band fronted by Jada Pinkett Smith, with former Fishbone drummer Philip 'Fish' Fisher keeping the beat. As good as their name suggests.
- **JC Chasez**: Former NSYNCer. On the road with Britney to support his 2004 debut solo album, *Schizophrenic*.

TOUR: The M+M's Tour
YEAR: 2007
LOCATION: United States
ASSOCIATED ALBUM: None
START DATE: 1 May 2007
END DATE: 20 May 2007
NUMBER OF SHOWS: 6

The M+M's Tour was a series of six short shows performed at House of Blues clubs across the US. Each show lasted between twelve and sixteen minutes and consisted of five shortened versions of classic Britney tracks. Spears was joined on stage by four female backing dancers as she lip-synced to her hits. There were no support acts.

TOUR: The Circus Starring Britney Spears
YEAR: 2009
LOCATIONS: North America; Europe; Oceania
ASSOCIATED ALBUMS: *Circus*; *Blackout*
START DATE: 3 March 2009
END DATE: 29 November 2009
NUMBER OF SHOWS: 97
OPENING ACTS:

- **Cascada:** German dance-music trio. Most likely to be found on a high-energy mix for a Peloton spin class.
- **Pussycat Dolls:** Originally founded as a burlesque group. Performed at Hollywood hotspot the Viper Room before signing to Interscope Records.
- **Slimmy:** Sub-Eurovision Portuguese androgynous glam rocker.
- **One Call:** Manufactured boy-band foursome whose own parents would probably struggle to pick them out of a line-up.
- **Jordin Sparks:** Teen winner of the sixth season of *American Idol*.
- **Kristinia DeBarge:** Worked with Kenneth 'Babyface' Edmonds from the age of fourteen before appearing on *American Idol* spin-off *American Juniors*. Progeny of the (moderately-sized-in-the-'80s) DeBarge family singers.

- **Girlicious:** After the success of the Pussycat Dolls, group founder Robin Antin created a reality TV show to construct the next great female pop group. This didn't happen, but she did end up with Girlicious.
- **DJ Havana Brown:** Australian DJ who supported Spears for both the European and Australian legs of the tour. She was a veteran of being on the road, having already played the opening slots for Rihanna and the Pussycat Dolls before joining Britney.
- **Ciara:** Known for songs like 'Goodies' and '1, 2 Step', the singer was already a star in her own right when she landed the Spears support role. However, it was perhaps a waning star in need of a fame-adjacent boost since her third album was not performing as well as the previous two.

TOUR: Femme Fatale Tour
YEAR: 2011
LOCATIONS: North America; Europe; Asia; South America
ASSOCIATED ALBUMS: *Circus*, *Blackout*
START DATE: 16 June 2011
END DATE: 10 December 2011
NUMBER OF SHOWS: 79
OPENING ACTS:

- **Nicki Minaj:** This slot could not have come at a better time for the self-proclaimed 'black Barbie'. Britney's core fanbase were now old enough to appreciate the subtle art of

Minaj's debut album, *Pink Friday*, which was released in 2010.

- **DJ Pauly D:** Fresh off the MTV reality smash hit *Jersey Shore*, Pauly brought some urban flavour to the opening set.
- **Destinee & Paris:** Sister duo rising from the ashes of former girl group Clique Girlz. Provided poppy yet utterly anonymous top-forty fare.
- **Nervo:** Twin-sister DJ duo from Australia.
- **The Wanted:** Cheeky British/Irish boy band formed via mass auditions.
- **Howie Dorough:** The 'nice' member of the Backstreet Boys taking a stab at going solo.
- **Jessie and the Toy Boys:** Lead singer Jessica Eden Malakouti living it up as a trashier, more fun version of Gwen Stefani, backed by boy dancers.
- **Joe Jonas:** The middle Jonas brother breaking away to go it alone.

TOUR: Piece of Me Tour
YEAR: 2018
LOCATIONS: North America; Europe
ASSOCIATED ALBUMS: None
START DATE: 12 July 2018
END DATE: 21 October 2018
NUMBER OF SHOWS: 31
OPENING ACT:

- **Pitbull:** By the time Armando Christian Pérez – better known by the stage name Pitbull – took the opening spot on Britney's most recent tour, he had already worked with an impressive roster of A-listers, including Jennifer Lopez, Flo Rida and Britney's frenemy Christina Aguilera.

PIECE 36

How #FreeBritney Started

While some may think that the #FreeBritney hashtag came about in 2021 with the premiere of the *New York Times* documentary *Framing Britney Spears*, the actual inception of the slogan – and the idea that all was not well in Spears' life – predates the film by more than a decade. The origins of #FreeBritney can be traced back to January 2009, less than a year after Britney was put into a permanent conservatorship by father Jamie. Jordan Miller was in college at the time while running the Breathe Heavy fan site. In response to a blog post asserting that Britney's dad had taken her mobile phone away, Miller wrote, 'Open your eyes! Free Britney!' After a deluge of criticism, he claims he received a letter from Jamie Spears demanding that he take his website down. Besides the mobile phone comment, Miller had also reproduced Britney lyrics on Breathe Heavy, leading Spears senior to call him out on copyright infringement. 'I felt censored,' Miller told

The Independent. 'In my opinion, it's not about lyrics. It's because I was speaking out about an injustice and they didn't like that and they wanted to control everything about Britney, including entities that they didn't technically own.'

Yet the site remained online. Over the next ten years, things went rather quiet in the media regarding Britney's plight. Concerns about her legal situation were a topic mostly relegated to die-hard fan forums. The singer continued to work, putting out four records, starring as a judge on *The X Factor* and performing a four-year Las Vegas residency totalling 248 shows. Yet her massive audience became worried when she suddenly and unexpectedly backed out of her Domination residency in January 2019, citing her father's deteriorating health as the reason for the cancellation. Then came the anonymous voicemail left for the *Britney's Gram* podcast in April 2019 claiming that Spears wanted out of her conservatorship. #FreeBritney was suddenly a thing again – and this time, it blew up.

The first #FreeBritney protesters gathered later that month outside West Hollywood's City Hall. In May 2019, the focus moved to the Stanley Mosk Courthouse – the place where activists have since congregated for each conservatorship hearing. Then, when COVID-19 hit, people found themselves with more free time to commit to the #FreeBritney cause. Thousands of fans across the world soon began advocating for Britney, running dedicated social media accounts, carrying out in-depth investigative research and organising support rallies. That is how Megan Radford, aged thirty-four, Leanne Simmons, thirty-one, Junior Olivas, thirty-two, and Kevin Wu, thirty-seven, first met and began planning their next move as the #FreeBritneyLA contingent.

Radford, Simmons, Olivas and Wu were all interviewed by director Samantha Stark for *Framing Britney Spears* after Spears 'gave a statement through her court-appointed lawyer, Samuel Ingham, that seemingly endorsed #FreeBritney'. In a court filing from September 2020, Ingham wrote, 'At this point in her life when she is trying to regain some measure of personal autonomy, Britney welcomes and appreciates the informed support of her many fans,' adding that Britney is 'vehemently opposed to this effort by her father to keep her legal struggle hidden away in the closet as a family secret'.[344] The pop star's statement through her lawyer validated and vindicated the #FreeBritney movement and gave its members more impetus to help the singer.

Through all the ups and downs, there is a relatability between Britney and her fans that has never been broken. In *Framing Britney Spears*, former MTV VJ David Holmes addresses this, saying how Spears is uniquely 'approachable' in a way that has allowed her audience's connection with the singer to never be 'severed'. This connection arguably became stronger when Spears' humanity was revealed, bringing to light the very real young woman behind the marketing machine. 'The image of Britney that we were sold when she first hit the scene was this perfect all-American girl next door; but a lot of fans are not that,' Wu argues in *Framing Britney Spears*:

> They were people like myself who felt like they didn't fit in; I think there was some wanting to aspire to that image. We know now that Britney wasn't perfect. Britney

had to navigate being told who she could be and what she could do. I think that story of control and identity really resonates.[345]

Radford, Simmons, Olivas and Wu are a sharp contrast to the stereotype the word 'fan' can elicit. (Think: screaming mobs of teenage girls in black-and-white Beatles footage or overexcited tweens stampeding after One Direction.) Radford is strikingly beautiful, with long flaxen hair, alabaster skin and an ethereal calm tinged with a no-nonsense 'let's get down to business' attitude. Simmons comes across as bubbly and cute at first – her curly brown locks bobbing around her head – but, as the conversation gets rolling, a more thoughtful young woman emerges, a tinge of sadness sometimes peeking out from beneath the happy exterior. Olivas is charming yet quiet – his passion for Britney palpable – while Wu is serious but with a ready smile, his obvious intelligence coupled with the handsome good looks that California living affords. Together, their dedication to Britney is both heart-warming and uncomfortable. It is inspiring that two young women from the Midwest and two queer men – one from Virgina, one from LA – found personal empowerment through this movement, but it is also troubling that it took a pop singer's plight to make them feel they *could* act. For them, however, Britney *is* personal.

Olivas attended the very first rally in West Hollywood. 'I had no idea we'd still be here two years later,' he comments. Wu was next. 'It all blew up on 16 April 2019 when the *Britney's Gram* podcast got that voicemail from a person claiming to be a former member of Britney Spears' legal team,' he says. 'When that voicemail leaked, I tracked it online. I think it was someone in Boston who made a graphic saying meet at City Hall; it wasn't anyone in LA. It was very organic how it all came together.'[346]

Radford first went to a #FreeBritneyLA event in January 2020 and was introduced to Wu and Olivas. 'I flew from Oklahoma City because I decided that I had to be there in person,' she says:

> Even in January 2020, there was still a feeling that things would actually change in court. Now we tell people that they should never expect an outcome from a hearing. We're not there for any other reason than to raise awareness for the cause. It's no longer about trying to be there when something big may be decided.'[347]

Simmons says that she 'was a passive supporter of #FreeBritney for thirteen years' as she thought 'the whole situation was ridiculous'. 'When I felt like I needed to actually physically do something was in early 2020,' she contends.

It has not always been easy being a Britney aficionado. 'I had felt this shame and had been made fun of for liking Britney throughout my life,' Simmons confides. 'I would joke about being a closet Britney fan; there's a stigma around it because there's a stigma around Britney. As a fan, you've been reduced to that.' The #FreeBritney movement gave her a 'sense of empowerment':

> This is so much deeper than just Britney Spears, the pop star; this is a human-rights issue at the root of it; it's a women's-rights issue . . . I understand more about how the legal system works. I do not trust the system – not that I ever did – but I certainly do not now.

Simmons also asserts that Britney's predicament was specific to being female – a symptom of the patriarchy of our society:

> We've seen male celebrities do things that are violent or illegal or much worse than the things that Britney experienced; they've never lost their rights. There are people who went to jail for different things; Britney was never in jail. Britney never harmed anyone, never harmed herself. I think it was very much that idea of a woman needing help.[348]

Inspired by the recent awareness, a 2021 proposal was brought to the US House of Representatives – a bill dubbed the FREE Act (an acronym of 'Freedom and Right to Emancipate from Exploitation'). This legislation 'would allow a person bound by a conservatorship to petition to replace their court-appointed private conservator with a public conservator, family member or private agent without having to prove abuse.'[349] However, #FreeBritney advocates oppose the bill as they believe it would empower professional conservators without preventing the establishment of abusive conservatorships.

Meanwhile, for Spears herself, things began changing rapidly following her 23 June 2021 court testimony. Just three weeks after, she was granted approval to appoint her own legal representation for the first time since entering the conservatorship. Then, in September, it was reported that Jamie was filing to end his daughter's mandate completely. At the subsequent court date, he was formally suspended as Britney's conservator.

Wu is quick to underscore that the price paid for these victories has been time and sweat equity, not cash. 'It is incredible how much we were able to accomplish without spending much money,' he proclaims. Indeed, the #FreeBritney advocates have witnessed huge changes in Spears' case despite utilising low- or no-cost methods to battle the conservatorship and the people behind it, some of whom are 'being paid hundreds of thousands, if not millions, of dollars every year', they note.[350]

To have made such great strides with their campaigning – changing the trajectory of Britney's life, impacting the laws in California and raising unprecedented global awareness about conservatorships – is both impressive and empowering. Their accomplishments illustrate the extent to which individual voices can make a major difference in the wider world.

PIECE 37

Secret Coded Britney

The question of who is actually at the helm of Britney Spears' social media has been at the centre of several conspiracy theories, all leading back to the underlying controversy of controlled versus control. Spears is a frequent presence across her dedicated internet platforms, providing an apparent glimpse into what she is thinking on any given day. However, in recent years, fans have started dissecting Spears' use of specific words, phrases and emojis, becoming suspicious when a caption or post deviates from the 'language' commonly seen in 'Britney speak'.

In January 2019, Spears used Instagram to explain why she had cancelled her second Las Vegas residency, Britney: Domination. Blaming it on her father's hospitalisation, Britney posted, 'I had to make the difficult decision to put my full focus and energy on my family at this time. I hope you all can understand.' Then the usually-Instagram-omnipresent Spears went nearly silent. In April,

TMZ claimed that the singer had been in a mental-health facility since late March. This report prompted a new Instagram post from the singer's account, captioned with the words, 'We all need to take time for a little "me time",' followed by a ':)' emoticon.[351] Suspicion was once again raised among devout Britney-ites as Spears rarely, if ever, used emoticons – she was an emoji girl. Fans also started complaining that their comments were being deleted on Britney's sites, which led them to post fruit emojis instead of words to show their support for Spears.

For the most discerning fans, there seemed to be a pattern emerging in Britney's posts: a combination of words and images that some believed were a cry for help. One post from February 2021 focusing on a jumbled-up Scrabble board – 'Can you find a word that isn't actually a word ???? Sometimes it's fun to make ones up !!!' – had Spears' tens of millions of followers eagle-eyeing the image, with several claiming to see the word 'quit' spelled backwards, which was clearly a plea for assistance. Another post from the same month – a picture of a gold heart with the quote, 'We need to care less about whether our children are academically gifted and more about whether they sit with the lonely kid in the cafeteria' – had people arguing that Spears saw herself as the 'lonely kid' and that it was a thank-you to #FreeBritney supporters for their loyalty. One fan referred to Britney as the 'queen of subliminal messages', leaving 'breadcrumbs' for her followers about the true meaning of her posts.

In early 2021, Instagram videos featuring Spears seductively dancing around to tracks by Justin Timberlake in front of a Christmas tree well past its expiry date raised concern among the Britney devout once more. The combination of out-of-season jollity and former-flame celebration seemed peculiar and even alarming. Fans flooded to comment on the clips, with one saying, 'People who care about her safety can tell that something is wrong here.' Another chimed in, 'This is just awkward. I'm starting to think she is being filmed through a mirror and doesn't realize it. She def doesn't have control of this page either.' A final attentive follower wrote, 'Queen, I'm not judging that the tree is still up but it wasn't up on the Dec. 28th soo that's suspicious. You don't need to answer to anyone but girl, we're concerned.' In response to the worries (and trolling), a new post was uploaded to Spears' account – this one saying that Britney had 'little patience for technology' and that the 'videos were only meant to be a bit of fun'.

Yet that did not stem the tide of speculation. Even before those videos, fans had already been using social media as a way to try to communicate with their idol. In July 2020, a follower asked Spears to wear a yellow shirt in her next video if she needed help – a visual signal to the 'outside' world. The next video Spears posted featured the star wearing a yellow top and swirling around with a massive bouquet of flowers. The caption: 'HOLY HOLY C**P My florist surprised me today by making the flower arrangement all different colors . . . I was so excited I threw on my favorite yellow shirt and just had to SHARE.'[352] Since then, Spears has donned the shirt in several other posts and stated that yellow is her favourite colour.

Further fuel was added to the conspiracy fire just a week later after a fan asked Britney via Twitter to share a picture of doves if she was in trouble. The singer then posted a painting by Austrian artist Hans Zatzka. The image depicts two women in a flowery spring scene, accompanied by two cherubs and five doves. This only confirmed to many fans that Spears was trying to reach out across the keyboard.

The 2021 BBC documentary *The Battle for Britney* highlights several other fan 'discoveries'. One girl believes that each pose Spears strikes in individual images comprising a set of pictures represents a letter of the alphabet, thus spelling out a message for her followers. Another woman zooms in on the label of a hat Spears is holding in another video. 'WAIT A MINUTE,' the lady screeches to the camera. 'What is she pointing to right there, on her hat? What is that? Sooooo I zoomed in. And that shit literally says, "Help!" (A very blurry word that may or may not be 'help' is enlarged on the screen.) A third man, also looking to bust the Britney code, reads out the caption of a Spears post: 'Natural light always reveals the magic in the eyes.' He then scrolls down and notes, 'A couple of comments said that you can see "Call 911" in her bottom eyelashes.'[353]

Team Britney asserted in a *New Yorker* article that Spears has almost complete control over her online platforms, with only a slim 1 per cent of her posts getting censored by handlers for liability reasons. Of Spears' seemingly random uploads, the source asked incredulously:

Would anyone be telling her to put that stuff up? It's detrimental to the brand. Trust me, if I had my way, that's not what she would be posting. But the point is that she's not the prisoner with no rights that some people in the #FreeBritney movement are trying to make her out to be.[354]

However, the controversy came under even harsher criticism following the February 2021 debut of *Framing Britney Spears*. Numerous media outlets ran articles about Spears 'breaking' her silence over a month and a half after the documentary first aired. Taking to Instagram once again, Spears posted:

> My life has always been very speculated . . . watched . . . and judged really my whole life !!! I have been exposed my whole life performing in front of people 😵😵😵 !!! It takes a lot of strength to TRUST the universe with your real vulnerability cause I've always been so judged . . . insulted . . . and embarrassed by the media . . . and I still am till this day 👎 👎 👎 !!!! As the world keeps on turning and life goes on we still remain so fragile and sensitive as people !!!

She went on to confess that she 'didn't watch the documentary', but what she did manage to glean from it made her 'embarrassed by the light they put me in', causing the star to cry 'for two weeks'.[355]

However, such heartfelt sentiments did not convince everyone that Spears was calling the shots online. Make-up artist Billy Brasfield, who worked with the singer on the US version of *The X Factor* and on the video for her 2013 single, 'Scream & Shout', claimed that Spears told him she was not fully in control of her social media. After seeing the response to the documentary posted on the star's Instagram account, Brasfield contended that he 'immediately knew it was not her'. He went on to say:

> I texted her about it and she texted me back last night. What was upsetting [about the Instagram post] – it was basically a narrative denouncing her fans and the #FreeBritney movement and people now taking a very conscious look at the facts and what is going on. Although it might be complicated for her, of course she is invested. It's her life. She does not like being a victim, she never wanted to be a victim and doesn't see herself as a victim. She sees herself as a survivor and has navigated this with patience and strategy.[356]

Brasfield denounced the Instagram response as simply an attempt to distract the public from the reality of Britney's conservatorship.

Almost immediately, the inevitable backlash against Brasfield's supposed conversation with Spears began, with various unnamed 'sources' – all 'close' to the star – reporting that the singer had not spoken to the make-up artist in years. *Page Six* even wrote, 'The rep told us that Spears reiterated: "I write my own posts, I don't know why he is saying that."'[357] These attempts to explain away Brasfield piggybacked on earlier assertions made by Britney's social media manager, Crowd-Surf's Cassie Petrey, in February 2021. On her personal Instagram account, Petrey started off her soliloquy by claiming to 'absolutely adore the Britney Spears fanbase'. 'They are incredible, loyal, and passionate,' Petrey gushed, continuing,

'I admire them. I know everything they do and say is because they truly love her.' She then cited this admiration as the reason she has overlooked 'some of the nasty comments that have been thrown my way over the years – because I know deep down it's all out of love for one of the greatest pop stars of all time'.

According to Petrey, it is Spears – and Spears alone – who creates all the posts and captions for Instagram. 'She finds the Google images, Pinterest images, quotes, memes, and everything else herself,' Petrey asserted:

> Nobody is suggesting any of that stuff to her. She generally edits the videos herself. If a video she sends in is edited by her social media team, it's because she gave specific instructions and asked for it to be edited that way. Then she sees it and decides if she wants to post it or not.

Petrey then denied any suggestion of Spears using Instagram as an SOS for support: 'She is literally just living her life and trying to have fun on Instagram. She has a team to help strategize, like any major celebrity generally does at this point in her career.' Petrey concluded by urging fans to stop hypothesising 'inaccurate theories', insisting that there were no secrets to uncover.[358]

This did not stop some fans from voicing their concerns when, on 14 September 2021, just days after the announcement of her engagement to long-term boyfriend Sam Asghari, Britney's Instagram account appeared to have been deleted. However, Spears' lawyer soon confirmed that it was the singer's decision to take a break from social media and Britney's final post before her hiatus openly praised her #FreeBritney supporters, proclaiming, 'You guys fucking kick ass!!!!! Love you so much and God bless.' The break was short-lived, though, with Spears returning to Instagram less than a week later.

As much as social media may create a sense of connection with Spears, her online platforms are really just another means for Britney's audience to project their own hopes, experiences and ideas onto the star, rather than being a true representation of her life or mental state. In *Framing Britney Spears*, former MTV VJ David Holmes perfectly summarised this notion. Speaking specifically about Spears' TikTok and Instagram content, Holmes said, 'It's impossible to know her . . . we never knew her. We know her even less now. She is kind of unknowable.'[359]

PIECE 38

The Business of Britney

When Britney Spears had her day in court on 23 June 2021, she had a lot to say about the previous thirteen years spent under a conservatorship. 'It's been a long time since I've owned my money,' Spears said. 'I shouldn't be in a conservatorship if I can work and provide money and work for myself and pay other people – it makes no sense.' Directly addressing the judge, she added, 'Ma'am, my dad and anyone involved in this conservatorship and my management who played a huge role in punishing me when I said no – ma'am, they should be in jail.'

An attorney representing the conservatorship asked the judge to clear the courtroom and have the transcripts of Spears' testimony sealed. Britney objected. 'Somebody's done a good job at exploiting my life,' she said. 'I feel like it should be an open-court hearing – they should listen and hear what I have to say.'[360]

Upon becoming a conservatee, Britney lost all control over her own money. In 2008, before being placed under the mandate,

Britney had amassed a huge fortune of $125 million – the combined total of her touring, record sales, sponsorships, appearance fees and a fragrance deal with Elizabeth Arden. Her monthly income alone was estimated to be $737,000.[361] *Forbes* listed her as one of the twenty richest women in entertainment. Former self-described manager Sam Lutfi claimed that, in 2008 alone, Britney earned over $9 million just from song royalties.

While under the conservatorship, Britney made four albums, went on four world tours, completed a four-year Las Vegas residency and released twenty-six fragrances. Yet documents revealed in 2021 place the singer's fortune at a comparatively low $60 million – less than half of what it was before she entered into the legal arrangement. To give further context, Jennifer Lopez (who also held a Las Vegas residency) is valued at over $100 million, while Beyoncé (who broke into the charts at around the same time as Britney) is worth over $700 million, independent of any wealth belonging to husband Jay-Z.

A rough estimate of Britney's total record sales and concert earnings comes to $193 million. This considers an industry standard of 10 per cent agent fees, 15 per cent management fees and 40 per cent tax payments. With these deductions factored in, Britney should have brought home at least $25 million for her Vegas residency. Meanwhile, her perfumes are rumoured to make $50 million each upon release. Even if this figure is hugely inflated and Spears only gets 1 per cent of it, there is still a large chunk of change missing from her bank account.

On top of this, there are other income streams to consider. These include Spears' stint as a judge on *The X Factor*, which came with a cool $15 million salary, as well as books, dolls, video games, merchandise, sponsorships and endorsement deals.

Between 2013 and 2017, Jamie Spears took 1.5 per cent of all gross ticket and merchandise sales from Britney's Piece of Me residency, tucking away a tidy nest egg of at least $2.1 million. Two years before, he paid himself a 2.95 per cent commission from Britney's Femme Fatale Tour, bagging himself a payday in the region of $500,000.

After Britney's devastating statement in court, mother Lynne and sister Jamie Lynn both took to social media to defend their public silence regarding the conservatorship. Lynne quoted a Bible verse from John 1:5: 'The light shines in the darkness and the darkness has not overcome it.'[362] Jamie Lynn, meanwhile, was a bit more direct, posting:

> The only reason I haven't [said anything] before is because I felt like, until my sister could speak for herself and say what she felt she needed to say publicly, it wasn't my place and it wasn't the right thing to do . . . If ending the conservatorship or whatever the hell else she wants to do to be happy, I support that 100 per cent . . . I have nothing to gain or lose either way.

Britney did not seem pleased with either of these messages. Though not calling anyone out by name, Brit watchers were convinced that Spears' 17 July Instagram offering was directed at her mother and sibling:

> There's nothing worse than when the people closest to you who never showed up for you post things in regard to your situation whatever it may be and speak righteously for support . . . How dare you make it public that NOW

you CARE . . . did you put your hand out when I was drowning ???? Again . . . NO.

Overall, Spears' income streams do not match up with her wealth. In 2018, Britney's total living costs came to $400,000. In a report by *E! News*, Britney's main personal expenses appeared to be her full-time bodyguard and repairs to the elevator in her home. Her penchant for retail therapy consisted of cheap and (relatively) cheerful high-street retailers – incongruous for a star of her wealth and status – including Target, Old Navy, Macy's and TJ Maxx (TK Maxx to UK shoppers).

Even the $20,000 a month in child support paid to ex-husband Kevin Federline pales in comparison to Britney's conservatorship and legal fees, which come to $1.1 million yearly. Jamie alone was the recipient of $128,000 for his role as conservator. In 2018, Jamie's co-conservator, attorney Andrew Wallet, negotiated a pay rise for his work on the star's case, increasing his Britney bucks to an annual sum of $426,000. Britney's own lawyer (until July 2021), Samuel Ingham, was not far off Wallet's salary. According to the *New York Times*, Ingham earned at least $3 million in legal fees from the singer since 2008.

Though Britney's current wealth of $60 million is nothing to sniff at, there are still some question marks surrounding her worth. In a court filing from 2018, an attorney representing Jamie claimed that Britney's estate had been 'nearly out of funds and cash equivalents' when the conservatorship took hold. It is thanks to her father, the attorney argued, that Britney has been able to build up what is now in the kitty. 'Extraordinary skills have been employed by all in order to achieve the results enjoyed at the present time,' the court filing stated. Jamie Spears 'has had many months at a time where all of his professional time was spent in services rendered exclusively to the conservatee'.[363]

However, a discrepancy remains between the cash Britney *did* hold at the start of the mandate, the cash she *should* hold after her various tours, deals and business ventures, and the cash she *actually* holds at present. Indeed, this discrepancy is one that Britney's lawyer – the recently appointed Mathew Rosengart – has made it clear he will look into. Responding to the announcement that Jamie Spears would be stepping down from his conservator role, Rosengart stated: 'We look forward to continuing our vigorous investigation into the conduct of Mr Spears, and others, over the past thirteen years, while he reaped millions of dollars from his daughter's estate, and I look forward to taking Mr Spears' sworn deposition in the near future.'[364]

Yet, on 7 September 2021, news broke that Jamie Spears was filing to shut down his daughter's conservatorship. While Rosengart acknowledged that this termination request was a 'victory and vindication' for Britney, he also highlighted a potentially troubling motive behind Spears senior's decision to abandon the arrangement he has held onto for so long. 'It appears that Mr Spears believes he can try to avoid accountability and justice, including sitting for a sworn deposition and answering other discovery under oath,' Rosengart suggested, adding, 'but, as we assess his filing (which was inappropriately sent to the media before it was served on counsel), we will also continue to explore all options.'[365] No doubt numerous revelations will come to light as Rosengart sifts through the many years of allegedly nefarious deals made during the conservatorship era.

Ultimately, though, with her father removed and an end to the mandate on the horizon, perhaps Britney might finally be able to – quite literally – mind her own business.

PIECE 39

The Handmaid

Margaret Atwood's *The Handmaid's Tale* was an immediate hit when it was published in 1985. The novel tells the story of a dystopian world in which an unquestioning obedience to the patriarchal society is valued above all else and women's rights, individuality and self-expression have been stripped away. Females of reproductive age are viewed as no more than vessels for producing children for high-ranking officers in the government; getting pregnant outside of this arrangement is illegal. Protagonist Offred and the other Handmaids do not have control over their own bodies; their physicality belongs to their 'commanders' to do with as they please, whenever they please. Once a Handmaid is done being useful, she is discarded.

Handmaid was a stark warning of what a seemingly distant future could look like if the important foundational rights taken for granted in western governments were not protected.

Decades before the phrase 'fake news' had even entered the lexicon, *Handmaid* encouraged readers to question what they heard, saw and read and to become part of the conversation and decision-making process of the world around them. *Handmaid* illustrates a society in which freedoms have been slowly chipped away until a nightmarish but believable reality exists. In this cautionary system, a woman is little more than chattel to churn out children, rendering her worthless once her 'use' expires.

Shades of Atwood's terrifying classic came to mind when Britney Spears spoke in court in June 2021 as part of her conservatorship trial. It was as though she were reading from an updated, 21st-century, autobiographical version of the story. For Spears, her worth is as a money-making machine, rather than a baby-making one. Instead of being a vessel for producing offspring, Britney has been a vessel for producing cash, with the conservatorship forcing her to take part in tours, performances and other profitable deals. Deemed legally incapable of making any decisions on her own, Britney had been stripped of the right to control even her most intimate physicality.

As Spears made her statement, her voice was audibly shaking with rage. She seemed completely alienated from her own being, as though – somewhat fittingly – it belonged to someone else. 'My precious body, who has worked for my dad for the past fucking thirteen years, trying to be so good and pretty . . . so perfect . . . when he works me so hard,' Britney said.[366] From the beginning of the conservatorship, it has been claimed that Jamie Spears 'understood his role as conservator to require prioritising not his daughter's mental health so much as her Barbie-doll public image'. A crucial part of this was taking control of Britney's body. Just days after the mandate was put in place in 2008, family friend Jacqueline Butcher said she witnessed a startling exchange between father and daughter, which she recounted in an interview with the *New Yorker*: 'Jamie said, "Baby. . ." – I thought he was going to say, "We love you, but you need help" – but what he said was, "You're fat. Daddy's gonna get you on a diet and a trainer and you're gonna get back in shape."' Butcher also alleged that, when anyone questioned Jamie about a decision made on behalf of Britney, he would scream, 'I am Britney Spears!'

In her testimony, Britney went on to talk about being forced to sign contracts, not being able to choose her own choreography, being placed on lithium by a therapist after she said no to performing at a show in Las Vegas, and not feeling heard or believed – all while her father was her conservator. 'The control he had over someone as powerful as me – he loved the control to hurt his own daughter, 100,000 per cent,' Spears proclaimed, voice trembling with anger.[367]

While all of Britney's allegations were shocking, one statement in particular felt like it could have been lifted directly from *Handmaid*:

> I was told right now in the conservatorship, I'm not able to get married or have a baby, I have an IUD inside of myself right now so I don't get pregnant. I wanted to take the IUD out so I could start trying to have another baby, but this so-called team won't let me go to the doctor to take it out because they don't want me to have children.

Britney concluded by saying, 'I deserve to have the same rights as anybody does, by having a child, a family, any of those things and more.'[368] However, as much as American women are led to believe that they have control and choice over their bodies, in legislative terms, they do not. Every year, more and more rights are being chipped away, *Handmaid*-style.

What few people know is that a 1927 Supreme Court ruling in the US made it legal and acceptable to forcibly sterilise a woman. In *Buck v. Bell*, 'the court argued that imbecility, epilepsy and feeblemindedness are hereditary and that inmates should be prevented from passing these defects to the next generation'. Inmate Carrie Buck, who the court called 'a feebleminded daughter of a feebleminded mother and herself the mother of a feebleminded child', was ordered to be sterilised to stop her from having any more children. The rationalisation, written by one Judge Holmes, said, 'Instead of waiting to execute degenerate offspring for crime or to let them starve for their imbecility, society can prevent those who are manifestly unfit from continuing their kind . . . Three generations of imbeciles are enough.' Holmes went on to state that, 'if public welfare may demand the lives of its best citizens, then surely the lowest members of society should be prevented from propagating their kind at the expense of everyone else'.[369]

Based on *Buck v. Bell*, if a woman is deemed to be one of the 'lowest members of society' (e.g., without access – be that from lack of money, status, representation or intellect), she can legally be made infertile. Adding further horror to the ruling, historian Paul Lombardo noted in his 2002 book, *Three Generations,*

No Imbecile, that Carrie had actually achieved good grades at school and that her pregnancy was the result of being raped by her foster mother's nephew.

While *Buck v. Bell* could easily be brushed off as an antiquated relic from a long-ago past, it has clear parallels with Britney's situation. Moreover, it is not just this century-old decision that is threatening control over women's bodies. Since the landmark 1973 *Roe v. Wade* ruling gave women the right to legally have an abortion, the rate of such procedures has steadily declined, reaching its lowest level on record in recent years.[370] Though a 2019 Pew Research poll showed that the majority of Americans believe that abortion should be legal in all or most cases, conservative activists and politicians have tried to overturn and limit the parameters provided by *Roe v. Wade* for decades.[371] Distressingly, in three US states, reproductive rights have already been radically diminished. In 2021, Arkansas banned all abortions except in medical emergencies, regardless of whether a pregnancy is the result of rape or incest. Meanwhile, Texas outlawed abortion after the detection of a foetal heartbeat. (This typically happens at about six weeks – often before a woman even realises she is pregnant.) Finally, Republican governor Kevin Stitt of Oklahoma signed an outright ban on abortion.[372] With the Supreme Court stacked with a 6–3 conservative majority after Donald Trump's presidency, right-to-choose groups are fearful that parts of the 1973 ruling could be overturned, further restricting access for women to terminate pregnancies.

Though Jamie has since been suspended as Britney's conservator and stated that he wants to let his daughter 'have a baby, if she so chooses', the singer's account of being forcibly denied the freedom to control her own body outraged many. However, it also raised a valid question: why does it take a pop star in an unacceptable situation for the world to object?

Television series *The Handmaid's Tale*, based on Atwood's novel, was such a global hit that the show's creators had to start creating new plots and ideas going beyond the book's original storylines. Millions of people followed the plight of Offred and her fellow Handmaids yet few picked up on the connection to what is going on in the world right now. Why was it not until Britney shared her suffering that the public took notice and got angry?

There is a scene in the 2004 movie *Hotel Rwanda* that is mortifying in its truism. Rwandan hotel manager Paul Rusesabagina, played by Don Cheadle, is thrilled that United Nations worker Jack Daglish, portrayed by Joaquin Phoenix, has captured some footage of the Rwandan genocide and is going to be sharing it with news outlets. The dialogue is still as apt as ever:

Paul: I am glad that you have shot this footage and that the world will see it. It is the only way we have a chance that people might intervene . . . How can they not intervene when they witness such atrocities?

Jack: If people see this footage, they'll say, 'Oh my god, that's horrible.' And then go on eating their dinner.[373]

PIECE 40

Britney by Numbers

Since her very first studio album, Britney Spears has been a sales phenomenon, making and breaking records of all kinds. Britney's career has bridged the transition from a music industry dependent on sales of physical products to a new world order in which albums are little more than promotional tools to sell the overall brand of an artist. By creating a devout fanbase with her initial releases, Britney laid the foundation for other standalone, financially viable ventures, too (e.g. tours, perfumes and merchandise). Consumers bought into Britney as a package, not just one specific album. When . . . *Baby One More Time* debuted, the music industry was on the brink of a huge transformation – an evolution that would, in many ways, parallel Britney's career itself.

Rewind to 1999: CDs were the format du jour, easy to transport from car to Walkman to home stereo and marketed as indestructible. Record companies were flush with cash as people were replacing their vinyl with the 'better-sounding' compact disc. However, things were about to change dramatically. As Britney's first album was introduced to the world, another cultural rupture tore through the music industry: file-sharing computer service Napster. This new network meant people could share their music libraries with each other free of charge. The beginning of the file-sharing, MP3-downloading, CD-burning, song-streaming evolution had begun, changing the way fans consumed music for ever.

The title track from . . . *Baby One More Time* drove the album's success, selling more than 10 million copies worldwide and becoming one of the biggest-selling singles of all time. The performance of the full-length album also broke previous sales records, with an unprecedented volume of units flying off the shelves.

. . . *Baby One More Time*

- Sold over 10.6 million copies in the US to date, making it the seventeenth best-selling album of all time (since the Nielsen Charts were first established in 1991).
- Made Britney the first new artist ever to have a single and an album both go to number one the week of release, as well as the youngest female artist in the history of *Billboard* to have a single and an album at number one in the same week.
- Entered the top ten in charts across the globe, speeding to number one in Canada, Germany and Switzerland and number two in the UK and Australia.

- Saw Britney usurp Alanis Morissette as the youngest artist ever to receive diamond status for an album in the US (an award given for the sale of over 10 million albums).
- Sold an eye-watering global total of 25 million copies.[374]

After the success of . . . *Baby One More Time*, Britney's follow-up, 2000's *Oops!. . . I Did It Again*, was greatly anticipated and, like its predecessor, set a new high-water mark for sales.

Oops! . . . I Did It Again

- Sold 1.39 million copies in its first week in the US and 2.5 million around the world, breaking previous records for highest debut-week album sales. (Britney held this record until Adele released her third studio album, *25*, in 2015, though she is still second only to the British songstress for having the highest first-week sales by a female artist worldwide.)
- Debuted at number one in charts across the globe and attained the coveted diamond status, making Britney, aged eighteen, the youngest artist ever to have two albums sell 10 million copies each.
- Is the thirty-second best-selling record of all time in the US.
- Sold a total of 20 million copies internationally.

When Britney dropped her namesake album in 2001, controversy about her more provocative image was starting to heat up. Tracks from the record like 'I'm a Slave 4 U' only stoked the fire. The sale numbers for *Britney* reflect the changing temperature of not only the media, but also the music economy: CD-burning had become a real threat to the sales of albums, and Napster was gaining popularity as younger fans balked at the high prices of new releases.

Britney

- Became Spears' third album to debut at the top of the *Billboard* chart, making her the first female artist ever to achieve this feat.
- Sold almost 5 million copies in the US and a total of 9 million copies worldwide.

In the Zone saw a Justin Timberlake-free Britney emerge, with themes of masturbation, sex and other more adult topics woven through the record. By the time the album was released in 2003, iTunes and the iPod had been introduced to the world, while Napster competitors like LimeWire were acquiring an even stronger toehold in the music arena, eroding the sales numbers of albums everywhere.

In the Zone

- Was Britney's fourth album in a row to top the *Billboard* chart upon release, making her the first female artist ever to claim this accomplishment.
- Entered the top ten in more than fifteen countries worldwide.
- Sold half a million copies in the UK and 3 million copies in the US.

When *Blackout* dropped in 2007, physical sales of music were in precipitous decline and the industry was trying to recalibrate just to survive. In less than a decade, their entire business model had changed. Albums – the traditional profit-driver for an artist – were now freely available to those willing to risk illegally downloading them from file-sharing services. The result was a dramatic downturn in LP purchases for artists of all genres – and Britney was no exception.

Blackout

- Peaked at number one in Canada and Ireland and number two in the US, the UK and France.
- Debuted at number two on the *Billboard* chart, selling 290,000 copies in its first week.
- Sold a million copies in the US, just under 300,000 in the UK and 3.1 million worldwide.

Circus – Britney's sixth studio album, released just a year after *Blackout* – fared slightly better than its predecessor. This could be attributed to the worldwide tour promoting its existence – a factor that was almost completely absent from *Blackout*'s PR.

Circus

- Debuted at number one on the *Billboard* chart.
- Attained platinum status in both the UK and the US.
- Hit global sales of 4 million.

The shift towards a singles-based, playlist-centred culture (encouraged by Spotify and other streaming services) was evident in the performance of Britney's 2011 album, *Femme Fatale*. While the overall sales of the record paled in comparison to Spears' previous releases, the success of its individual tracks highlighted the evolution of the industry. Consumers were now picking and mixing instead of immersing themselves in an entire full-length album experience.

Femme Fatale

- Attained platinum status in the UK and the US.
- Was Britney's first album to have three top-ten singles in the US charts ('Hold It Against Me', 'Till the World Ends' and 'I Wanna Go').
- Groovalicious track 'Criminal' was a global hit, reaching the top twenty in several countries upon release. It saw a huge resurgence in popularity in 2020 due to a video that went viral on social media site TikTok, helping make the single one of Britney's most-streamed songs.

By the time *Britney Jean* appeared in 2013, large physical sales were a thing of the past. Artists were depending on touring, merchandise and other revenue opportunities for income. Britney herself was about to embark on what would become a four-year residency in Las Vegas – an endeavour that would make millions of dollars. The performance of Britney's eighth album reflected these new trends. Sales for records were also calculated from three components: purchases of the traditional physical-format full album; streams from platforms like Spotify; and 'album equivalents' – jargon that was introduced in the mid-2010s to encapsulate the consumption of music from downloading and other means equalling 'an album in total'.

Britney Jean

- Entered the US *Billboard* chart at number four, selling 107,000 copies in its first week, making it both the lowest debut and the lowest-selling album Britney had ever released.
- Sold just under 13,000 copies in the UK.
- Was eventually granted gold status in the US for sales of 500,000 units (when factoring in combined album sales, streams and 'album equivalents').

Three years later, when *Glory* hit stores, 'album equivalents' were one of the main tools for evaluating a release's performance, aggregating streams, downloads and physical-format purchases to obtain a total sales number.

Glory

- Debuted at number two in the UK, making it Britney's highest-charting album since *Blackout*.
- Went to number three in Germany, the highest chart position there for Spears since *In the Zone*.
- Was Britney's first album to go to number one in Italy.
- Premiered at number one in Taiwan and Ireland.

- Entered at number three in the US chart, selling the 'album equivalent' of 111,000. The breakdown for *Glory* to reach that 111,000 'album equivalent' illustrates how detrimental to album economics music-streaming services like Spotify can be. It comprised:
  - 88,000 pure album sales (full-album downloads and physical-format purchases);
  - 113,000 song sales (from download platforms);
  - 18.1 million streams.[375]

CONCLUSION

Born to Make You Happy?

The unrelenting obsession with Britney Spears reveals America's reverence for itself. She acts as a distorted mirror, allowing public and press alike to scrutinise their own reflection. By picking apart someone seemingly familiar, we are not forced to look directly at our own fundamental wrongs. When worth is only ascribed to those who garner great fame and monetary wealth, prosperity and achievements of other kinds are not intrinsically valued or regarded as aspirational. Analysing Britney gives us an opportunity to fleetingly examine our own national and personal identity. Yet any potential commitment to change we may feel as a result rarely lingers beyond a blog post on a celebrity gossip site. Consideration lasts only as long as the momentary anger, entertainment, disgust or envy that a Britney update delivers – it is an emotion quickly expended and then forgotten.

Britney's appearance and sexuality have been crucial monetised products since the start of her professional career. Early on, there was an inherent and intriguing tension between her chaste innocence and overt libido, each defining the other by its juxtaposition. One of the reasons Britney's breakout video, '. . . Baby One More Time', was such a sensation was because it played on this intangible balance. Indeed, the Britney quandary is one faced by many young women; the very lexicon used around virginity – 'lost', 'given away' – creates an unescapable and confusing dynamic wherein sex is both a burden and a gift, something to get rid of and something to keep. Once virginity is 'lost', it is unclear what is to be 'found' or 'gained' in its place. When Britney was forced to admit to having been physically intimate with her long-term boyfriend Justin Timberlake, there was seemingly nowhere for her to go but to 'sexy seductress'. Yet, as she turned to a more adult image to complement her deflowered status, Britney was crucified for leaving behind her loveable girl-next-door innocence. Essentially, she was punished for growing up.

There is an expectation that celebrities should be positive role models, especially if they have a young following. However, for people like Spears, maturing as a consumer entity under the unrelenting glare of the public eye, it is impossible to remain an evergreen good girl. Being a polished marketable paragon does not allow for any inwardly personal – yet publicly facing – journeys of experimentation, exploration or self-engagement. When a person is forced to inhabit a two-dimensional idealised representation of perfection, rather than openly existing as a fallible human being, it not surprising when they stumble and fall. Britney's experience was inevitable within the toxic broth of ingrained misogyny, puritan righteousness and hypocritical standards directed at women. It was an all-too-familiar path, well-trod by many before her.

The fact that Spears was silenced for over a decade under a legally mandated conservatorship is also terrifying, though the emergence of the #FreeBritney movement has provided hope that normal people can raise awareness and effect change. However, the fact that it is has taken the plight of a celebrity to mobilise a vocal contingent is disheartening when we live in a world already so divided and divisive.

Being Britney is the fulfilment of the American Dream – the ultimate metamorphosis from working-class southern girl to globally worshipped icon. Yet the price paid by the woman behind the multi-million-dollar brand has been extreme. Her story is symptomatic of the injustice present in a society idle for change and rabid to consume those they exalt.

Britney is, in many ways, just a cultural vessel for our own projections, comprising the very characters she has embodied in her music videos – from naive schoolgirl to femme fatale to kinky housewife. The Britney most often seen is an enigma, allowing her to be anyone to everyone – a cobbled-together pastiche of social media posts, carefully choreographed interviews and the remnants of young adulthood splayed out and picked over for all the world to see. Yet, when Britney has offered us a glimpse of her unedited self, she has been rejected or abused. Though she is applauded by her fans for being 'authentic', the 'real' parts of Britney are often *too* real for the wider public. They don't want their star to look, act or sound like the person she is underneath the mediated polish because the likeness is too unsettling: she is a girl many of us know or embody ourselves.

However, while this version of Britney may be at odds with the flawless, airbrushed image constructed by content providers and industry executives since her childhood, it may also be the last piece of herself that she can still truly call her own.

Acknowledgements

Thank you to everyone who has supported me in so many different ways. I feel lucky every day.

Biggest bow of gratitude to Pete Selby for being an inspiring, thoughtful, wonderful human being. Your encouragement, belief and unyielding fabness are breathtaking. You are a true legend.

Thank you to Melissa Bond for all your editorial help and guidance. You are a rock!

Big high fives to Lizzie Dorney-Kingdom for the hard grind in bringing this book to the masses and I would be remiss not to mention Francesca Eades for her dedication to the Britney cause.

Thank you to my agent, Matthew Hamilton.

This book would not have been possible without all the wonderful folks who kindly gave their time and thoughts. Thank you to Jude Clay, Courtney, Jocasta Hamilton, Michael Levine, Sadie Smith, Pandora Sykes and Sasha Yevtushenko.

Huge love for the #FreeBritneyLA crew – Leanne Simmons, Kevin Wu, Junior Olivas and especially my girl Megan Radford.

You've shown me that change is possible. And all of the love to my ride-or-die Adam Oliver at #FreeBritneyLondon for making me a believer.

Thank you to Nicola and Trevor Collins for sharing the story of your brother, Keith.

Mary Close, you are divine.

Big hugs to Finn Longhurst, Rich Dawes, Marina Stavropoulou, Julie Foxen, Alan Gonzales, Vaseema Hamilton, Jackie Jeffries, Krystal Kalikala MacKnight, Ben Smith, Laurence Tritton, Alex White, Terry Currier, Janeen Rundle, Bill Frith, Oregon Music Hall of Fame, Rough Trade, G. Scott Barrett, Scott Klopfenstein, Dana Palmer, Zoe Alexander, Dave Navarro, Stuart Braithwaite, Henry Rollins, Mark and Shell Gilbert, Cosey Fanni Tutti, Sam Allison, Amoeba Records, Marc Weinstein, Marsha Janestski, Megan Page, Record Store Day, Jordan Hill, Allyson Baker, William Badgley, Roisin O'Connor, Pat Mandell and the Mandell family, Natasha Middlecote, Peter Katsis, Izzy Bee Phillips, Black Honey, Dan Potts, Meredith Aleandri, Big Freedia, Leigh Anne Lewis, Jason Feinberg, Nina Budden, Calyx Clagg, Nicole Balin, Justin Loeber at Mouth Digital + Public Relations, Kristen Carranza, Celeste Faraola Perie, Jo Whitty and Audrey Faine.

I am forever indebted to the wonderful, wise and inspiring goddess Shirley Manson. Thank you for being my friend and cheerleader. You are incredible and I adore you to pieces.

Thank you to Debbi Peterson for offering humour and humanity during this intense task.

Thank you to my writing godmother, Susanna Hoffs, for believing in me and supporting me, even though you have your own crazy schedule.

ACKNOWLEDGEMENTS

Huge love to Vicki Peterson for listening to my Diet Coke rants and being such a great therapist throughout the writing of this book. I am so happy I wrote that letter.

Thank you to my boss and mentor, David O'Connor. You are the best and I am lucky to know you. Your unerring support means more than I can ever say.

I am so grateful to have Richard Novak in my life. I love you to bits and am honoured to call you a friend and adviser on all aspects of my crazy existence.

All my love to my aunt Janet Pucci and my uncle Ray Santana.

I love you more than words can say, my two bestest friends in the universe: Tami 'VP' Cady and Lynne 'Billy Hufsey' Collins.

I have the best family of friends in the world. I love you to Santa Cruz and back, Alix Brodie-Wray, Andrea Fincham, Hayley Jordan, Margareth Ainley, Sheri Siegfried, Julie Weir, Julia Ruzicka and Stacy Horne.

The biggest thanks of all to my husband, James. I love you so much; I could not do anything without you. Thank you for being my tower of strength, my wonderwall and my boo.

Notes

1. Strauss, A. (2014) *Britney Spears: An Unauthorized Biography*. St Martin's Press (Kindle edition).

2. Dennis, S. (2009) *Britney: Inside the Dream*. HarperCollins (Kindle edition).

3. Strauss, A. (2014) *Britney Spears: An Unauthorized Biography*. St Martin's Press (Kindle edition).

4. DeDecker, B. (2016) 'Hidden Louisiana: It's Britney, Bitch'. Available at anti-gravitymagazine.com/column/hidden-louisiana-its-britney-bitch. Accessed 5 May 2021. Also: Grigoriadis, V. (2008) 'The Tragedy of Britney Spears'. Available at rollingstone.com/feature/the-tragedy-of-britney-spears-2-254735. Accessed 6 May 2021.

5. DeDecker, B. (2016) 'Hidden Louisiana: It's Britney, Bitch'. Available at anti-gravitymagazine.com/column/hidden-louisiana-its-britney-bitch. Accessed 5 May 2021.

6. Eliscu, J. (2011) 'Britney Spears Returns'. Available at rollingstone.com/music/music-news/britney-spears-returns-254594. Accessed 5 May 2021.

7. C., J. (2004) 'Britney Spears Barefoot in a Gas Station Bathroom'. Available at popdirt.com/britney-spears-barefoot-in-a-gas-station-bathroom/32138. Accessed 6 May 2021.

8. Traister, R. (2004) 'Don't do it, Britney!'. Available at salon.com/2004/08/23/britney_9. Accessed 4 May 2021.

NOTES

9. No author (2021) 'Britney Spears criticizes documentaries made about her life'. Available at explica.co/britney-spears-criticizes-documentaries-made-about-her-life.html. Accessed 27 May 2021.

10. Grigoriadis, V. (2008) 'The Tragedy of Britney Spears'. Available at rollingstone.com/feature/the-tragedy-of-britney-spears-2-254735. Accessed 6 May 2021.

11. YouTube (2010) 'Britney Spears Graces the Star Search Stage, 1992'. Available at youtube.com/watch?v=01moeH2mfmY. Accessed 4 May 2021.

12. Parker, L. (2014) 'Losing to Win: Remembering the Real Stars of "Star Search"'. Available at rollingstone.com/music/music-news/losing-to-win-remembering-the-real-stars-of-star-search-117560. Accessed 8 April 2021.

13. YouTube (2010) 'Britney Spears Graces the Star Search Stage, 1992'. Available at youtube.com/watch?v=01moeH2mfmY. Accessed 4 May 2021.

14. ABC News (2006) '"Star Search" Losers Who Made It Big'. Available at abcnews.go.com/2020/story?id=123814&page=1. Accessed 8 April 2021.

15. YouTube (2010) 'Britney Spears Graces the Star Search Stage, 1992'. Available at youtube.com/watch?v=01moeH2mfmY. Accessed 4 May 2021.

16. ABC News (2006) '"Star Search" Losers Who Made It Big'. Available at abcnews.go.com/2020/story?id=123814&page=1. Accessed 8 April 2021.

17. Slovacek, R. (2019) 'Marty Thomas's Journey from Small-Town Dances To "Dreamlover"'. Available at instinctmagazine.com/marty-thomas-journey-from-small-town-dances-to-dreamlover. Accessed 9 April 2021.

18. OurScene TV interview (2009) 'Broadway Babe Marty Thomas Talks Britney Spears, Xanadu & the Great White Way'. Available at youtube.com/watch?v=AfjfGU_bRRA. Accessed 10 April 2021.

19. Heard, C. (2014) *Britney Spears: Little Girl Lost*. Cogito America Inc. (Kindle edition).

20. Macatee, R. (2018) 'Ready to Launch: Inside Britney Spears, Justin Timberlake, Christina Aguilera & Ryan Gosling's Darling *Mickey Mouse Club* Days'. Available at eonline.com/uk/news/969561/ready-to-launch-inside-britney-spears-justin-timberlake-christina-aguilera-ryan-gosling-s-darling-mickey-mouse-club-days. Accessed 22 April 2021.

21. Dennis, S. (2009) *Britney: Inside the Dream*. HarperCollins (Kindle edition).

22. Macatee, R. (2018) 'Ready to Launch: Inside Britney Spears, Justin Timberlake, Christina Aguilera & Ryan Gosling's Darling *Mickey Mouse Club* Days'. Available at eonline.com/uk/news/969561/ready-to-launch-inside-britney-spears-justin-timberlake-christina-aguilera-ryan-gosling-s-darling-mickey-mouse-club-days. Accessed 22 April 2021.

23. Care, R. (date unknown) 'The Mouseketeers'. Available at encyclopedia.com/media/encyclopedias-almanacs-transcripts-and-maps/mouseketeers. Accessed 22 April 2021.

24. YouTube (2020) 'The Untold Truth of Annette Funicello'. Available at youtube.com/watch?v=c_fflAbJvBA. Accessed 22 April 2021.

25. No author (no date) 'Suppressed Mammaries'. Available at allthetropes.fandom.com/wiki/Suppressed_Mammaries. Accessed 22 April 2021.

26. Yarrow, A. (2018) 'How the '90s Tricked Women into Thinking They'd Gained Gender Equality'. Available at time.com/5310256/90s-gender-equality-progress. Accessed 22 April 2021.

27. Seabrook, J. (2015) 'Blank Space: What Kind of Genius Is Max Martin?'. Available at newyorker.com/culture/cultural-comment/blank-space-what-kind-of-genius-is-max-martin. Accessed 16 June 2021.

28. Goldstein, J. M. (2018) '"Britney Spears wanted to be a star": An oral history of ". . . Baby One More Time"'. Available at ew.com/music/2018/10/23/baby-one-more-time-britney-spears-oral-history. Accessed 16 June 2021.

29. Levine, N. (2019) 'Max Martin: the secrets of the world's best pop songwriter'. Available at bbc.com/culture/article/20191119-max-martin-the-secrets-of-the-worlds-best-pop-songwriter. Accessed 16 June 2021.

30. Cragg, M. (2019) '"Britney Spears is a genius": Max Martin, the powerhouse of pure pop'. Available at theguardian.com/music/2019/oct/25/were-not-made-to-be-famous-max-martin-the-powerhouse-of-pure-pop. Accessed 16 June 2021.

31. Lhooq, M., Myers, O. & Tanzer, M. (2018) 'It's Britney, Bitch!'. Available at thefader.com/2017/09/27/britney-spears-blackout-interview-10-year-anniversary-2007. Accessed 16 June 2021.

32. Goldstein, J. M. (2018) '"Britney Spears wanted to be a star": An oral history of ". . . Baby One More Time"'. Available at ew.com/music/2018/10/23/baby-one-more-time-britney-spears-oral-history. Accessed 16 June 2021.

33. Grady, C. (2021) 'Why Britney Spears' fans are convinced she's being held captive'. Available at vox.com/culture/22280627/britney-spears-conservatorship-free-britney-explained-framing-britney-spears. Accessed 16 June 2021.

34. Goldstein, J. M. (2018) '"Britney Spears wanted to be a star": An oral history of ". . . Baby One More Time"'. Available at ew.com/music/2018/10/23/baby-one-more-time-britney-spears-oral-history. Accessed 16 June 2021.

35. Goldstein, J. M. (2018) '"Britney Spears wanted to be a star": An oral history of ". . . Baby One More Time"'. Available at ew.com/music/2018/10/23/baby-one-more-time-britney-spears-oral-history. Accessed 16 June 2021.

36. Daly, S. (1999) 'Britney Spears: Inside the Mind (and Bedroom) of America's Teen Queen'. Available at rocksbackpages.com/Library/Article/britney-spears-inside-the-mind-and-bedroom-of-americas-teen-queen. Accessed 6 July 2021.

37. Fratti, K. (2018) '11 Wild Facts about Britney's Iconic "Baby One More Time" Video (It Was Almost Animated!)'. Available at bustle.com/p/britney-spears-baby-one-more-time-video-was-almost-animated-10-other-surprising-facts-about-the-20-year-old-clip-12596305. Accessed 2 July 2021.

38. YouTube (2014) 'Britney Spears – Making of . . . Baby One More Time'. Available at youtube.com/watch?v=WVlL5Bv0z0A. Accessed 2 July 2021.

39. Dennis, S. (2009) *Britney: Inside the Dream*. HarperCollins (Kindle edition).

40. Goldstein, J. M. (2018) '"Britney Spears wanted to be a star": An oral history of ". . . Baby One More Time"'. Available at ew.com/music/2018/10/23/baby-one-more-time-britney-spears-oral-history. Accessed 16 June 2021.

41. YouTube (2014) 'Britney Spears – Making of . . . Baby One More Time'. Available at youtube.com/watch?v=WVlL5Bv0z0A. Accessed 2 July 2021.

42. Hutchins, R. (2013) 'Myrna Loy: Hero On and Off Screen'. Available at blog.richmond.edu/heroes/2012/03/13/myrna-loy-hero-in-both-fact-and-fiction. Accessed 2 July 2021.

43. Heard, C. (2014) *Britney Spears: Little Girl Lost*. Cogito America Inc. (Kindle edition).

44. Goldstein, J. M. (2018) '"Britney Spears wanted to be a star": An oral history of ". . . Baby One More Time"'. Available at ew.com/music/2018/10/23/baby-one-more-time-britney-spears-oral-history. Accessed 16 June 2021.

45. Heard, C. (2014) *Britney Spears: Little Girl Lost*. Cogito America Inc. (Kindle edition).

46. Nashawatv, C. (2001) 'Britney Spears: Sex & the Singles Girl'. Available at ew.com/music/2001/11/09/sex-singles-girl. Accessed 7 July 2021.

47. Daly, S. (1999) 'Britney Spears: Inside the Mind (and Bedroom) of America's Teen Queen'. Available at rocksbackpages.com/Library/Article/britney-spears-inside-the-mind-and-bedroom-of-americas-teen-queen. Accessed 6 July 2021.

48. Goldstein, J. M. (2018) '"Britney Spears wanted to be a star": An oral history of ". . . Baby One More Time"'. Available at ew.com/music/2018/10/23/baby-one-more-time-britney-spears-oral-history. Accessed 16 June 2021.

49. Morgan, K. (1999) 'Why we let little Britney pose like a Lolita; NO REGRETS: SINGING STAR'S PARENTS ARE HAPPY WITH THE PHOTOS THAT HAVE SPARKED OUTRAGE'. Available at https://www.thefreelibrary.com/Why+we+let+little+Britney+pose+like+a+Lolita%3B+NO+REGRETS%3A+SINGING. . .-a060420191. Accessed 6 July 2021.

50. Heard, C. (2014) *Britney Spears: Little Girl Lost*. Cogito America Inc. (Kindle edition).

51. Montgomery, J. (2008) 'Justin Timberlake, Beyonce, Eminem, Fall Out Boy Mark End of an Era at "TRL" Finale'. Available at mtv.com/news/1599452/justin-timberlake-beyonce-eminem-fall-out-boy-mark-end-of-an-era-at-trl-finale. Accessed 7 July 2021.

52. Kenney, D. (2019) *The Unknown Keyboard Player* (Kindle edition).

53. Heard, C. (2014) *Britney Spears: Little Girl Lost*. Cogito America Inc. (Kindle edition).

54. Stark, S. (2021) *Framing Britney Spears*. New York Times Company & Left/Right Productions.

55. *People* (2000) 'Too Sexy Too Soon?'.

56. Wolk, J. (1999) 'Britney Spears debunks rumors of breast implants'. Available at ew.com/article/1999/10/04/britney-spears-debunks-rumors-breast-implants. Accessed 14 April 2021.

57. Biggers, A. (2019) 'Height in Girls: When Do They Stop Growing, What's the Median Height, and More'. Available at healthline.com/health/when-do-girls-stop-growing#qa:-breast-growth. Accessed 14 April 2021.

58. Google (1999) 'Britney Spears breast implants? Available at groups.google.com/g/alt.tv.dawsons-creek/c/NTzHF5CR6D8?pli=1. Accessed 14 April 2021.

59. Grigoriadis, V. (2008) 'The Tragedy of Britney Spears'. Available at rolling-stone.com/feature/the-tragedy-of-britney-spears-2-254735. Accessed 6 May 2021.

60. Bond, N. (2021) 'Dutch interviewer Ivo Niehe defends shocking Britney Spears interview'. Available at news.com.au/entertainment/tv/flashback/dutch-interviewer-ivo-niehe-defends-shocking-britney-spears-interview/news-story/76c68333baf63b45830eb1750791b68f. Accessed 14 April 2021.

61. PSP Team (2018) 'DID BRITNEY SPEARS HAVE COSMETIC SURGERY?'. Available at plasticsurgerypeople.com/britney-spears-cosmetic-surgery. Accessed 14 April 2021.

62. Dubrow, T. (2013) 'What is the best age for breast augmentation?'. Available at drdubrow.com/what-age-is-best-for-breast-augmentation. Accessed 14 April 2021.

63. Gold, C. (2019) 'A BRIEF HISTORY OF BOOB JOBS'. Available at dazeddigital.com/beauty/body/article/45520/1/a-brief-history-of-boob-jobs. Accessed 14 April 2021.

64. Jeny (2020) 'One Woman's Hunt for Britney Spears and Justin Timberlake's Matching Denim Outfits'. Available at womanlynews.com/woman/2020/06/11/one-womans-hunt-for-britney-spears-and-justin-timberlakes-matching-denim-outfits. Accessed 13 July 2021.

65. YouTube (2020) 'Justin Timberlake – Lance Bass Daily POPcast, 2020'. Available at youtube.com/watch?v=7S4SK3_71gY. Accessed 13 July 2021.

66. Jeny (2020) 'One Woman's Hunt for Britney Spears and Justin Timberlake's Matching Denim Outfits'. Available at womanlynews.com/woman/2020/06/11/one-womans-hunt-for-britney-spears-and-justin-timberlakes-matching-denim-outfits. Accessed 13 July 2021.

67. No author (no date) 'True Love Waits'. Available at encyclopedia.com/religion/legal-and-political-magazines/true-love-waits. Accessed 19 April 2021.

68. Heard, C. (2014) *Britney Spears: Little Girl Lost*. Cogito America Inc. (Kindle edition).

69. No author (2003) 'Epidemiology of HIV/AIDS in the United States'. Available at hivinsite.ucsf.edu/insite?page=kb-01-03. Accessed 18 April 2021.

70. Deneson, A. (2017) 'True love waits? The story of my purity ring and feeling like I didn't have a choice'. Available at theguardian.com/lifeandstyle/2017/feb/18/purity-ring-virginity-abstinence-sexual-education. Accessed 18 April 2021.

71. Cills, H. (2018) 'The Rise and Fall of the Pop Star Purity Ring'. Available at themuse.jezebel.com/the-rise-and-fall-of-the-pop-star-purity-ring-1822170318. Accessed 18 April 2021.

72. Dominus, S. (2001) 'Abstinence Minded: Does know-nothing sex ed help kids say no? It depends on what the question is'. Available at archive.nytimes.com/nytimes.com/library/magazine/home/20010121mag-wwln.html. Accessed 18 April 2021.

73. Williams, Z. (2002) 'Legacy of the virgin queen'. Available at standard.co.uk/hp/front/legacy-of-the-virgin-queen-6328707.html. Accessed 18 April 2021.

74. Deneson, A. (2017) 'True love waits? The story of my purity ring and feeling like I didn't have a choice'. Available at theguardian.com/lifeandstyle/2017/feb/18/purity-ring-virginity-abstinence-sexual-education. Accessed 18 April 2021.

75. Stark, S. (2021) *Framing Britney Spears*. New York Times Company & Left/Right Productions.

76. Papisova, V. (2015) 'Find Out When Most Teens Are Losing Their Virginity'. Available at teenvogue.com/story/teens-losing-virginity-age. Accessed 19 April 2021.

77. Vernon, P. (2000) 'Like a virgin?'. Available at theguardian.com/world/2000/jun/06/gender.uk1. Accessed 20 April 2021.

78. Rennex, M. (2021) 'Justin Timberlake Is Finally Getting Called Out for His Terrible Mistreatment of Britney Spears'. Available at junkee.com/justin-timberlake-britney-spears-documentary/287585. Accessed 20 April 2021.

79. No author (2003) 'Britney's boast busts virgin myth'. Available at news.bbc.co.uk/1/hi/entertainment/3052143.stm. Accessed 20 April 2021.

80. Rennex, M. (2021) 'Justin Timberlake Is Finally Getting Called Out for His Terrible Mistreatment of Britney Spears'. Available at junkee.com/justin-timberlake-britney-spears-documentary/287585. Accessed 20 April 2021.

81. No author (2003) 'Britney's boast busts virgin myth'. Available at news.bbc.co.uk/1/hi/entertainment/3052143.stm. Accessed 20 April 2021.

82. Susman, G. (2003) 'Britney Spears discusses her sex life'. Available at ew.com/article/2003/07/08/britney-spears-discusses-her-sex-life. Accessed 20 April 2021.

83. No author (2003) 'Britney's boast busts virgin myth'. Available at news.bbc.co.uk/1/hi/entertainment/3052143.stm. Accessed 20 April 2021.

84. *NME* (2007) 'Britney Spears lost virginity as teen? – Tabloid Hell'. Available at nme.com/news/music/tabloid-hell-341-1337959. Accessed 20 April 2021.

85. Grigoriadis, V. (2008) 'The Tragedy of Britney Spears'. Available at rollingstone. com/feature/the-tragedy-of-britney-spears-2-254735. Accessed 6 May 2021.

86. Cills, H. (2018) 'The Rise and Fall of the Pop Star Purity Ring'. Available at themuse.jezebel.com/the-rise-and-fall-of-the-pop-star-purity-ring-1822170318. Accessed 20 April 2021.

87. Lee, M. (2013) 'Joe Jonas Talks about Relationship with God, Frustration with Purity Rings in Raw, Revealing Interview'. Available at christianpost.com/ news/joe-jonas-talks-about-relationship-with-god-frustration-with-purity-rings-in-raw-revealing-interview-109886. Accessed 20 April 2021.

88. *Daily Record* (2001) 'OTR . . . Off the Record: Your Time Is Up, Jacko; Britney Wants Album Top Slot'.

89. Reid, S. (2001) 'Britney, J. Lo, NSYNC Turn to Jungle, Ja Rule, Jacko for VMA Performances'. Available at mtv.com/news/1448715/britney-j-lo-nsync-turn-to-jungle-ja-rule-jacko-for-vma-performances. Accessed 15 June 2021.

90. Fiasco, L. (2001) 'PETA Asks Britney Not to Use Live Animals for VMA'. Available at idobi.com/news/peta-asks-britney-not-to-use-live-animals-for-vma. Accessed 15 June 2021.

91. Orfanides, E. (2020) 'Why PETA Came After Britney Spears' Iconic Python Dance'. Available at heavy.com/entertainment/britney-spears/peta-britney-spears-python-snake-dance. Accessed 15 June 2021.

92. Fiasco, L. (2001) 'PETA Asks Britney Not to Use Live Animals for VMA'. Available at idobi.com/news/peta-asks-britney-not-to-use-live-animals-for-vma. Accessed 15 June 2021.

93. Orfanides, E. (2020) 'Why PETA Came After Britney Spears' Iconic Python Dance'. Available at heavy.com/entertainment/britney-spears/peta-britney-spears-python-snake-dance. Accessed 15 June 2021.

94. Holland, O. (2020) 'PETA ends "I'd Rather Go Naked" anti-fur campaign after three decades'. Available at edition.cnn.com/style/article/peta-naked-fur-campaign-ends/index.html. Accessed 15 June 2021.

95. No author (2008) 'PETA slams Britney over animals in video'. Available at accessonline.com/articles/britneys-circus-video-slammed-by-peta-66594. Accessed 15 June 2021.

96. Freeman, H. (2018) 'Times move pretty fast! Rewatching 80s favourites in the age of #MeToo'. Available at theguardian.com/film/2018/apr/13/80s-films-molly-ringwald-john-hughes-metoo. Accessed 10 August 2021.

97. Goldfarb, C. (2016) 'Not a Hit, Not Yet a Cult Classic: Shonda Rhimes on the Making of "Crossroads"'. Available at vice.com/en/article/vv5w59/shonda-rhimes-on-the-making-of-crossroads-britney-spears. Accessed 24 July 2021.

98. Lumenick, L. (no date) *Crossroads* review. Available at metacritic.com/movie/crossroads/critic-reviews. Accessed 24 July 2021.

99. Kaltenbach, C. (no date) *Crossroads* review. Available at metacritic.com/movie/crossroads/critic-reviews. Accessed 24 July 2021.

100. Holden, S. (no date) *Crossroads* review. Available at metacritic.com/movie/crossroads/critic-reviews. Accessed 24 July 2021.

101. Cohen, A. (2020) '*Crossroads* Hinted at Britney Spears' Future Problems – But We Didn't Listen'. Available at refinery29.com/en-gb/2020/03/9533324/crossroads-britney-spears-real-life-movie. Accessed 24 July 2021.

102. No author (no date) 'Why Do Singers Use Autotune? The Four Main Reasons'. Available at indiepanda.net/why-do-singers-use-autotune. Accessed 4 June 2021.

103. Hampp, A. (2012) 'Christina Aguilera: *Billboard* Cover Story'. Available at billboard.com/articles/news/474983/christina-aguilera-billboard-cover-story. Accessed 4 June 2021.

104. Grossbart, S. (2018) 'The Complete History of Christina Aguilera and Britney Spears' Long-Running Rivalry – Including Everything You Forgot'. Available at eonline.com/uk/news/933845/the-complete-history-of-christina-aguilera-and-britney-spears-long-running-rivalry-including-everything-you-forgot. Accessed 4 June 2021.

105. Tobi, B. (2017) 'Who's Trashier? Christina Aguilera vs Britney Spears in Their Prime'. Available at therichest.com/world-entertainment/whos-trashier-christina-aguilera-vs-britney-spears-in-their-prime. Accessed 4 June 2021.

106. Grossbart, S. (2018) 'The Complete History of Christina Aguilera and Britney Spears' Long-Running Rivalry – Including Everything You Forgot'. Available at eonline.com/uk/news/933845/the-complete-history-of-christina-aguilera-and-britney-spears-long-running-rivalry-including-everything-you-forgot. Accessed 4 June 2021.

107. Cozens, C. (2001) 'Britney to front global Pepsi campaign'. Available at theguardian.com/media/2001/feb/07/advertising3. Accessed 5 June 2021.

108. Whitehead, J. (2003) 'Christina follows in Britney's steps with Skechers deal'. Available at campaignlive.co.uk/article/christina-follows-britneys-steps-skechers-deal/188548. Accessed 5 June 2021.

109. Bonin, L. (2001) 'Christina Aguilera's Coke ad debuts'. Available at ew.com/article/2001/05/17/christina-aguileras-coke-ad-debuts. Accessed 5 June 2021.

110. Gutowitz, J. (2018) 'How the Madonna–Britney–Christina Kiss Became a Benchmark for Lesbian Visibility'. Available at intomore.com/culture/how-the-madonna-britney-christina-kiss-became-a-benchmark-for-lesbian-visibility. Accessed 17 June 2021.

111. Tobi, B. (2017) 'Who's Trashier? Christina Aguilera vs Britney Spears in Their Prime'. Available at therichest.com/world-entertainment/whos-trashier-christina-aguilera-vs-britney-spears-in-their-prime. Accessed 4 June 2021.

112. Grossbart, S. (2018) 'The Complete History of Christina Aguilera and Britney Spears' Long-Running Rivalry – Including Everything You Forgot'. Available at eonline.com/uk/news/933845/the-complete-history-of-christina-aguilera-and-britney-spears-long-running-rivalry-including-everything-you-forgot. Accessed 4 June 2021.

113. Lee, C. (2015) 'Christina Aguilera and Britney Spears' Rivalry through the Years: What They've Said about Each Other'. Available at usmagazine.com/celebrity-news/news/christina-aguilera-britney-spears-friendship-what-theyve-said-2015242. Accessed 4 June 2021.

114. Grossbart, S. (2018) 'The Complete History of Christina Aguilera and Britney Spears' Long-Running Rivalry – Including Everything You Forgot'. Available at eonline.com/uk/news/933845/the-complete-history-of-christina-aguilera-and-britney-spears-long-running-rivalry-including-everything-you-forgot. Accessed 4 June 2021.

115. Brodsky, R. (2021) 'People spent years taking photos of Britney Spears. But did they ever actually look?'. Available at independent.co.uk/arts-entertainment/music/features/britney-spears-framing-documentary-conservatorship-b1800182.html. Accessed 20 July 2021.

116. Margaret, M. (2012) 'Christina Aguilera on Britney Spears Joining "X Factor": "The More the Merrier"'. Available at parade.com/124070/marymargaret/13-the-voice-christina-aguilera-on-britney-spears-x-factor. Accessed 5 June 2021.

117. Quinn, D. (2018) 'Christina Aguilera Says She Would Record a Song with Britney Spears: It's "Not Too Late"'. Available at people.com/music/christina-aguilera-open-to-duet-with-britney-spears. Accessed 5 June 2021.

118. No author (2021) 'Bible Belt States 2021'. Available at worldpopulationreview.com/state-rankings/bible-belt-states. Accessed 17 June 2021.

119. Fahmy, D. (2019) '7 facts about Southern Baptists'. Available at pewresearch.org/fact-tank/2019/06/07/7-facts-about-southern-baptists. Accessed 17 June 2021.

120. Walsch, N. D. (2000) 'Neale Donald Walsch on CNN's "Larry King Live"'. Available at cs.cmu.edu/~zechner/cwg/lkl-ndw.html. Accessed 17 June 2021.

121. Dennis, S. (2009) *Britney: Inside the Dream*. HarperCollins (Kindle edition).

122. Bailey, F. & Barbato R. (2013) *I Am Britney Jean*. World of Wonder Productions.

123. Boorstin, D. (1962) *The Image: A Guide to Pseudo-Events in America*. Vintage Books.

124. YouTube (2019) 'Britney Spears on meeting Janet Jackson and Madonna (2001)'. Available at youtube.com/watch?v=MDna_aqtfys. Accessed 17 August 2021.

125. Grigoriadis, V. (2008) 'The Tragedy of Britney Spears'. Available at rollingstone.com/feature/the-tragedy-of-britney-spears-2-254735. Accessed 6 May 2021.

126. *Marie Claire* (2011) 'Britney Spears: Madonna helped me through the bad times'. Available at marieclaire.co.uk/news/celebrity-news/britney-spears-madonna-helped-me-through-the-bad-times-210711. Accessed 17 June 2021.

127. Griffin, P. (2008) *Britney: For the Record*. Radical Media.

128. Dennis, S. (2009) *Britney: Inside the Dream*. HarperCollins (Kindle edition).

129. No author (2005) '"Elle" Magazine Speaks to Britney about Babies and More'. Available at ukbritney.tv/2005/09/06/elle-magazine-speaks-to-britney-about-birth-babies-and-more. Accessed 17 June 2021.

130. Dennis, S. (2009) *Britney: Inside the Dream*. HarperCollins (Kindle edition).

131. Walls, J. (2006) 'Forget Kabbalah, Britney's baby is her religion'. Available at today.com/popculture/forget-kabbalah-britneys-baby-her-religion-wbna12920032. Accessed 17 June 2021.

NOTES

132. Bailey, S. P. (2021) 'Church membership in the US has fallen below the majority for the first time in nearly a century'. Available at washingtonpost.com/religion/2021/03/29/church-membership-fallen-below-majority. Accessed 17 June 2021.

133. Otter Bickerdike, J. (2015) *The Secular Religion of Fandom: Pop Culture Pilgrim.* Sage Publications.

134. Bailey, S. P. (2021) 'Church membership in the US has fallen below the majority for the first time in nearly a century'. Available at washingtonpost.com/religion/2021/03/29/church-membership-fallen-below-majority. Accessed 17 June 2021.

135. Boorstin, D. (1962) *The Image: A Guide to Pseudo-Events in America.* Vintage Books.

136. Lynch, J. (2020) 'Turns out Britney Spears' "Toxic" was originally written for another star, not Kylie Minogue'. Available at tonedeaf.thebrag.com/britney-spears-toxic-janet-jackson-kylie-minogue. Accessed 28 July 2021.

137. Wootton, D. (2019) 'Songwriter Cathy Dennis reveals she didn't write Toxic for Britney Spears'. Available at thesun.co.uk/tvandshowbiz/8853107/cathy-dennis-britney-spears-toxic-lucky. Accessed 28 July 2021.

138. Lynch, J. (2020) 'Turns out Britney Spears' "Toxic" was originally written for another star, not Kylie Minogue'. Available at tonedeaf.thebrag.com/britney-spears-toxic-janet-jackson-kylie-minogue. Accessed 28 July 2021.

139. Krishna, P. (2016) 'The Curious Staying Power of Britney's Perfume Empire'. Available at racked.com/2016/10/20/13260722/curious-britney-spears-perfume-fantasy-fragrance. Accessed 8 July 2021.

140. Gardner, E. (2013) 'The 10 Best-Selling Celebrity Perfumes'. Available at hollywoodreporter.com/news/general-news/jennifer-lopez-britney-spears-best-427374. Accessed 10 August 2021.

141. McIntosh, S. (2018) 'Why success still smells sweet for Britney Spears'. Available at bbc.co.uk/news/entertainment-arts-43211613. Accessed 8 July 2021.

142. Syme, R. (2018) 'How Britney Spears Built a Billion-Dollar Business Without Selling a Single Record'. Available at instyle.com/celebrity/britney-spears-perfume-billion-dollar-business. Accessed 8 July 2021.

143. Young, K. (2012) 'Listen to Marilyn Monroe talk about Chanel No. 5'. Available at fashion.telegraph.co.uk/beauty/news-features/TMG9680298/Listen-to-Marilyn-Monroe-talk-about-Chanel-No.-5.html. Accessed 8 July 2021.

144. No author (2015) 'Actress Beauty Tip #35: Youth Dew Perfume – An Actress Favorite'. Available at cometoverhollywood.com/tag/joan-crawford-perfume. Accessed 8 July 2021.

145. Vesilind, E. (2009) 'Elizabeth Taylor's perfumes led the way for others'. Available at latimes.com/archives/la-xpm-2009-nov-29-la-ig-liz29-2009nov29-story.html. Accessed 8 July 2021.

146. Lubitz, R. (2018) 'Why celebrity fragrances wouldn't exist without Elizabeth Taylor'. Available at mic.com/articles/188527/why-celebrity-fragrances-wouldnt-exist-without-elizabeth-taylor. Accessed 8 July 2021.

147. Vesilind, E. (2009) 'Elizabeth Taylor's perfumes led the way for others'. Available at latimes.com/archives/la-xpm-2009-nov-29-la-ig-liz29-2009nov29-story.html. Accessed 8 July 2021.

148. Lubitz, R. (2018) 'Why celebrity fragrances wouldn't exist without Elizabeth Taylor'. Available at mic.com/articles/188527/why-celebrity-fragrances-wouldnt-exist-without-elizabeth-taylor. Accessed 8 July 2021.

149. Krishna, P. (2016) 'The Curious Staying Power of Britney's Perfume Empire'. Available at racked.com/2016/10/20/13260722/curious-britney-spears-perfume-fantasy-fragrance. Accessed 8 July 2021.

150. Lawrence, K. (2019) 'A Brief History of the Most Successful Celebrity Perfumes'. Available at cools.com/most-successful-celebrity-perfumes. Accessed 8 July 2021.

151. Syme, R. (2018) 'How Britney Spears Built a Billion-Dollar Business Without Selling a Single Record'. Available at instyle.com/celebrity/britney-spears-perfume-billion-dollar-business. Accessed 8 July 2021.

152. Krishna, P. (2016) 'The Curious Staying Power of Britney's Perfume Empire'. Available at racked.com/2016/10/20/13260722/curious-britney-spears-perfume-fantasy-fragrance. Accessed 8 July 2021.

153. Syme, R. (2018) 'How Britney Spears Built a Billion-Dollar Business Without Selling a Single Record'. Available at instyle.com/celebrity/britney-spears-perfume-billion-dollar-business. Accessed 8 July 2021.

154. Vineyard, J. (2005) 'Reality-TV Britney Asks Fans: Can You Handle the Truth?'. Available at mtv.com/news/1501849/reality-tv-britney-asks-fans-can-you-handle-the-truth. Accessed 23 June 2021.

155. Gonzalez, E. (2005) 'Review: *Britney and Kevin: Chaotic*'. Available at slantmagazine.com/tv/britney-and-kevin-chaotic. Accessed 23 June 2021.

156. Wolk, J. (2005) '"Britney and Kevin": Career suicide by videocam'. Available at ew.com/article/2005/05/18/britney-and-kevin-career-suicide-videocam. Accessed 23 June 2021.

157. Asare, A. (2013) 'Britney Spears is right: 5 reasons "Chaotic" is her worst career move'. Available at ew.com/article/2013/12/09/britney-spears-chaotic. Accessed 23 June 2021.

158. Wolk, J. (2005) '"Britney and Kevin": Career suicide by videocam'. Available at ew.com/article/2005/05/18/britney-and-kevin-career-suicide-videocam. Accessed 23 June 2021.

159. Rabin, N. (2012) 'Crossing the Federline Case File #9: *Britney & Kevin: Chaotic*'. Available at avclub.com/crossing-the-federline-case-file-9-britney-kevin-c-1798229882. Accessed 23 June 2021.

160. Gonzalez, E. (2005) 'Review: *Britney and Kevin: Chaotic*'. Available at slantmagazine.com/tv/britney-and-kevin-chaotic. Accessed 23 June 2021.

161. Jamdog (2005) '*Chaotic* review, VH1'. Available at aerialtelly.co.uk/britney-chaotic-2.php. Accessed 14 July 2021.

162. Rabin, N. (2012) 'Crossing the Federline Case File #9: *Britney & Kevin: Chaotic*'. Available at avclub.com/crossing-the-federline-case-file-9-britney-kevin-c-1798229882. Accessed 23 June 2021.

163. Wolk, J. (2005) '"Britney and Kevin": Career suicide by videocam'. Available at ew.com/article/2005/05/18/britney-and-kevin-career-suicide-videocam. Accessed 23 June 2021.

164. Gonzalez, E. (2005) 'Review: *Britney and Kevin: Chaotic*'. Available at slantmagazine.com/tv/britney-and-kevin-chaotic. Accessed 23 June 2021.

165. McNeilage, R. (2019) 'Britney Spears was the OG vlogger and her reality show proves it'. Available at i-d.vice.com/en_uk/article/bjwmz3/britney-spears-kevin-federline-reality-show. Accessed 23 June 2021.

166. Rabin, N. (2012) 'Crossing the Federline Case File #9: *Britney & Kevin: Chaotic*'. Available at avclub.com/crossing-the-federline-case-file-9-britney-kevin-c-1798229882. Accessed 23 June 2021.

167. Jamdog (2005) '*Chaotic* review, VH1'. Available at aerialtelly.co.uk/britney-chaotic-2.php. Accessed 14 July 2021.

168. Copsey, R. (2013) 'Britney Spears: "*Chaotic* documentary was my worst career move"'. Available at digitalspy.com/music/a536786/britney-spears-chaotic-documentary-was-my-worst-career-move. Accessed 23 June 2021.

169. Nash, M. (2006) 'Oh Baby, Baby: (Un)Veiling Britney Spears' Pregnant Body'. *Michigan Feminist Studies*, Vol. 19.

170. Fiasco, L. (2002) 'Britney Spears Named Sexiest Woman in the World'. Available at idobi.com/news/britney-spears-named-sexiest-woman-in-the-world. Accessed 1 June 2021.

171. Nash, M. (2006) 'Oh Baby, Baby: (Un)Veiling Britney Spears' Pregnant Body'. *Michigan Feminist Studies*, Vol. 19.

172. DeDecker, B. (2016) 'Hidden Louisiana: It's Britney, Bitch'. Available at antigravitymagazine.com/column/hidden-louisiana-its-britney-bitch. Accessed 5 May 2021.

173. Nash, M. (2006) 'Oh Baby, Baby: (Un)Veiling Britney Spears' Pregnant Body'. *Michigan Feminist Studies*, Vol. 19.

174. DeDecker, B. (2016) 'Hidden Louisiana: It's Britney, Bitch'. Available at antigravitymagazine.com/column/hidden-louisiana-its-britney-bitch. Accessed 5 May 2021.

175. Nash, M. (2006) 'Oh Baby, Baby: (Un)Veiling Britney Spears' Pregnant Body'. *Michigan Feminist Studies*, Vol. 19.

176. *Harper's Bazaar* (2011) 'Britney Spears: 2006 Cover Photos'. Available at harpersbazaar.com/celebrity/latest/news/g1521/britney-spears-pregnancy-pictures. Accessed 2 June 2021.

177. Ahlgrim, C. (2019) '24 times celebrity moms were refreshingly honest about their post-pregnancy bodies'. Available at insider.com/celebrity-moms-talk-about-their-post-baby-bodies-2018-6. Accessed 2 June 2021.

178. Dennis, S. (2009) *Britney: Inside the Dream*. HarperCollins (Kindle edition).

179. Tiegel, E. (2008) *Overexposed: The Price of Fame – The Troubles of Britney, Lindsay, Paris and Nicole*. Phoenix Books Inc. (Kindle edition).

180. Coleman, E. (2018) 'The Ideal Weight and Body Fat Percentage for a 5'4" Female'. Available at livehealthy.chron.com/ideal-weight-body-fat-percentage-5-4-female-5585.html. Accessed 2 June 2021.

181. Endres, L. K., Straub, H., McKinney, C., Plunkett, B., Minkovitz, C. S., Schetter, C. D., Ramey, S., Wang, C., Hobel, C., Raju, T., Shalowitz, M. U. & Community Child Health Network of the Eunice Kennedy Shriver National Institute of Child Health and Human Development (2015) 'Postpartum weight retention risk factors and relationship to obesity at 1 year'. *Obstetrics & Gynecology*, Volume 125, Issue 1.

182. Tiegel, E. (2008) *Overexposed: The Price of Fame – The Troubles of Britney, Lindsay, Paris and Nicole*. Phoenix Books Inc. (Kindle edition).

183. No author (2007) 'Britney escaped to Las Vegas "for liposuction"'. Available at dailymail.co.uk/tvshowbiz/article-493433/Britney-escaped-Las-Vegas-liposuction.html. Accessed 2 June 2021.

184. LondonNet (2007) 'Britney Spears addicted to plastic surgery'. Available at londonnet.co.uk/entertainment/britney-spears-addicted-to-plastic-surgery. Accessed 2 June 2021.

185. Sphinx, K. (2013) 'Britney Spears $150,000 Diet, Plastic Surgery, Liposuction Makeover'. Available at celebdirtylaundry.com/2013/britney-spears-diet-plastic-surgery-liposuction-makeover-0103. Accessed 2 June 2021.

186. Grossberg, J. (2006) 'NBC Spears Britney's "Will & Grace" Story Line'. Available at eonline.com/news/51596/nbc-spears-britney-s-will-grace-story-line. Accessed 24 June 2021.

187. NBC (2006) 'Buy, Buy Baby'. *Will & Grace*, Series 8, Episode 18.

188. Associated Press (2014) 'Harris: Britney bad for "How I Met Your Mother"'. Available at latimes.com/entertainment/gossip/la-et-howimetyourmother-britney-harris10april10-story.html. Accessed 24 June 2021.

189. Zeegers, M. (2021) '"How I Met Your Mother" Was Saved by Britney Spears'. Available at cheatsheet.com/entertainment/how-i-met-your-mother-was-saved-by-britney-spears.html. Accessed 24 June 2021.

190. Vineyard, J. (2008) 'Britney Spears Has "Great Comic Timing", Say the Stars of "How I Met Your Mother"'. Available at mtv.com/news/1583848/britney-spears-has-great-comic-timing-say-the-stars-of-how-i-met-your-mother. Accessed 24 June 2021.

191. Zeegers, M. (2021) '"How I Met Your Mother" Was Saved by Britney Spears'. Available at cheatsheet.com/entertainment/how-i-met-your-mother-was-saved-by-britney-spears.html. Accessed 24 June 2021.

192. Associated Press (2014) 'Harris: Britney bad for "How I Met Your Mother"'. Available at latimes.com/entertainment/gossip/la-et-howimetyourmother-britney-harris10april10-story.html. Accessed 24 June 2021.

193. NBC (2006) 'Matt Lauer Interview with Britney Spears'. *Dateline*.

194. Bailey, F. & Barbato, R. (2013) *I Am Britney Jean*. World of Wonder Productions.

195. Grigoriadis, V. (2008) 'The Tragedy of Britney Spears'. Available at rollingstone.com/feature/the-tragedy-of-britney-spears-2-254735. Accessed 6 May 2021.

196. Price, C. (2008) 'The Britney economy: is Spears a one-woman economic force?'. Available at salon.com/2008/01/22/britney_economy. Accessed 23 July 2021.

197. Grigoriadis, V. (2008) 'The Tragedy of Britney Spears'. Available at rolling-stone.com/feature/the-tragedy-of-britney-spears-2-254735. Accessed 6 May 2021.

198. Tiegel, E. (2008) *Overexposed: The Price of Fame – The Troubles of Britney, Lindsay, Paris and Nicole*. Phoenix Books Inc. (Kindle edition).

199. BBC (2021) *The Battle for Britney: Fans, Cash and a Conservatorship*. Forest.

200. Grigoriadis, V. (2008) 'The Tragedy of Britney Spears'. Available at rolling-stone.com/feature/the-tragedy-of-britney-spears-2-254735. Accessed 6 May 2021.

201. Stark, S. (2021) *Framing Britney Spears*. New York Times Company & Left/Right Productions.

202. Alexander, D. (2021) 'The paparazzi who stalked Britney Spears have no regrets'. Available at insider.com/the-paparazzi-who-stalked-britney-spears-have-no-regrets-2021-2/ . Accessed 21 July 2021.

203. BBC (2021) *The Battle for Britney: Fans, Cash and a Conservatorship*. Forest.

204. Maddick, E. (2021) 'Photographer who trailed Britney Spears, but quit over her terrible treatment, reveals what he witnessed – and it's shocking'. Available at glamourmagazine.co.uk/article/britney-spears-paparazzi-interview. Accessed 21 July 2021.

205. Sykes, P. (2021) 'Chaotic'. *Pieces of Britney*, Episode 5.

206. Grigoriadis, V. (2008) 'The Tragedy of Britney Spears'. Available at rollingstone.com/feature/the-tragedy-of-britney-spears-2-254735. Accessed 6 May 2021.

207. Free Britney (2008) 'Now There's the Britney Spears We Love'. Available at thehollywoodgossip.com/2008/09/britney-spears-news-womanizer-released-online. Accessed 22 July 2021.

208. No author (2007) 'Want to buy Brit's locks on eBay?'. Available at today.com/popculture/salon-selling-britney-s-shorn-locks-wbna17229991. Accessed 12 August 2021.

209. Hoffman, A. (2007) 'Spears gives brief concert at SoCal club'. Available at web.archive.org/web/20070505081512/http://fe19.news.sp1.yahoo.com/s/ap/20070502/ap_en_mu/britney_spears. Accessed 5 August 2021.

210. Arnold, T. (2007) 'WHAT A YEAR FOR SPEARS'. Available at usatoday30. usatoday.com/life/music/news/2007-04-26-britney-hob_N.htm. Accessed 5 August 2021.

211. Erlewine, S. (no date) '*Blackout* – Britney Spears'. Available at allmusic.com/album/blackout-mw0000487827. Accessed 7 June 2021. Also: Grigoriadis, V. (2008) 'The Tragedy of Britney Spears'. Available at rollingstone.com/feature/the-tragedy-of-britney-spears-2-254735. Accessed 6 May 2021.

212. Griffin, P. (2008) *Britney: For the Record*. Radical Media.

213. McBride, C. (2013) 'Britney Spears opens up on bipolar disorder: "I turn into a different person"'. Available at independent.ie/entertainment/britney-spears-opens-up-on-bipolar-disorder-i-turn-into-a-different-person-29861547.html. Accessed 7 June 2021.

214. Bailey, F. & Barbato, R. (2013) *I Am Britney Jean*. World of Wonder Productions.

215. No author (2012) 'The many faces of Britney: troubled singer may have "multiple personality disorder"'. Available at standard.co.uk/showbiz/the-many-faces-of-britney-troubled-singer-may-have-multiple-personality-disorder-7260079.html. Accessed 7 June 2021.

216. Forrest, E. (2008) 'Britney's tragic descent into mania is a journey I know all too well'. Available at theguardian.com/uk/2008/feb/03/world.musicnews. Accessed 7 June 2021.

217. Vineyard, J. (2007) 'Britney Back in Rehab Yet Again'. Available at mtv.com/news/1552993/britney-back-in-rehab-yet-again. Accessed 7 June 2021.

218. *People* (2006) 'COVER STORY: Inside Britney & Kevin's Split'. Available at people.com/celebrity/cover-story-inside-britney-kevins-split. Accessed 7 June 2021.

219. Griffin, P. (2008) *Britney: For the Record*. Radical Media.

220. No author (no date) 'Overview – Postnatal depression'. Available at nhs.uk/mental-health/conditions/post-natal-depression/overview. Accessed 7 June 2021.

221. Manes, Y. (2020) '23 celebrity moms who opened up about having postpartum depression after their kids were born'. Available at insider.com/celebrities-who-had-postpartum-depression-ppd-2017-12. Accessed 8 June 2021.

222. No author (no date) 'Overview – Postnatal depression'. Available at nhs.uk/mental-health/conditions/post-natal-depression/overview. Accessed 7 June 2021.

223. Griffin, P. (2008) *Britney: For the Record*. Radical Media.

224. BBC (2021) *The Battle for Britney: Fans, Cash and a Conservatorship*. Forest.

225. Volpe, A. (2017) '"Leave Britney Alone": Chris Crocker on the Viral YouTube Clip'. Available at rollingstone.com/culture/culture-features/leave-britney-alone-chris-crocker-10-years-later-111918. Accessed 13 July 2021.

226. YouTube (2007) 'Leave Britney Alone'. Available at youtube.com/watch?v=WqSTXuJeTks. Accessed 13 July 2021.

227. Volpe, A. (2017) '"Leave Britney Alone": Chris Crocker on the Viral YouTube Clip'. Available at rollingstone.com/culture/culture-features/leave-britney-alone-chris-crocker-10-years-later-111918. Accessed 13 July 2021.

228. Kelleher, P. (2021) 'Chris Crocker hopes to begin transition after selling NFT of iconic "leave Britney alone" video'. Available at pinknews.co.uk/2021/04/13/chris-crocker-leave-britney-alone-nft-video-bid-transgender-transition. Accessed 8 May 2021.

229. Maurice, L. F. (2021) 'Here's What Chris Crocker, The "Leave Britney Alone" Person, Has To Say After "Framing Britney Spears"'. Available at buzzfeed.com/larryfitzmaurice/chris-crocker-leave-britney-alone-on-framing-britney-spears. Accessed 5 May 2021.

230. Grigoriadis, V. (2008) 'The Tragedy of Britney Spears'. Available at rolling-stone.com/feature/the-tragedy-of-britney-spears-2-254735. Accessed 6 May 2021.

231. Petridis, A. (2007) 'Britney Spears, Blackout'. Available at theguardian.com/music/2007/oct/26/popandrock.shopping. Accessed 17 July 2021.

232. Lim, D. (2007) 'Britney Spears: Blackout'. Available at web.archive.org/web/20071112165702/http:/www.blender.com/guide/reviews.aspx?id=4852. Accessed 17 July 2021.

233. Armstrong, J. K. (2017) 'Britney Spears' "Blackout" Turns 10: How Her Worst Year Gave Us Her Best Album'. Available at billboard.com/articles/columns/pop/8014074/britney-spears-blackout-anniversary. Accessed 17 July 2021.

234. Ewing, T. (2007) 'Britney in the Black Lodge (Damn Fine Album)'. Available at pitchfork.com/features/poptimist/6734-poptimist-10. Accessed 17 July 2021.

235. Lhooq, M., Myers, O. & Tanzer, M. (2018) 'It's Britney, Bitch!'. Available at thefader.com/2017/09/27/britney-spears-blackout-interview-10-year-anniversary-2007. Accessed 16 June 2021.

236. Kheraj, A. (2017) 'Britney's Blackout ten years on – a mutant pop classic'. Available at dazeddigital.com/music/article/37874/1/britney-spears-blackout-10th-anniversary-retrospective. Accessed 17 July 2021.

237. Vineyard, J. (2007) 'Britney Spears' New Album, *Blackout*: A Track-By-Track Report'. Available at mtv.com/news/1571813/britney-spears-new-album-blackout-a-track-by-track-report. Accessed 17 July 2021.

238. Lhooq, M., Myers, O. & Tanzer, M. (2018) 'It's Britney, Bitch!'. Available at thefader.com/2017/09/27/britney-spears-blackout-interview-10-year-anniversary-2007. Accessed 16 June 2021.

239. Reuters (2007) 'Britney Spears names new album "Blackout"'. Available at reuters.com/article/us-spears-idUSN0328342220071006. Accessed 17 July 2021.

240. Petridis, A. (2007) 'Britney Spears, Blackout'. Available at theguardian.com/music/2007/oct/26/popandrock.shopping. Accessed 17 July 2021. Also: Wilson, M. (2007) 'Blackout'. Available at ew.com/article/2007/10/26/blackout-2. Accessed 17 July 2021.

241. Alexander, E. (2018) 'Ellen Von Unwerth talks selfies, sexual harassment and her ultimate muse'. Available at harpersbazaar.com/uk/fashion/fashion-news/a20159172/ellen-von-unwerth-interview. Accessed 17 July 2021.

242. *Ottawa Citizen* (2007) 'Britney's latest album: Two views on Blackout'. Available at web.archive.org/web/20121110155603/http://www.canada.com/ottawacitizen/news/arts/story.html?id=5c1b742b-7d58-4ce8-852c-d37141ba5caa. Accessed 17 July 2021.

243. Kaufman, G. (2007) 'Britney Spears Slammed by Catholic League For *Blackout*'s Religious-Themed Photos'. Available at mtv.com/news/1573060/britney-spears-slammed-by-catholic-league-for-blackouts-religious-themed-photos. Accessed 17 July 2021.

244. Sheffield, R. (2017) 'Britney Spears' "Blackout": A Salute to Her Misunderstood Punk Masterpiece'. Available at rollingstone.com/music/music-news/britney-spears-blackout-a-salute-to-her-misunderstood-punk-masterpiece-121525. Accessed 17 July 2021.

245. Kheraj, A. (2017) 'Britney's Blackout ten years on – a mutant pop classic'. Available at dazeddigital.com/music/article/37874/1/britney-spears-blackout-10th-anniversary-retrospective. Accessed 17 July 2021.

246. Kenney, D. (2019) *The Unknown Keyboard Player* (Kindle edition).

247. Dennis, S. (2009) *Britney: Inside the Dream*. HarperCollins (Kindle edition).

248. O'Connor, R. (2021) '"What was wrong with you at lunch? You were mean": Britney Spears' letters to high-school boyfriend up for auction'. Available at independent.co.uk/arts-entertainment/music/news/britney-spears-letters-boyfriend-auction-b1864628.html. Accessed 22 July 2021.

249. Susman, G. (2004) 'Dancer comes clean about sharing a bed with Britney'. Available at ew.com/article/2004/02/19/dancer-comes-clean-about-sharing-bed-britney. Accessed 22 July 2021.

250. Boren, J. (2015) '"Scandal" Star Columbus Short Claims He Hooked Up with Britney Spears after "A Wild Party" in the Early '00s'. Available at latestnews-post.com/news/entertainment/scandal-star-columbus-short-confesses-he-hooked-up-with-britney-spears-after-a-wild-party-in-the-early-00s. Accessed 22 July 2021.

251. Dangelo, J. (2003) 'Durst Furthers Britney Romance Rumors with Online Post'. Available at mtv.com/news/1459522/durst-furthers-britney-romance-rumors-with-online-post. Accessed 22 July 2021.

252. Kaufman, G. (2003) 'Durst Dishes Alleged Britney Nookie on Howard Stern Show'. Available at mtv.com/news/1470210/durst-dishes-alleged-britney-nookie-on-howard-stern-show. Accessed 22 July 2021.

253. No author (2003) 'LIMP BIZKIT's DURST Dishes Dirt on BRITNEY'. Available at blabbermouth.net/news/limp-bizkit-s-durst-dishes-dirt-on-britney. Accessed 22 July 2021.

254. Kaufman, G. (2003) 'Durst Dishes Alleged Britney Nookie on Howard Stern Show'. Available at mtv.com/news/1470210/durst-dishes-alleged-britney-nookie-on-howard-stern-show. Accessed 22 July 2021.

255. No author (2009) 'Fred Durst on Alleged 2003 Relationship with Britney Spears: "Taboo for a Guy Like Me To Be Associated with a Gal Like Her"'. Available at accessonline.com/articles/fred-durst-on-alleged-2003-relationship-with-britney-spears-taboo-for-a-guy-like-me-to-be-associated-with-a-gal-like-her-69018. Accessed 22 July 2021.

256. Taylor, T. (2018) 'Hollyweird: Britney Spears Briefly Dated Colin Farrell'. Available at papermag.com/hollyweird-britney-spears-colin-farrell-2610075030.html?rebelltitem=4#rebelltitem4. Accessed 22 July 2021.

257. Free Britney (2007) 'Isaac Cohen Speaks: Britney Spears' Newest Ex Tells of Marathon Sex Romps, Booze, Insecurities'. Available at thehollywoodgossip. com/2007/02/isaac-cohen-britney-spears-sex-romps-insecurities-more. Accessed 22 July 2021.

258. No author (2007) 'Britney is a limp rag doll after sex'. Available at hindustan-times.com/india/britney-is-a-limp-rag-doll-after-sex/story-oNiuEjDWNM-mI4e9ZrdzxKM.html. Accessed 22 July 2021.

259. Free Britney (2007) 'Report: Isaac Cohen Dumps Britney over Phone'. Available at thehollywoodgossip.com/2007/02/this-just-in-britney-spears-is-smoking. Accessed 22 July 2021.

260. Grigoriadis, V. (2008) 'The Tragedy of Britney Spears'. Available at rollingstone. com/feature/the-tragedy-of-britney-spears-2-254735. Accessed 6 May 2021.

261. Vineyard, J. (2008) 'Britney Spears "Happily Dating" Paparazzi Photographer, His Photo Agency Claims'. Available at mtv.com/news/1579490/britney-spears-happily-dating-paparazzi-photographer-his-photo-agency-claims. Accessed 22 July 2021.

262. Hilton, B. (2008) 'Britney Spears expecting third baby?'. Available at digitalspy. com/showbiz/a85740/britney-spears-expecting-third-baby. Accessed 22 July 2021.

263. Feehan, C. (2008) 'Britney dumps boyfriend over pregnancy test stunt'. Available at independent.ie/woman/celeb-news/britney-dumps-boyfriend-over-pregnancy-test-stunt-26346516.html. Accessed 22 July 2021.

264. Free Britney (2008) 'Adnan Ghalib: I Will Sell a Britney Spears Sex Tape!'. Available at thehollywoodgossip.com/2008/09/the-hollywood-gossip-caption-contest-49. Accessed 22 July 2021.

265. Eibeinde, C. (2008) 'Adnan Ghalib: There's No Britney Sex Tape'. Available at justjared.com/2008/10/01/adnan-sex-tape. Accessed 22 July 2021.

266. Dennis, S. (2009) *Britney: Inside the Dream*. HarperCollins (Kindle edition).

267. Google (2011). Available at archive.google.com/jobs/britney.html. Accessed 17 August 2021.

268. David (2012) 'Britney Spears "Most Searched Celebrity" Since Creation of Internet'. Available at thatgrapejuice.net/2012/12/britney-spears-most-searched-celebrity-creation-internet. Accessed 14 June 2021.

269. Zambas, J. (2021) '50+ Most Popular & Trending Celebrities of 2021'. Available at telltalesonline.com/26925/popular-celebs. Accessed 14 June 2021.

270. Harris, P. (2008) 'No freedom and treated like a child – how Britney's dad took control'. Available at theguardian.com/lifeandstyle/2008/dec/07/britney-spears-music-celebrity. Accessed 5 May 2021.

271. Eliscu, J. (2011) 'Britney Spears Returns'. Available at rollingstone.com/music/music-news/britney-spears-returns-254594. Accessed 5 May 2021.

272. No author (2009) 'Britney Spears Voicemail: Save Me from My Dad!'. Available at justjared.com/2009/03/30/britney-spears-voicemail-save-me-from-my-dad. Accessed 27 May 2021.

273. Eliscu, J. (2011) 'Britney Spears Returns'. Available at rollingstone.com/music/music-news/britney-spears-returns-254594. Accessed 5 May 2021.

274. Harris, P. (2008) 'No freedom and treated like a child – how Britney's dad took control'. Available at theguardian.com/lifeandstyle/2008/dec/07/britney-spears-music-celebrity. Accessed 5 May 2021.

275. Spears, L. (2008) *Through the Storm: A Real Story of Fame and Family in a Tabloid World.* Thomas Nelson.

276. Schaefer, K. (2021) 'New documentary "Framing Britney Spears" released, reviving discussion of conservatorship'. Available at berkeleybeacon.com/new-documentary-framing-britney-spears-released-reviving-discussion-of-conservatorship. Accessed 5 May 2021.

277. Eliscu, J. (2011) 'Britney Spears Returns'. Available at rollingstone.com/music/music-news/britney-spears-returns-254594. Accessed 5 May 2021.

278. Ross, M. (2019) 'Britney Spears is now #FreeBritney: Singer alleges her father forced her into hospital, report says'. Available at mercurynews.com/2019/05/13/britney-spears-is-now-freebritney-alleges-her-father-forced-her-into-the-hospital-report-says. Accessed 5 May 2021.

279. Song, S. (2020) 'Inside #FreeBritney: A Stan Movement to Help Their Pop Savior'. Available at papermag.com/inside-free-britney-2647769346.html?rebelltitem=1#rebelltitem1. Accessed 5 May 2021.

280. Ross, M. (2019) 'Britney Spears is now #FreeBritney: Singer alleges her father forced her into hospital, report says'. Available at mercurynews.com/2019/05/13/britney-spears-is-now-freebritney-alleges-her-father-forced-her-into-the-hospital-report-says. Accessed 5 May 2021.

281. Miller, K. & Shiffer, E. (2021) 'The Full Timeline of Britney Spears' Conservatorship and the #FreeBritney Movement, Explained'. Available at womenshealthmag.com/life/a33336398/britney-spears-conservatorship-timeline. Accessed 5 May 2021.

282. BBC (2021) *The Battle for Britney: Fans, Cash and a Conservatorship.* Forest.

283. Kirkpatrick, E. (2020) 'Britney Spears' Dad Says the #FreeBritney Movement "Is a Joke"'. Available at vanityfair.com/style/2020/08/britney-spears-jamie-spears-free-britney-movement. Accessed 5 May 2021.

284. Vincent, M. (2021) 'Britney Spears' dad requesting pop star to pay nearly $2 million of his legal fees'. Available at newsbreak.com/news/2195562396483/britney-spears-dad-requests-pop-star-to-pay-nearly-2-million-of-his-legal-fees. Accessed 5 May 2021.

285. Levin, S. (2021) 'Britney Spears' father files to shut down conservatorship that controls his daughter's life'. Available at theguardian.com/music/2021/sep/07/britney-jamie-spears-father-conservatorship-end. Accessed 9 September 2021.

286. Griffin, P. (2008) *Britney: For the Record.* Radical Media.

287. YouTube (2019) 'Alanis Morissette on Britney Spears' "You Oughta Know" Cover, WWHL'. Available at youtube.com/watch?v=zAJwqRT4qSU. Accessed 21 July 2021.

288. *NME* (2000) 'The Queen of Pop – and England?'. Available at nme.com/news/music/britney-spears-383-1398735. Accessed 9 June 2021.

289. Berk. S., Spears, B. & Spears, L. (2000) *Britney Spears' Heart to Heart.* Three Rivers.

290. No author (no date) 'Britney and William "set up date"'. Available at dailymail.co.uk/tvshowbiz/article-96505/Britney-William-set-date.html. Accessed 9 June 2021.

291. ABC News (2002) 'Britney Spears: Prince Wills Stood Me Up'. Available at abcnews.go.com/international/story?id=80207&page=1. Accessed 9 June 2021.

292. Dennis, S. (2009) *Britney: Inside the Dream.* HarperCollins (Kindle edition).

293. Hughes, I. (2014) 'Britney Spears wants Kate Middleton to model her new LINGERIE collection'. Available at mirror.co.uk/3am/celebrity-news/britney-spears-wants-kate-middleton-4313645. Accessed 9 June 2021.

294. Banks, K. (2014) 'Britney Spears: "I'll get Kate Middleton in my undies!"'. Available at closeronline.co.uk/celebrity/news/britney-spears-ll-get-kate-middleton-undies. Accessed 9 June 2021.

295. Dennis, S. (2009) 'Tragic Blondes: The Diana–Britney Connection'. Available at vanityfair.com/news/2009/10/britney-vs-diana. Accessed 9 June 2021.

296. Grady, C. (2020) 'The pop cultural obsession with Princess Diana's innocence, explained'. Available at vox.com/culture/21593569/princess-diana-explainer-crown-netflix-marilyn-monroe-britney-spears-innocence. Accessed 9 June 2021.

297. No author (2021) 'Princess Diana interview: What did Martin Bashir and the BBC do?'. Available at bbc.co.uk/news/explainers-57163815. Accessed 9 June 2021.

298. Faulkner, D. & Lee, J. (2021) 'BBC's deceit over Diana interview worsened my parents' relationship – William'. Available at bbc.co.uk/news/uk-57195046. Accessed 9 June 2021.

299. Trock, G. (2021) 'Britney Spears Shows Love for Late Princess Diana amid Interview Drama'. Available at theblast.com/6490947/britney-spears-shows-love-for-late-princess-diana-amid-interview. Accessed 9 June 2021.

300. Hull, S. (2012) 'Britney's Diana death fear'. Available at standard.co.uk/showbiz/britney-s-diana-death-fear-7248416.html. Accessed 9 June 2012.

301. Friedman, J. (2008) 'Britney Spears May Face the Same Fate as Princess Diana'. Available at cbsnews.com/news/britney-spears-may-face-the-same-fate-as-princess-diana. Accessed 9 June 2021.

302. Dahlgren, W. (2014) '"Ghosts exist", say 1 in 3 Brits'. Available at yougov.co.uk/topics/politics/articles-reports/2014/10/31/ghosts-exist-say-1-3-brits. Accessed 30 June 2021.

303. Scott, H. A. (2019) 'More than 45 Per Cent of Americans Believe Demons and Ghosts'. Available at newsweek.com/more-45-percent-americans-believe-demons-ghosts-are-real-survey-1466743. Accessed 30 June 2021.

304. Zaborowski, J. (2021) 'Britney's Haunted House with Heather Auble and John E. L. Tenney'. *We Need to Talk About Britney*.

305. Schmelzer, C. (2016) 'The Dark History of Brittany Murphy's House'. Available at nickiswift.com/17695/dark-history-brittany-murphys-house. Accessed 30 June 2021.

306. No author (no date) 'Kentwood, Louisiana facts for kids'. Available at kids.kiddle.co/Kentwood,_Louisiana. Accessed 5 May 2021.

307. Dennis, S. (2009) *Britney: Inside the Dream*. HarperCollins (Kindle edition).

308. No author (no date) 'Kentwood Historical and Cultural Arts Museum'. Available at atlasobscura.com/places/kentwood-historical-and-cultural-arts-museum. Accessed 4 May 2021.

309. DeDecker, B. (2016) 'Hidden Louisiana: It's Britney, Bitch'. Available at anti-gravitymagazine.com/column/hidden-louisiana-its-britney-bitch. Accessed 5 May 2021.

310. Author interview with Nicola and Trevor Collins, 2021.

311. Roach, A. (2019) 'Britney Spears superfan from Hornchurch who died from brain tumour will have his story retold in New York pop-up event'. Available at romfordrecorder.co.uk/news/health/new-york-show-to-feature-hornchurch-britney-fan-s-story-3218784. Accessed 4 May 2021.

312. Author interview with Nicola and Trevor Collins, 2021.

313. Roach, A. (2019) 'Britney Spears superfan from Hornchurch who died from brain tumour will have his story retold in New York pop-up event'. Available at romfordrecorder.co.uk/news/health/new-york-show-to-feature-hornchurch-britney-fan-s-story-3218784. Accessed 4 May 2021.

314. Author interview with Nicola and Trevor Collins, 2021.

315. No author (2012) 'Britney Spears "excited" to join *X Factor* judges'. Available at bbc.co.uk/news/av/entertainment-arts-18071160. Accessed 11 August 2021.

316. Kaufman, G. (2013) 'Simon Cowell Says Britney Spears "Couldn't Talk" on "X Factor"'. Available at mtv.com/news/1713830/simon-cowell-britney-spears-x-factor-interview. Accessed 11 August 2021.

317. Hautman, N. (2021) 'Louis Walsh: Britney Spears "was on so much medication" on "X Factor"'. Available at pagesix.com/2021/06/14/louis-walsh-britney-spears-was-on-medication-on-x-factor. Accessed 11 August 2021.

318. Bower, T. (2021) 'How Britney Spears got her X Factor back thanks to Simon Cowell – before she fell into despair'. Available at thesun.co.uk/tvandshowbiz/15386679/how-simon-cowell-saved-britney-spears. Accessed 11 August 2021.

319. *Elle* (2012) 'Britney Spears: The Brit Factor'. Available at elle.com/culture/celebrities/g18288/britney-spears-cover-shoot-october-2012. Accessed 13 August 2021.

320. Twitter (2018). Available at twitter.com/femalepopfacts/status/989975539099295744?lang=en. Accessed 26 June 2021.

321. Coogin, D. (2020) 'How Much Was Britney Spears Paid for Her Las Vegas Residency?'. Available at thethings.com/how-much-was-britney-spears-paid-for-her-las-vegas-residency. Accessed 26 June 2021.

322. Chilton, M. (2021) 'Viva Las Vegas: A History of Sin City's Musical Residencies'. Available at udiscovermusic.com/in-depth-features/las-vegas-residencies-history. Accessed 26 June 2021.

323. McIntyre, H. (2015) 'Britney Spears' Vegas Residency Was a Game Changer'. Available at forbes.com/sites/hughmcintyre/2015/11/27/britney-spears-vegas-residency-was-a-game-changer/?sh=7bbc1414536f. Accessed 26 June 2021.

324. Coogin, D. (2020) 'How Much Was Britney Spears Paid for Her Las Vegas Residency?'. Available at thethings.com/how-much-was-britney-spears-paid-for-her-las-vegas-residency. Accessed 26 June 2021.

325. Ramos, A. (2018) 'Britney Spears to be honored at the 29th Annual GLAAD Media Awards for LGBTQ support and allyship'. Available at glaad.org/blog/britney-spears-be-honored-29th-annual-glaad-media-awards-lgbtq-support-and-allyship. Accessed 22 June 2021.

326. Harwood, E. (2018) 'Britney Spears Nearly Broke the GLAAD Media Awards'. Available at vanityfair.com/style/2018/04/britney-spears-nearly-broke-the-glaad-media-awards. Accessed 22 June 2021.

327. No author (2009) 'Britney Spears is the new icon for gay community'. Available at indianexpress.com/article/entertainment/entertainment-others/britney-spears-is-the-new-icon-for-gay-community. Accessed 22 June 2021.

328. Peeples, J. (2013) 'Britney Spears: A (Queer) Piece of Me'. Available at advocate.com/arts-entertainment/music/2013/12/03/britney-spears-queer-piece-me. Accessed 22 June 2021.

329. Twitter (2020). Available at twitter.com/britneyspears/status/1275554414829252608?lang=en. Accessed 17 August 2021.

330. No author (no date) 'Britney Spears #1 Gay Icon in California'. Available at navsi100.com/en/news/532-Britney-Spears-1-Gay-Icon-in-California. Accessed 22 June 2021.

331. Lister, D. (1992) 'Alluring qualities that make a gay icon'. Available at independent.co.uk/news/uk/alluring-qualities-that-make-a-gay-icon-1555024.html. Accessed 22 June 2021.

332. Kaiser, C. (1997) *The Gay Metropolis: The Landmark History of Gay Life in America*. Mariner Books.

333. Betancourt, M. (2017) 'Why Do Gay Men Love Britney Spears?'. Available at vice.com/en/article/8qkqnk/why-do-gay-men-love-britney-spears. Accessed 22 June 2021.

334. Appel, B. (2017) 'Lest We Forget Why Gay Men Love Britney and Madonna'. Available at huffpost.com/entry/lest-we-forget-why-gay-men-love-britney-and-madonna_b_59beedfee4b02c642e4a17e8. Accessed 22 June 2021.

335. Spears, B. (2017) 'Britney Spears: Love Letter to the LGBTQ Community'. Available at assets.billboard.com/articles/news/pride/7809846/britney-spears-gay-pride-month-love-letter. Accessed 22 June 2021.

336. Crowley, P. (2018) '7 Times Britney Spears Earned Her Gay Icon Status'. Available at billboard.com/articles/news/pride/8099507/britney-spears-gay-icon-best-moments. Accessed 22 June 2021.

337. Megarry, D. (no date) 'Drag Race star Derrick Barry thinks drag queens are "too censored" now'. Available at gaytimes.co.uk/culture/drag-race-star-derrick-barry-thinks-drag-queens-are-too-censored-now. Accessed 22 June 2021.

338. Goble, G. (2020) 'Gay iconography and lesbian omission'. Available at varsity.co.uk/music/19635. Accessed 22 June 2021.

339. Peeples, J. (2013) 'Britney Spears: A (Queer) Piece of Me'. Available at advocate.com/arts-entertainment/music/2013/12/03/britney-spears-queer-piece-me. Accessed 22 June 2021.

340. Azzopardi, C. (2013) 'Britney Spears Talks Gay Fans: "They're Somewhat Girls"'. Available at pridesource.com/article/63493-2. Accessed 22 June 2021.

341. Goldstein, N. (2013) 'Why is Britney Spears so appealing to gay fans?'. Available at theguardian.com/commentisfree/2013/dec/12/britney-jean-spears-new-album-gay-fans. Accessed 22 June 2021.

342. Goble, G. (2020) 'Gay iconography and lesbian omission'. Available at varsity.co.uk/music/19635. Accessed 22 June 2021.

343. Simon, M. (2011) 'Britney Spears Accused of Exploiting Gays for Her Big Comeback'. Available at queerty.com/britney-spears-accused-of-exploiting-gays-for-her-big-comeback-20110325. Accessed 22 June 2021.

344. Linder, E. (2021) 'FreeBritney: How the Britney Spears fan movement actually started'. Available at independent.co.uk/arts-entertainment/music/news/free-britney-fans-conservatorship-b1816671.html#r3z-addoor. Accessed 29 April 2021.

345. Stark, S. (2021) *Framing Britney Spears*. New York Times Company & Left/Right Productions.

346. Author interview with Kevin Wu, 2021.

347. Author interview with Megan Radford, 2021.

348. Author interview with Leanne Simmons, 2021.

349. Snapes, L. (2021) 'Britney Spears: US House of Representatives introduces bill to end conservatorship abuse'. Available at theguardian.com/music/2021/jul/21/britney-spears-us-house-of-representatives-introduce-bill-to-end-conservatorship-abuse. Accessed 21 July 2021.

350. Author interview with Kevin Wu, 2021.

351. Read, B. (2019) 'Britney Spears Responds to Fans Concerned about Her Well-Being in Instagram Video'. Available at vogue.com/article/britney-spears-instagram-video-mental-health-response. Accessed 4 May 2021.

352. Richardson, H. (2021) 'Britney's Insta-code: Fans insist star is using her social media to send cries for help, from a photo of a dying rose to a cryptic image of a Scrabble board – as new documentary delves into her conservatorship'. Available at dailymail.co.uk/femail/article-9270243/Britneys-Insta-code-Fans-insist-star-using-social-media-send-secret-cries-help.html. Accessed 4 May 2021.

353. BBC (2021) *The Battle for Britney: Fans, Cash and a Conservatorship*. Forest.

354. Farrow, R. & Tolentino, J. (2021) 'Britney Spears' Conservatorship Nightmare'. Available at newyorker.com/news/american-chronicles/britney-spears-conservatorship-nightmare. Accessed 14 July 2021.

355. Instagram (2021). Available at instagram.com/tv/CND5B1RArtK/?utm_source=ig_embed. Accessed 4 May 2021.

356. Kirkpatrick, E. (2021) 'Britney Spears' Former Makeup Artist Claims Her Instagram "Content Is Her, But the Words Are Not"'. Available at vanityfair.com/style/2021/04/britney-spears-instagram-former-makeup-artist-conservatorship-not-in-charge-of-account. Accessed 4 May 2021.

357. Fikse, A. (2021) 'Britney Spears Claps Back at Claims She Doesn't Run Her Instagram Account'. Available at popculture.com/celebrity/news/britney-spears-claps-back-at-claims-she-doesnt-run-her-instagram-account. Accessed 4 May 2021.

358. Instagram (2021). Available at instagram.com/p/CKzHQ5jhXL4. Accessed 4 May 2021.

359. Stark, S. (2021) *Framing Britney Spears*. New York Times Company & Left/Right Productions.

360. Aswald, J. (2021) 'Read Britney Spears' Full Statement Against Conservatorship: "I Am Traumatized"'. Available at variety.com/2021/music/news/britney-spears-full-statement-conservatorship-1235003940. Accessed 14 July 2021.

361. Tiegel, E. (2008) *Overexposed: The Price of Fame – The Troubles of Britney, Lindsay, Paris and Nicole*. Phoenix Books Inc.

362. Kirkpatrick, E. (2021) 'Britney Spears' Mom and Sister Both Share Subtle Messages of Support after Latest Conservatorship Hearing'. Available at vanityfair.com/style/2021/07/britney-spears-conservatorship-hearing-lynne-spears-jamie-lynn-spears-instagram-messages. Accessed 25 July 2021.

363. Shoaib, A. (2021) 'Britney Spears appears to criticize her sister and mother, calling out those closest to her "who never showed up"'. Available at insider.com/britney-spears-criticizes-people-closest-to-her-who-never-showed-up-2021-7. Accessed 25 July 2021.

364. Levin, S. (2021) 'Britney Spears' father agrees to step down as conservator "when the time is right"'. Available at theguardian.com/music/2021/aug/12/britney-jamie-spears-father-conservator-step-down. Accessed 13 August 2021.

365. Levin, S. (2021) 'Britney Spears' father files to shut down conservatorship that controls his daughter's life'. Available at theguardian.com/music/2021/sep/07/britney-jamie-spears-father-conservatorship-end. Accessed 9 September 2021.

366. Aswad, J. (2021) 'Read Britney Spears' Full Statement Against Conservatorship: "I Am Traumatized"'. Available at variety.com/2021/music/news/britney-spears-full-statement-conservatorship-1235003940. Accessed 14 July 2021.

367. Grady, C. (2021) 'What we've learned about Britney Spears' conservatorship case changes everything'. Available at vox.com/culture/22565683/britney-spears-conservatorship-testimony. Accessed 21 July 2021.

368. Aswad, J. (2021) 'Read Britney Spears' Full Statement Against Conservatorship: "I Am Traumatized"'. Available at variety.com/2021/music/news/britney-spears-full-statement-conservatorship-1235003940. Accessed 14 July 2021.

369. Antionios, N. & Raup, C. (2012) 'Buck v. Bell (1927)'. Available at embryo.asu.edu/pages/buck-v-bell-1927. Accessed 21 July 2021.

370. Murray, C. (2021) 'What is Roe v. Wade and could a new case overturn US abortion rights?'. Available at news.trust.org/item/20210518181318-t2h4j. Accessed 21 July 2021.

371. Pew Research Center (2019) 'US Public Continues to Favor Legal Abortion, Oppose Overturning Roe v. Wade'. Available at pewresearch.org/politics/2019/08/29/u-s-public-continues-to-favor-legal-abortion-oppose-overturning-roe-v-wade. Accessed 21 July 2021.

372. Batha, E. (2021) 'US states making 2021 moves on abortion rights and access'. Available at news.trust.org/item/20201231112641-qfynt. Accessed 21 July 2021.

373. George, T. (2005) *Hotel Rwanda*. United Artists/Lions Gate Films.

374. Trust, G. (2019) 'Ask *Billboard*: Britney Spears' Career Album & Song Sales, on the 20th Anniversary of ". . . Baby One More Time"'. Available at billboard.com/articles/columns/chart-beat/8493258/britney-spears-career-sales-baby-one-more-time-20th-anniversary-ask-billboard. Accessed 24 July 2021.

375. Ryan, P. (2016) 'Britney Spears basks in "Glory" of number-three debut'. Available at eu.usatoday.com/story/life/music/2016/09/06/britney-spears-barbra-streisand-sales/89883410. Accessed 24 July 2021.

Credits

Page numbers refer to plate section.

p. 1: dpa picture alliance/Alamy Stock Photo

p. 2 (top): Everett Collection Inc./Alamy Stock Photo

p. 2 (bottom, left to right): Everett Collection Inc./Alamy Stock Photo; ZUMA Press Inc./Alamy Stock Photo

p. 3 (top, left to right): Lester Cohen/WireImage/Getty Images; Trinity Mirror/Mirrorpix/Alamy Stock Photo

p. 3 (bottom): Dave Hogan/Getty Images

p. 4: Frank Trapper/Corbis via Getty Images

p. 5 (top): Timothy A. Clary/AFP via Getty Images

p. 5 (bottom): Paul Bergen/Redferns/Getty Images

p. 6 (top): Kevin Kane/WireImage/Getty Images

p. 6 (bottom, left and right): Retro AdArchives/Alamy Stock Photo

p. 7 (top): Jeffrey Mayer/WireImage/Getty Images

p. 7 (bottom): Monty Brinton/CBS via Getty Images

p. 8 (top): Francis Specker/Alamy Stock Photo

p. 8 (bottom): ZUMA Press Inc./Alamy Stock Photo

p. 9 (top): WENN Rights Ltd/Alamy Stock Photo